Nigeria

Nigeria

Dancing on the Brink

Updated Edition

John Campbell

A COUNCIL ON FOREIGN RELATIONS BOOK
ROWMAN & LITTLEFIELD PUBLISHERS, INC.
Lanham • Boulder • New York • Toronto • Plymouth, UK

The Council on Foreign Relations (CFR) is an independent, nonpartisan membership organization, think tank, and publisher dedicated to being a resource for its members, government officials, business executives, journalists, educators and students, civic and religious leaders, and other interested citizens in order to help them better understand the world and the foreign policy choices facing the United States and other countries. Founded in 1921, CFR carries out its mission by maintaining a diverse membership, with special programs to promote interest and develop expertise in the next generation of foreign policy leaders; convening meetings at its headquarters in New York and in Washington, DC, and other cities where senior government officials, members of Congress, global leaders, and prominent thinkers come together with CFR members to discuss and debate major international issues; supporting a Studies Program that fosters independent research, enabling CFR scholars to produce articles, reports, and books and hold roundtables that analyze foreign policy issues and make concrete policy recommendations; publishing *Foreign Affairs*, the preeminent journal on international affairs and U.S. foreign policy; sponsoring Independent Task Forces that produce reports with both findings and policy prescriptions on the most important foreign policy topics; and providing up-to-date information and analysis about world events and American foreign policy on its website, www.cfr.org.

THE COUNCIL ON FOREIGN RELATIONS TAKES NO INSTITUTIONAL POSITION ON POLICY ISSUES AND HAS NO AFFILIATION WITH THE U.S. GOVERNMENT. ALL STATEMENTS OF FACT AND EXPRESSIONS OF OPINION CONTAINED IN ITS PUBLICATIONS ARE THE SOLE RESPONSIBILITY OF THE AUTHOR OR AUTHORS.

Published by Rowman & Littlefield Publishers, Inc.
A wholly owned subsidiary of The Rowman & Littlefield Publishing Group, Inc.
4501 Forbes Boulevard, Suite 200, Lanham, Maryland 20706
www.rowman.com

10 Thornbury Road, Plymouth PL6 7PP, United Kingdom

British Library Cataloguing in Publication Information Available

Library of Congress Cataloging-in-Publication Data
Campbell, John, 1944–
Nigeria : dancing on the brink / John Campbell.
p. cm.
"A Council on Foreign Relations book."
Includes bibliographical references and index.
ISBN 978-1-4422-2156-7 (cloth : alk. paper) — ISBN 978-1-4422-2157-4 (pbk. : alk. paper) — ISBN 978-1-4422-2158-1 (electronic) 1. Nigeria—Politics and government—2007– 2. Nigeria—Economic conditions—1970– 3. Social conflict—Nigeria. 4. Ethnic conflict—Nigeria. I. Title.
JQ3090.C36 2013
966.9054—dc23
2013008131

♾™ The paper used in this publication meets the minimum requirements of American National Standard for Information Sciences Permanence of Paper for Printed Library Materials, ANSI/NISO Z39.48-1992.

Printed in the United States of America

Contents

Preface

Nigeria, home to about 20 percent of the people living in Africa south of the Sahara, has a population about the size of the Russian Federation's. The United States is increasingly dependent on it for imported oil and natural gas, though that could change as its own oil and gas production increases with the new oil shale technologies. Nigeria's government contributes large numbers of troops to United Nations and other peacekeeping operations, and it has lobbied vigorously for a permanent seat on the UN Security Council. A regional leader, Nigeria is one of the founders of the African Union and is the linchpin of the Economic Community of West African States.

With its large population, natural resource endowment, and tradition of international engagement, Nigeria was perhaps the most important African strategic partner of George W. Bush's administration. But Nigeria at present faces challenges that put its partnership with the United States at risk, and Nigeria's international role has declined under presidents Umaru Yar'Adua and Goodluck Jonathan.

In the Niger Delta, the heartland of Nigeria's natural resource wealth, an insurgency against the federal government continues despite an amnesty now more than two years old. In the North, currents of radical Islam have taken hold, and bloody uprisings against government authorities are increasing in frequency. Ostensibly a democracy since the end of military dictatorship in 1998, executive authority in Abuja was paralyzed by the illness and subsequent death of the president, Umaru Yar'Adua, in May 2010.

President Jonathan successfully ran for election in 2011, thereby ending the informal arrangement under which the presidency alternated between candidates from the South and the North, exacerbating the latter's alienation from the Abuja government and encouraging the rise of radical Islam. Growing numbers of Nigerians, not just in the North, are alienated from their government and believe their nation is failing as a state.

For a country of such importance, Nigeria is little known in the United States. Only one book intended for the nonspecialist reader has appeared in English in the past decade, Karl Maier's *This House Has Fallen: Nigeria in Crisis* (2002). Few Americans visit. Internal travel is difficult with the deterioration of Nigeria's infrastructure and escalating violence. My hope is that *Nigeria: Dancing on the Brink* will introduce the nonspecialist reader to the complexity and challenges of contemporary Nigeria and foster an appreciation for those Nigerians working against state failure in Africa's most important country.

Despite the regular abrogation of the rule of law, the high levels of violence, and official corruption and incompetence, Nigerians regard themselves as fundamentally free, and they have never been afraid to express their opinions, even during the years of military dictatorship. And they like to talk to foreign diplomats. Much of this book is based on conversations and personal experiences I had during my thirty months (February 1988 through July 1990) as political counselor based in Lagos and my thirty-eight months as ambassador (May 2004 through July 2007) in Abuja. This second edition addresses Nigerian developments since the death of President Yar'Adua.

In *Nigeria: Dancing on the Brink*, I argue that U.S. policy makers should pay greater attention to Nigeria's internal developments, which affect its ability to partner with the United States. With its other preoccupations, the United States can play only a marginal role in Nigeria. At the time the first edition appeared, there were hopeful developments. Alas, Nigeria faces even greater challenges now, and this edition has two new chapters, one on political developments and the other on the grassroots radical Islamic insurgency in the North called Boko Haram. I close the book with modest policy recommendations as to what the Obama administration might do to support Nigerians working for democracy and the rule of law.

Acknowledgments

I knew nothing firsthand about Africa until the U.S. Foreign Service quixotically transferred me from Geneva to Lagos in 1988. My sole African experience had been a stop at the Dakar airport during a flight from London to Buenos Aires. Once I arrived in Nigeria, however, Ambassador Princeton N. Lyman patiently introduced me to Africa's fascinating complexities. Ever since, he has been a source of encouragement and wisdom.

Nigeria: Dancing on the Brink is based on what I saw and heard from Nigerians during two tours, one in Lagos, the other in Abuja, during which I traveled all over the country. But what did it all mean? Talking with those who know Nigeria well helped shape my understanding—hence my gratitude to Judith Asuni, Pauline H. Baker, Anthony Carroll, Frances D. Cook, Thomas P. Furey, Louis W. Goodman, Russell Hanks, Jean Herskovits, Michael Higgins, Darren Kew, Peter M. Lewis, Deirdre LaPin, Matthew Page, John Paden, James Sanders, Sue Ann Sandusky, Patrick Ukata, and Jacob Zenn.

I wrote the first draft of *Nigeria: Dancing on the Brink* during the 2007–8 academic year at the Division of International Studies at the University of Wisconsin, Madison. I am grateful to Dean Gilles Bousquet for the invitation to Madison and for the hospitality after I arrived. I am grateful, too, for the support of Cynthia P. Williams and Cheryl Woodards. I benefited enormously from discussions with Wisconsin faculty members and students. I am particularly grateful to Crawford Young, who commented on the entire manuscript, and to Paul Beckett for his insights. Jeff Keepman, my student assistant, performed yeoman service in tracking down references and the multiple other chores associated with starting a book.

Draft in hand, I attended the 2009 International Politics Summer School at Oxford where I benefited from the insights of Nicholas Cheeseman and my fellow students in his Africa seminar. I am grateful to all of them.

At the Council on Foreign Relations (CFR), I am indebted to Richard N. Haass, James M. Lindsay, and Janine Hill for their support, encouragement, and criticism. Patricia Dorff was my guide to the new world of publishing. Lisa Shields and her team in Communications were a great help. Irina Faskianos organized my discussion of draft chapters with CFR members across the United States. I am grateful to her and the chairs of those sessions: Cedric Suzman in Atlanta, Walter C. Carrington in Boston, Richard Joseph in Chicago, Edmond J. Keller in Los Angeles, Susan B. Levine in San Francisco, and Ted Van Dyk in Seattle. Richard Joseph read the entire manuscript and provided detailed comments, for which I am deeply grateful.

CFR-sponsored study groups of Africa experts in New York and Washington provided feedback on specific chapters. I am grateful to the chairs, Mahesh K. Kotecha in New York and Pauline H. Baker in Washington. Other participants in New York were Tade Aina, Jonathan E. Berman, Craig Charney, Helima L. Croft, Donald B. Easum, Jean Herskovits, and James R. Silkenat. In Washington, they were Herman J. Cohen, Peter M. Lewis, Olav Ljosne, George E. Moose, Sola Omole, John N. Paden, and James Sanders. Many of them subsequently provided written comments on the manuscript. I am indebted to them all.

I am grateful to Susan McEachern, Carrie Broadwell-Tkach, and Janice Braunstein at Rowman & Littlefield for their crucial role in bringing this book to publication.

Finally, Asch C. Harwood, my research associate at CFR, was an editor and critic of intelligence, patience, and diligence leavened with humor and good cheer. His suggestions and ideas made *Nigeria* a better book. Ably assisted by our intern, Mohamed Jallow, Harwood also ensured that the facts were checked and the formats were followed.

For the second edition, Asch Harwood, Emily Mellgard, and Jay Chittooran did yeoman service in editing and fact checking, for which I am grateful. I have also corrected factual errors in the first edition, which readers kindly called to my attention.

Among Nigeria's friends and observers, there are differing perspectives on the country's history and situation. Those who have so patiently provided me with help and advice do not necessarily share my point of view or agree with my conclusions. The responsibility for the interpretations and judgments in this book is entirely my own.

Introduction

An Ambassadorial Credential Presentation

Within two days of being sworn in as the U.S. ambassador to Nigeria in Washington, DC, I arrived in Abuja, Nigeria's capital, on May 20, 2004.[1] Five weeks later, I presented my credentials as U.S. ambassador "Extraordinary and Plenipotentiary" to Nigeria's President Olusegun Obasanjo at Aso Villa, the presidential executive compound. Until that ceremony, like any other newly arrived ambassador in Nigeria, I was a diplomatic nonperson: no public appearances or media and no official calls. As the chief of protocol told me, "Your Excellency, you must be very, very quiet."[2]

For elite Nigerians, ceremony and protocol are valued and enjoyed. Under diplomatic practice codified in seventeenth-century Europe, an ambassador "stands in" for the chief of state and outranks all others of his nationality in the host country, except when his own chief of state visits.[3] Nigerians are punctilious about observing this protocol and often treat ambassadors with exaggerated courtesy. So they saw an ambassadorial credentials presentation as the appropriate occasion for an affirmation of Nigeria's international importance.

The practice in Nigeria is that groups of three to five ambassadors on the same day sequentially present to the president their own chief of state's letters of credence and recall,[4] their "credentials." The new Russian ambassador was already waiting when I arrived in Nigeria, and when our Dutch colleague came, the Ministry of Foreign Affairs and the president's office set an early date for the three of us.

On the big day, the ministry collected me in a black Mercedes with a friendly protocol officer charged with the care of foreign diplomats. A separate Mercedes collected my accompanying party. The vehicles arrived at our chancery forty-five minutes late. I had already learned that, while diplomats must always be on time, Nigerian official events almost never were during the Obasanjo presidency.

The three ambassadorial parties joined up at the Officers' Mess adjacent to Aso Villa. We waited together in a large room in need of a paint job. African proverbs flashed across a huge television screen. The lighting was fluorescent, and out-of-date wall calendars were the principal decoration. The furniture was reminiscent of Chairman Mao photo ops. "Minerals" (soft drinks) were set out on a table, accompanied by a bottle opener but no ice. A soon-to-be ambassadorial colleague observed that the scene "was not what he had expected." After an hour or so of waiting together, each ambassador and his party in turn were driven to Aso Villa for individual credentials presentations. The contrast to the Officers' Mess was complete. The crisp uniforms and salutes, the national anthem played beautifully by a military band, presentation of arms, and inspection of troops would have done proud the Fort Myer Headquarters of the Military District of Washington. Leather and brass had a high shine. Nothing needed paint or a scrub. I found the same dignity and military precision inside the hall of the Villa, where the actual presentation took place. The president and the foreign minister were magnificent in full Yoruba[5] regalia, while we diplomats looked like pin-striped sparrows. Following the ceremony so reflective of the military essence of this ostensibly civilian government, each newly accredited ambassador had a private conversation with the president. It was all over by noon, and then I went to work in public. That afternoon I gave my first press conference.

NIGERIA'S PRESIDENCY SINCE THE 1980s

I had first served in Nigeria in the late 1980s as political counselor to Ambassador Princeton Lyman and subsequently to Ambassador Lannon Walker.[6] At that time Lagos was the capital, and optimism was in the air among the embassy's contacts,[7] despite the overthrow of Nigeria's Second Republic in 1983 by the military, failing oil prices, and high inflation. In its mood of optimism and hope, both the diplomatic community and Nigerians themselves failed to see that military governance was creating an increasingly ubiquitous culture of corruption that would sap Nigeria of its developing potential.[8]

The president at that time was Ibrahim Babangida, who had come to power in a military coup in 1985 and ruled until he stepped down in 1993 under pressure from elements within the military. In the late 1980s, he appeared to be actively pursuing the restoration of civilian, democratic government and a concomitant economic reform initiative called the Structural Adjustment Program (SAP). Babangida's SAP owed much to reform programs advocated by the World Bank and the International Monetary Fund. Nevertheless, he could assert that his SAP was indigenous and not imposed by outsiders. Babangida's SAP appeared to accomplish what a conventional structural adjustment program of an international financial institution would do. For example, it largely eliminated the black market in Nigeria's currency. Today, Babangida is blamed by Nigerians for the destruction of the country's middle class by his austerity measures during a period of relatively low oil prices. Then, however, among Nigeria's friends in the diplomatic community, the disquiet was only that another military coup might oust Babangida and set back both the political and economic reform programs.[9] There was widespread confidence in his intentions, as long as he could hold on to power.

This optimism proved premature. Nobody foresaw that Babangida would annul the democratic elections of 1993, regarded as the most free and fair in Nigeria's history.[10] In hindsight, observers from Nigerian civil society and the diplomatic community overestimated Babangida's commitment, and that of the military, to democracy. The reality proved to be that the military and the security services intended to remain in charge. Through his annulment of the 1993 elections, Babangida paved the way for the dictatorship of General Sani Abacha, who took power in 1993 and ruled until his death in 1998. Abacha made Nigeria an international pariah, in large part because of well-publicized human rights abuses.

Abacha's military dictatorship was followed by a transition to an ostensibly civilian government under Olusegun Obasanjo in 1999. Obasanjo served for two terms, leaving office in 2007. By the time I returned to Nigeria as ambassador in 2004, fourteen years after I had left, the country had been portraying itself as a civilian democracy for five years. The judicial murder of enemies of the regime that so marred Nigeria's international reputation under Abacha had ended.[11] Politically motivated jailings had also declined. Yet the national mood seemed pessimistic.[12] The population looked visibly poorer than I remembered. Personal security seemed worse.[13] In 1998–99, Nigerians and foreign friends believed that a democratic, civilian government would transform the country. By 2004, the new political dispensation had apparently changed less than had been hoped for in the heady days after Abacha's suspicious death.[14] In fact, there was significant continuity of personnel between the Abacha regime through Obasanjo's Fourth Republic (1999–2007) and into the subsequent Yar'Adua administration.[15] Under President Goodluck Jonathan (2010–present), however, this continuity was largely broken when he surrounded himself with his fellow Ijaws rather than those with a military background.

While Obasanjo's government was civilian and democratic in outward appearance and the military had "returned to the barracks," the president surrounded himself with retired military officers. The "command" political culture at Aso Villa resembled a military installation, as illustrated by our ambassadorial credentials presentation ceremony.

Obasanjo's style and quality of governance appeared to be little different from the military norm since the end of Nigeria's devastating 1967–70 civil war.[16] Widespread, popular disillusionment with the federal government would subsequently manifest itself in the low voter turnout for the elections of April 2007, probably the least credible in Nigeria's history, as well as the indifference to the electoral outcome. The contrast between Nigerian apathy and Kenyan popular protests over electoral fraud only eight months later was noteworthy.

The presidential elections of 1999 and 2003 that put Obasanjo in power and kept him there had been flawed. On the heels of the 2003 election, the president (or his close associates) started work to repeal constitutionally mandated term limits so he could retain the presidency through rigged elections for another term, to start in 2007. The prospect was that he would remain in office indefinitely, the "Robert Mugabe" option, as it was sometimes called.[17] If a regime is democratic if it holds credible elections in which the opposition has some chance of winning or taking office, Obasanjo's Nigeria was far from democratic, and the possibility of change anytime soon appeared remote.[18] This has remained the reality under his successors, Umaru Yar'Adua and Goodluck Jonathan. Nonetheless, as of 2013, Nigeria's government has been civilian, if not democratic, for fourteen years. This is by far the longest period in its history without overt military rule.

THE TRADITION OF ZONING IN NIGERIAN POLITICS

One of the most important features of Nigerian politics since the restoration of civilian government has been the informal arrangement of power alternation known as zoning. Zoning was a tacit agreement among the country's elite to alternate the presidency between candidates from the Christian South and Muslim North. Although not without its problems, zoning did provide a degree of political stability, and it guaranteed access to oil revenue by all the major elite groups.

This consensus fractured after the death in office of the Northern Muslim president Umaru Yar'Adua. Yar'Adua's vice president, southerner Goodluck Jonathan, finished Yar'Adua's term and should have stepped aside at the end of that term to return the presidency to a Northern candidate. Instead Jonathan ran again in the 2011 elections. Those elections, unduly praised by the international community because polling was marginally better than it had been in 2007, were characterized by heightened appeals to ethnic and religious identities and by an avalanche of money intended to manipulate the political process.

The result—a Jonathan victory by a large margin—was not seen as credible by many in the North. Worse, the election campaign released the religious and ethnic genie from the political bottle—the zoning system—that had contained it, leading to the country's worst outbreak of post-electoral violence since the civil war of 1967–70. This was characterized by tit-for-tat ethnic and religious killings. Leading up to the 2011 elections, Presidents Yar'Adua and Goodluck Jonathan had made strides in dissipating the insurgency in the oil-rich Niger Delta that had arisen over poverty and the political process. In that region, an amnesty program established by President Yar'Adua and continued by President Jonathan largely co-opted the old leadership of the loosely organized insurgency known as the Movement for the Emancipation of the Niger Delta (MEND). But neither president established a political process that would address the deep sense of grievance in the region over the distribution of oil revenue and environmental depredations. Consequently, a new cycle of violence now appears to be in its early stages, and the oil production that provides the fiscal glue holding the country together is already beginning to decline. Oil theft is again on the upswing.

Taking advantage of this sense of grievance and anger in the North over Jonathan's reelection, the radical Islamic group Boko Haram escalated its war on the Nigerian political economy. The Jonathan administration responded by treating Boko Haram solely as a security threat, not as a political challenge stemming from widespread poverty and marginalization. The heavy-handed response by the military and the police further alienated many in the North.

In these developments, we see the unintended legacy of Olusegun Obasanjo's presidency. His efforts in 2005 and 2006 to retain power indefinitely (by amending the constitution so that he could run for a third presidential term) failed because of elite and popular opposition to a "president for life." Subsequent to this failure, he handpicked as ruling party presidential and vice presidential candidates Umaru Yar'Adua, who was visibly ailing, and Goodluck Jonathan, a political novice. It was widely believed that with a weak president and vice president, he could continue to exercise power, if from behind the throne rather than on it. However, drawing on the powers of presidential incumbency, both Yar'Adua and Jonathan were able to throw off much of Obasanjo's influence. He could not rule from behind the throne.

Following Yar'Adua's predictable death, it was Jonathan's refusal to step aside in the presidential elections in 2011 and wait for the South's turn in 2015 that fractured the traditional elite consensus. The resulting political vacuum provided the space for Boko Haram to flourish and for renewed violence in the Delta.

CHALLENGES TO GOVERNANCE

Governance, let alone democracy, faces grievous, structural challenges in Nigeria. The country is home to about 250 different ethnic groups, each with its own language.[19] The three largest, the Hausa-Fulani, the Yoruba, and the Igbo, together are less than two-thirds of all Nigerians. Estimated at 170 million, the population is growing and urbanizing rapidly; a majority may now live in urban areas. (Greater Lagos, with a population estimated by former state governor Bola Tinubu and numerous demographers at 17 million, is already one of the largest cities in the world.) In terms of usual measurements of income, Nigerians are very poor, with wealth from oil concentrated among a miniscule number of *ogas* or "big men." The country is bifurcated between Christianity and Islam (similar to other African states bordering the Sahel such as Sudan, Côte d'Ivoire, and Ghana), with the South predominately Christian and the North primarily Muslim.[20] Both populations are religiously militant, and the explosive expansion of Christianity in the North has contributed both to destabilizing the Islamic political and social status quo and encouraged the emergence of the radical Islamist movements.

Nigeria has been run by competing and cooperating elites supported by their patron-client networks, ethnic interests, big business, and the military. With the withdrawal of the military from active governance, none of these sectors has been strong enough to impose a specific direction in governance. Consequences include a chronic inability of the political system to address Nigeria's problems and the progressive alienation of non-elite Nigerians. With honorable exceptions, the behavior of Nigerian elites has too often been self-interested, lacking a national focus, oriented almost solely toward short-term advantage, and distorted by competition for oil wealth. Whether military or civilian in form, the government has reflected the paralysis of the country's fragmented elites. This paralysis has at least provided for political stability and kept ethnic and religious rivalries under control, even if the power alternation that was an essential part of that stability ended with Jonathan's capture of the presidency in 2011.

Control of the federal government means access to oil riches by the political victors and their clients. That encouraged the elites to hang together, and motivated the Ijaw around Jonathan to cling to power as long as they could. Many Hausa-Fulani[21] told me that the North's escalating poverty has resulted from its declining access to oil starting after the loss of the presidency to Olusegun Obasanjo, a Southern Christian Yoruba, following the death of the Northern Muslim Kanuri, Sani Abacha. Northern elites recaptured the federal government with the rigged elections of 2007 and the presidency of Umaru Yar'Adua. But they lost it again when Yar'Adua died in May 2010 and the vice president, Goodluck Jonathan, a Christian Ijaw from the South, became president. Jonathan's presidential victory in 2011 appeared to many Northerners to mark their exclusion forever from the highest political office.

After the 2011 elections Nigeria appeared to be balkanizing, with national identity continuing to decline in the face of a renewed interest in ethnicity and religion. Federal institutions that in the past were a source of national pride were also in decline: the civil service, the educational system, the youth service corps, even the military. However, ethnic, religious, and political pressures are unlikely to lead to a formal split of the country. A more realistic alternative is that federal authority will continue to decline, while power will gravitate to the state governments. The danger is not the emergence of an independent Biafra or a Nigerian version of South Sudan with defined boundaries. Rather it is of national fragmentation in the context of hollowed-out or irrelevant federal institutions with the prospect of localized ethnic and religious conflict dominated by warlords.

Northern elites had played an important role in selecting Obasanjo to be the chief of state following Abacha's death. Their understanding had been that the presidency would revert to the North following one term. That did not happen in 2003, when Obasanjo, with some Northern support, manipulated the ruling political party to remain in office for a second term. By the time of my arrival as ambassador more than a year later, much of the Northern establishment felt politically marginalized and aggrieved by Obasanjo. Many feared that he intended to remain president for the rest of his life. That concern was a theme of Nigerian politics throughout my ambassadorial assignment.

In the oil-rich Niger Delta, there is also a deep sense of grievance against the Nigerian establishment in general and President Obasanjo in particular. The population has benefited little from the billions of dollars produced by oil and resents the federal government's insensitivity to its traditional patterns of local governance. And politicians are not above facilitating and exploiting Delta violence for their own, narrow interests.

RELIGION AND VIOLENCE

Popular alienation and a fragmented establishment have contributed to Nigeria becoming one of the most religious and, at the same time, one of the most violent countries in the world. In 2010, the International Society for Civil Liberties and the Rule of Law estimated that the number of those killed since 1999 "outside the law in Nigeria might have increased to 34,000." That total included 160 political assassinations and over 13,500 killings resulting from ethno-religious and intercommunal violence.[22] Earlier, Human Rights Watch, a respected nongovernmental organization (NGO), had estimated that at least 11,000 deaths between 1999 and 2006 in Nigeria could be attributed to religious and ethnic strife.[23] Officials usually understate such mortality statistics. One NGO-affiliated observer, referring to the sectarian conflict near Jos in 2010, told me to multiply the official statistics by at least five to approximate the true number of victims.

During the Obasanjo years, as it is today, violence was often sparked by competition for scarce resources such as water and land, or it was the result of a struggle between competing elites. It was exacerbated by weak governments that too often lacked the means or the will to control its spread. While most of the violence has appeared to be indigenous, Nigerian security operatives have argued in open court that there were al-Qaeda affiliates in the North. Some police told me that they were fearful that popular support would grow for radical Islamic groups such as Boko Haram that are opposed to the present system and possibly linked to al-Qaeda. Umar Farouk Abdulmutallab, the Nigerian arrested in Detroit for a failed terrorist attack on Christmas Day in 2009, is representative of what some in the security services feared, though he apparently had had no contact with al-Qaeda when he was in Nigeria. Since 2009, as Boko Haram violence has escalated and become more sophisticated, Nigerian security services reiterate the theme that it is part of the international jihadist movement rather than an essentially indigenous revolt against the Nigerian political economy.

The grievances that feed Boko Haram pose conundrums for official U.S. policy makers. The United States must calibrate its official relationship with a corrupt Nigerian political class and a federal government that is removed from the people it governs and is mishandling the challenges of the North. But the Goodluck Jonathan administration continues to remain closely aligned with Washington on a host of African issues of mutual concern. That requires a good official relationship between Washington and Abuja that undercuts the credibility of American claims to support democracy and good governance.

Even leaving aside Boko Haram–related incidents, officially sanctioned violence is shocking in its magnitude and reflects the weakness of government institutions. For example, then–acting inspector general of police Mike Okiro boasted to the press in mid-November 2007 that, during the three months he had been in office, 785 "suspected armed robbers" had been killed by the police, without any judicial procedure. He also said that, during the same period, an additional 1,600 suspected armed robbers had been arrested and charged.[24] It is widely believed that the police kill thousands each year, a reason they are so hated and so frequently targeted for murder by Boko Haram. Okiro's boast lends credibility to that belief. The Network on Police Reform, a nongovernmental organization, found that between 2008 and 2012, the security services had extra-judicially killed 7,198 persons.

STRATEGIC PARTNERS?

Despite growing alienation between the Nigerian people and their increasingly impotent government, by 2004 Nigeria had become crucial to the long-term well-being of the United States. It supplies almost 11 percent of U.S. imported oil, and its natural reserves are huge.[25] Some American policy makers have become intrigued with the possibility that Nigeria and the Gulf of Guinea could help reduce significantly U.S. dependence on Middle Eastern oil.[26] Consecutive American administrations have seen Abuja as the indispensable U.S. diplomatic and security partner in Africa on issues of mutual concern, including opposition to military coups, the ending of the civil wars, and the restoration of peace and stability in conflicted regions. Nigeria has long been one of the largest contributors of troops to UN peacekeeping missions around the world. The American expectation has continued, at least until recently, to be what it had been for more than a decade: that Nigeria would carry the water on African regional issues where the United States could not or would not.[27] Hence, Obasanjo's, Yar'Adua's, and Jonathan's friendship and cooperation have been seen as valuable, even indispensable. That era is coming to an end as Nigeria, bedeviled by Boko Haram and the prospect of renewed insurrection in the Delta, plays a reduced international role.

The bilateral relationship has become much more than oil, peacekeepers, and regional diplomacy. Beginning even before Nigeria's independence in 1960, American citizens interested in Africa had started to organize nongovernmental organizations. The Africa-America Institute, for example, was founded in 1953. Its mission has been African capacity building through advanced academic education and professional training. The African Studies Association was organized in 1957 to promote scholarly and professional interest in Africa. Over the next half-century, numerous other nonprofit organizations with a focus on Africa emerged. In addition, foundations with a worldwide reach, such as the MacArthur Foundation and the Carnegie Corporation, became active in Africa. While American organizations advocating for Africa have remained smaller than many of those focused on other parts of the world, they have come to constitute an important thread in the texture of America's relationship with Africa. They are particularly significant with respect to Nigeria because many of them focused on it their aspirations for the entire continent.

Nigeria and the United States have come to influence each other in myriad ways. I found the United States to be the standard against which many Nigerians judge their own country and find it wanting. They associate the United States with modernity, democracy, and respect for human rights. Nigerians regularly said to me that it is the "least racist" of the Western democracies and that "at least 1 million" of them had lived in the United

States and returned home. During their American sojourns, some acquired American spouses, linking extended families in the two countries. Popular culture from New York and Los Angeles is ubiquitous in Lagos. Nigeria's legions of unemployed university graduates dream of a U.S. visa.

That Nigeria also influences American culture is often only weakly acknowledged in the United States. Yet Fela Ransome-Kuti's "Afro-beat" and other musical styles of Nigerian origin have influenced American pop. Nigerians have also played successfully in the National Basketball Association and the National Football League, an important source of Nigerian national pride. Christianity also provides strong, sometimes controversial, linkages. The retired Anglican primate of Nigeria, Archbishop Peter Akinola, is a bitter critic of the Episcopal Church in the United States over gay and lesbian issues and has encouraged schism within that denomination, thereby sharpening the differences between American liberal and conservative approaches to Christianity.

Over the next decade the Nigerian factor in American life is likely to increase. Whatever the exact figure, Nigerians in the United States estimate their diaspora to be at least 2 million. It has been a successful immigrant community characterized by entrepreneurship, strong family ties, and an emphasis on education. Socially, it is generally conservative and evangelical or even Pentecostal in outlook.[28] It is just starting to flex its muscles in local American politics.

If it addresses successfully its governance and security issues, Nigeria has the potential to become an important U.S. trading and investment partner beyond oil and gas. Nigeria is currently the locus of the greatest U.S. investment in Africa. That is almost solely in the petroleum industry, and at present the level of nonoil and oil-related bilateral trade is low. The poverty of most of Nigeria's people has limited their ability to buy American-produced consumer goods, and the Nigerian government's trade and investment policies, often arbitrary and inconsistent, have discouraged American business. Nigerian enterprises have been slow to take advantage of U.S. programs, such as the African Growth and Opportunity Act (AGOA),[29] designed to promote exports to America. The causes are complex but include the Nigerian elite's preoccupation with oil and related enterprises to the exclusion of other economic possibilities. With the exception of the oil sector, the political, security, social, and cultural bilateral relationship is more developed than the economic.

Nevertheless, for the international business community, Nigeria is much less problematic than for those observers interested in democracy and security. The economy of the Lagos-Ibadan corridor is booming, and the size of the potential Nigerian market is huge. For investors in London, New York, or Johannesburg, the central reality is not an Islamic insurrection and a weak government. It is that Nigeria is poised to follow in the economic footsteps of China or India. For them, Boko Haram and governance issues are marginal.

Dense international linkages also mean that failing domestic institutions can have a global impact. Diseases that incubate in Nigeria, where the public health system has all but collapsed, could spread worldwide remarkably quickly. The 2003 state-government suspension of the World Health Organization (WHO)–sponsored polio vaccination campaign in the North led to the disease's re-infection—from Nigerian sources—of nineteen other countries as far away as Indonesia.[30] Against the backdrop of Boko Haram and radical Islam, the vaccination campaign was in trouble again in 2011, 2012, and 2013 because it was associated with the widely hated Abuja government and with the West. Avian influenza was ubiquitous, and the first human deaths from the disease in Africa were in Nigeria, as well as the probable first case on the continent of its human-to-human transmission. If the virus mutates so that it spreads readily from human to human in Lagos, its new form could likely be present in New York City within a week.

OLUSEGUN OBASANJO

Western friends of Africa thought they knew Obasanjo well from his first period as military chief of state from 1976 to 1979. He claimed as his legacy that he was the first African military ruler to voluntarily relinquish power to a civilian government.[31] While out of office, and before military chief of state Sani Abacha jailed him in 1995, he traveled extensively on behalf of the Commonwealth Eminent Persons Group in search of a strategy for a democratic transition in South Africa. He was also a principal of the African Leadership Forum, promoting democracy, good governance, and anticorruption. His imprisonment by Abacha followed by plots to have him murdered lent him an aura of potential martyrdom for democracy. Obasanjo has publicly stated that he survived only through God's grace and the publicizing of his plight by former president Jimmy Carter.

As president of Nigeria, Obasanjo publicly valued his relationship with President George W. Bush. In the aftermath of the September 11, 2001, terrorist attacks on New York and Washington, he was the first head of a major African state to come to Washington to show his support. Hence, it is no surprise that when Obasanjo was chairperson of the African Union, from 2004 to 2006, the Bush administration turned to him on a range of African issues. Some, abroad if not at home, believed he had the potential to fill Nelson Mandela's shoes as Africa's preeminent statesman.[32]

Yet Obasanjo's administration did little to address the threats to integrity of the Nigerian state: the North's alienation from his government, the Delta's anger over the distribution of oil revenue, and the pervasive poverty of most

Nigerians. Instead, his surrogates sought to amend the constitution through bribery and intimidation so he could remain in office for at least another presidential term. He participated in and supervised three corrupt elections, each worse than the last, in 1999, 2003, and 2007. While he created anticorruption agencies, he used them against his own political enemies. Nevertheless, their establishment bodes well for the future if they evolve into mainstays for the apolitical enforcement of the law.

When Obasanjo's attempt to retain presidential power by running for a third term failed, he succeeded in making his handpicked choices, Yar'Adua and Jonathan, the president and the vice president in 2007. Yar'Adua, the governor of the small state of Katsina dominated by a single ethnic group, the Hausa-Fulani, and with only a very small Christian minority, was shy, retiring, and in poor health. He had assiduously avoided the limelight. Nobody would have predicted that someday he would be president of Nigeria. Obasanjo could have had every expectation that he would remain in power behind the scenes. While Obasanjo was to be disappointed by Yar'Adua's growing independence the longer the latter held presidential office, for more than a year after Yar'Adua's inauguration the former president continued to exercise influence over the Nigerian government from his position as chairman "for life" of the ruling party's Board of Trustees. From his party perch, Obasanjo has successfully deflected calls by civil society for his indictment for personal corruption. In 2010, when Yar'Adua was dying, Obasanjo supported the National Assembly's extra-constitutional designation of Jonathan as acting president.

UNDERSTANDING NIGERIA

It has been unwise of friends of Nigeria to downplay internal developments in this perplexing country. Too often, American policy makers have alternated between ignoring or deprecating the "Giant of Africa" on the one hand and exaggerating its alleged achievements on the other. Then, too often, they turn their attention to Darfur or Somalia or whatever humanitarian crisis is being featured on network television that day.

More generally, the assets the international community devoted to understanding Nigeria have been limited. Consecutive American administrations have underresourced the American embassy in Abuja and the consulate general in Lagos for a generation. Because of realistic security concerns, the world's last remaining superpower has no diplomatic presence north of Abuja, despite the fact that Kano and Maiduguri are centers of important changes in Nigerian Islam, with possible implications for West Africa as a whole. Diplomatic travel in the Niger Delta continues to be curtailed because of an insurrection and expatriate kidnappings.[33]

The American foreign policy establishment's current preoccupation with Nigeria, particularly in the departments of State and Defense, is new. This turnabout is a direct outgrowth of the concern that Boko Haram might be, or might become, linked with international terrorist movements and thereby a threat to the United States. This has occurred with other radical Islamic groups such as al-Shabab in Somalia, al-Qaeda in the Islamic Maghreb (AQIM), and the Yemen-based al-Qaeda in the Arabian Peninsula.

Nigeria has been the African country of greatest importance to the United States, even as that reality was overshadowed in Washington by other concerns. Accordingly, during my thirty-eight-month tenure as ambassador, my goals were to strengthen democracy and the rule of law, reach out to Muslims and to civil society, encourage a resolution of the disputes in the Delta, and facilitate cooperation between the United States and Nigeria on regional issues and the global war on terrorism. The embassy managed an assistance program focused on health, education, democratization, and women that cost almost half a billion dollars per year by 2007. Though it was one of the largest U.S. assistance programs in sub-Saharan Africa, on a per capita basis it was the smallest, such is the size of Nigeria's population in comparison with other African nations. Subsequent to my departure, the relationship between the U.S. and Nigerian militaries has become closer. Nevertheless, the size of U.S. military assistance remains small compared with U.S. expenditures in Nigeria on health programs related to HIV/AIDS and malaria.

Much of the international community has overestimated its ability to influence through gentle persuasion the pace of democratization and social and economic development in Africa. In addition, there are many competing priorities for American attention, and for many years Nigeria has not received the sustained attention it deserves from senior policy makers. The bloodshed in southern Sudan, Darfur, and Somalia and the fate of Liberian ex-dictator Charles Taylor held their attention, not the shortcomings of elections preparations in Nigeria. As with former military chief of state Babangida, there was too much U.S. wishful thinking about the degree of Nigeria's political development and Obasanjo's personal commitment to fighting corruption and conducting free and fair elections. Worse, perhaps, American observers convinced themselves that Obasanjo and the Nigerian oligarchs wanted change and only needed U.S. expertise to bring it about, another echo of the U.S. view of Babangida in the 1980s. Too often, foreign friends of Nigeria preferred cheerleading to analysis. Instead of a healthy skepticism, there was a predisposition to take self-serving Nigerian official statements at face value, despite consistent embassy reporting to the contrary. Too many American observers saw Obasanjo as a beacon of hope on the bleak African landscape rather than as the military politician he proved to be. The United States provided substantial technical assistance for the country's 1999, 2003, and 2007 elections. But I am aware of no Bush administration high-level conversation with Obasanjo insisting that those elections must be credible, free, and fair.[34] The Obama administration made democracy and good governance its top African priority and, in view of the failure of 2007, reiterated regularly the necessity for improved Nigerian elections in 2011.

DANCING ON THE BRINK

In the meantime, Nigerians have mastered the art of dancing on the precipice without falling over. One bright spot is in the Lagos-Ibadan corridor. There, the economy is booming, spurred in part by foreign investment and encouraged by capable state governments. This vibrant economic activity owes much to capital generated by oil. Returnees from the Nigerian diaspora in the UK and the United States are often its public face. Unfortunately, the boom has had little impact on the general population, and levels of absolute poverty nationwide may have actually increased over the last five years. Especially in the North, chaos and state failure are gaining ground, and the same could happen in the Delta.

Many of Nigeria's elite are still convinced that Nigeria is "too big to fail." Such a view encourages their unwillingness to address the issues that so trouble the country and may even promote their irresponsible behavior, such as the manipulation of ethnic or religious conflict for their own narrow political ends, over which they soon lose control. Successfully addressing issues potentially fatal to the state will require a political process that has the confidence of the Nigerian people. Since the restoration of nominally civilian government in 1999, that opportunity thus far has been lost.

Yar'Adua's foreign minister, Ojo Maduekwe, in a 2005 public lecture given while he was secretary of the ruling party, spoke of the possibility that Nigeria could become a failed state.[35] Such a catastrophe would likely involve anarchy or bloody warlord competition leading to refugee flows that could destabilize the other, much smaller states in West Africa. Democracy and the rule of law, fragile in Africa at best, would be set back profoundly, if only by the negative example Nigerian failure would provide other multiethnic, religiously divided states wrestling with poverty and underdevelopment. The international community would face a much greater humanitarian disaster than in Darfur or Somalia, if for no other reason than Nigeria's population is exponentially larger.

Nigeria's importance requires greater U.S. engagement, not so much with the Abuja government as with civil society. It is in the long-term interest of the United States to do more to directly support those Nigerians and institutions that are working to establish a democratic polity and the rule of law. In the short term, this approach risks cooler relations with official Abuja. But closer U.S. identification with those working for democracy and the rule of law will, in the long run, strengthen the foundations of the U.S.-Nigeria bilateral relationship. Many Nigerians understood President Obama's declining to visit Nigeria during his 2009 presidential visit to Africa as a sign that the United States was distancing itself from the Nigerian government and its corruption. They took Obama's flyover as a gesture of support for those working for democracy and the rule of law. Secretary of State Hillary Clinton's speeches to Nigerian civil society during her subsequent visit were also taken as highly supportive of democracy and the rule of law. On the other hand, many Nigerians are puzzled by the Obama administration's embrace of Jonathan, himself the beneficiary of rigged elections as vice president and designated acting president by the National Assembly through an extra-legal process. The administration's stance appeared to contradict its principled support for democracy and the rule of law, and its over-eager embrace of the 2011 elections probably undermined American credibility in the North.

It is Nigerians who must build democracy and the rule of law in their own country. Their foreign friends can help only on the margins. It is axiomatic that credible elections and adherence to the rule of law would change for the better the relationship between Nigerians and their government and would be the best guarantee against state failure. At present, Nigeria ranks perilously high ("bad") on the Fund for Peace's Failed State Index and near the bottom (also "bad") of the United Nations Development Programme's Human Development Index. Whether Nigeria will survive as a democratizing state that can lift its people out of poverty or join the list of failed states must be of direct, immediate concern to the international community. Yet it is the Nigerians who must move the dance back from the brink and fulfill the country's image of itself at independence as a huge multiethnic nation governed according to democracy and the rule of law.

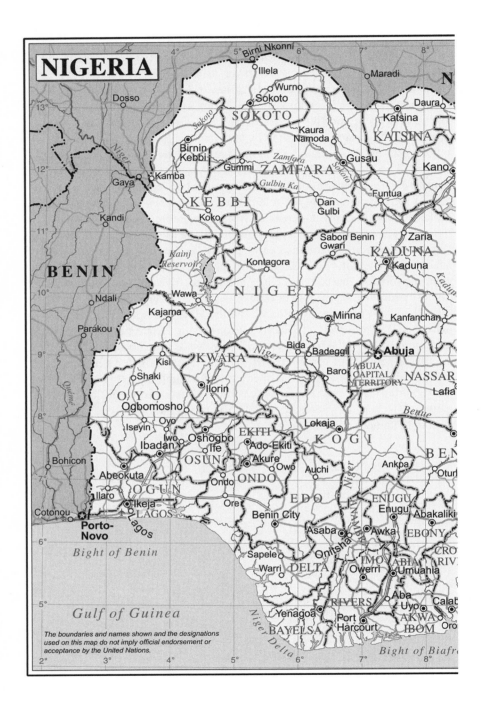

NIGERIA

The boundaries and names shown and the designations used on this map do not imply official endorsement or acceptance by the United Nations.

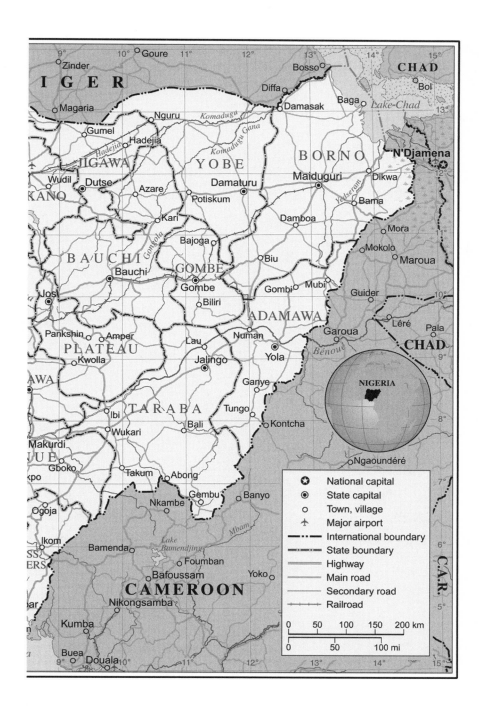

Chapter One

"Un Peu d'Histoire"

The *Guide Michelin* often includes for its readers a note called "un peu d'histoire" ("a little history") for a place to be visited. It provides just enough historical background to enhance the visitor's experience. That is the inspiration for this brief review of Nigeria's history from the colonial period to 1999. It provides the context for Nigeria's bilateral relationship with the United States and its current internal crises that are putting the country at risk for state failure. It also introduces many of the principal players in the Nigerian drama, as there has been little generational change in the country's leadership since the end of the civil war in 1970.

Parts of the current territory of Nigeria were the location of culturally rich, premodern civilizations. There was a succession of Hausa-Fulani, Yoruba, and other empires before the British completed their conquest of the present territory of Nigeria. The most recent was founded in 1804 by Usman Dan Fodio and became the Hausa-Fulani sultanate of Sokoto, which still exists today. Ancient civilizations and empires shaped the peoples where they held sway. But none of the early empires incorporated into a single political unit all of the territory of the present state—nor was there an overarching cultural unity among the hundreds of different ethnic groups that were later found in the state of Nigeria. The nation and the concept of a Nigerian national identity are British creations without indigenous roots.

For administrative expediency in 1914, the British cobbled together their Nigerian colony out of three disparate but adjacent territories they had acquired over a century as they moved inland from the Gulf of Guinea and the older Lagos colony. As was generally the case with colonial rule in Africa, British decisions about governance were made without reference to the indigenous populations. The British goal was to keep the costs of governance as low as possible. There appeared to be little consideration of the consequences

1

of amalgamating highly diverse populations and cultures into a single political entity. No one then was thinking that the territory would be sovereign and independent within a half-century.

The name "Nigeria" is credited to the colonial editor of the *Times* of London, Flora Shaw, who later married the new entity's first governor, Lord Frederick Lugard. The name stuck. But the new name was not accompanied by any sense of national unity. Other than the army, there were no real national institutions until near the end of the colonial period when the British established a small number of high-quality secondary schools that drew their students nationwide and a handful of university colleges. To make matters worse, governance was also varied within the new country; British rule in the North was very different from that in the South. In the North, the British ruled through the emirate system that had preceded them. To maintain the emirate system, they discouraged Christian missionary activity, which meant no Western schools in most areas and few hospitals or clinics. That, in effect, perpetuated much of the North's premodern backwardness. The political union did allow individuals from the South, especially traders and mechanics, to settle in the North. But they tended to settle in separate, unassimilated communities, sowing the seeds for postcolonial tensions and pogroms that continue to this day. Obafemi Awolowo, the revered Yoruba leader during the independence period, famously cautioned that Nigeria is a "mere geographical expression," not a nation.[1]

The British yoking together of so many different peoples into a huge state, and the Harold Macmillan government's subsequent decision to bring it to independence as a single entity in 1960, shaped the future of about a fifth of Africa's sub-Saharan population. While Awolowo's observation is still true for many of its inhabitants, the state of Nigeria has provided a political structure for hundreds of different ethnic groups to live together that has endured for more than fifty years. It has enabled its elites to play a significant role on the African and even the world stage that would have been closed to them if their base had been a smaller nation. Nevertheless, with civil war and repeated military dictatorships, an ethnically and religiously divided population, and a state identity created by the former colonial power, Nigeria has danced on the brink from its very beginning.

THE BRITISH AND STATE BUILDING

From the seventeenth century, the British traded along the Gulf of Guinea with indigenous middlemen, many of them members of the Ijaw ethnic group, first for slaves and subsequently for palm oil, an essential lubricant for the machines of the early Industrial Revolution. They made no permanent settlements other than small trading stations along a malarial coast. Westminster's hands-off approach changed when the breakup of the Oyo empire in Yorubaland resulted in a regional instability that was bad for trade. The British annexed Lagos in 1861 to protect their commercial interests and made it a royal colony. Lagos and subsequently the adjacent Yorubaland became the first of the three building blocks of colonial Nigeria. At the instigation of a private company aiming to facilitate trade, in 1878 the Congress of Berlin recognized British occupation of Oil Rivers,[2] then the center of palm oil and now Nigeria's petroleum patch, with the unenthusiastic acquiescence of Westminster. The Oil Rivers Protectorate thereby became the second building block.

The third building block, the Middle Belt and the North, came from the British defeat of the sultan of Sokoto and his emirs during the first decade of the twentieth century. British motives for the conquest of the North were a mix of commercial, strategic, and altruistic concerns, including suspicion of French intentions in that part of the Sahel and the desire to suppress the slave trade: by the turn of the twentieth century, the sultanate of Sokoto was probably the largest slaveholding empire remaining in the world.

These three blocks were profoundly different, though Yorubaland and Oil Rivers came to share a greater openness to Western influence, including Christianity and Western education, than the North. The latter remained within the orbit of emirate-based Islam. Such were the differences between the North and the rest of Nigeria that, despite the 1914 formal amalgamation, the British in effect governed Nigeria as two separate entities until the period of pre-independence constitution making.

Except in the Lagos colony, shortages of personnel and Westminster's insistence on running its empire on the cheap dictated that the British rule in Nigeria through native institutions and personalities as much as possible. In Northern Nigeria, where the caliphate had been strong, Lugard promoted a policy of indirect rule more systematically than elsewhere in Nigeria. He looked to preserve the defeated caliphate's traditional Islamic institutions. To that end, Lugard discouraged or banned Christian missionary activity in caliphate territory and recognized traditional Islamic sharia law, though he prohibited inhumane punishments such as mutilation or stoning.[3] One consequence of this approach was that the Sokoto caliphate has continued to evolve from its establishment by Sultan Dan Fodio in 1804 to the present despite its defeat.[4] Indirect rule preserved much that was precolonial and premodern in Northern Nigeria. Few missionaries meant little Western education and a resulting technological underdevelopment. The number of Northern university graduates at the time of independence was miniscule.

By contrast, the South lacked indigenous state structures, especially in village-centered Igboland, so the British introduced more Western institutions and structures. Christianity was widely adopted by the population, and British missionaries promoted modern education and business practices that led to comparative prosperity. It also fed ethnic resentments. The Igbo early mastered Western business practices and technology and became small traders and mechanics. They settled throughout the country. Their success was often resented, and they were sometimes dismissed as "the Jews of West Africa." In other areas, local politicians interacted successfully with the colonial administration. Those most successful became "big men," wielding significant power in their localities. The territories once part of Yorubaland and the Oil Rivers increasingly became part of the modern world, while the North remained largely premodern and apart. By the time of independence, Northern political leaders were acutely aware of their economic underdevelopment and feared Southern and Western domination in a united, independent Nigeria.

During the colonial period, the British presence in Nigeria remained thin. For example, in 1900, in the aftermath of the defeat of the Sokoto caliphate, the British ruled Northern Nigeria with 6 civilian administrators, 120 officers, and an indigenous army of 2,000 ex-slaves. The population of the North was then approximately 10 million.[5] When the colonial administration amalgamated the police forces of Northern and Southern Nigeria in 1930, the combined strength consisted of eighty-five British officers and some additional African chief inspectors to police a population of perhaps 20 million.[6]

Nigeria has the largest number of ethnic groups of any state in Africa. The Hausa-Fulani, Yoruba, and Igbo are the largest. Smaller ethnic groups are especially numerous in the southern part of the country and the borderlands with the North, the latter territory often called the Middle Belt.[7] As the twentieth century advanced, the British turned to federalism as the best means of responding to Nigeria's multiethnic reality. The pre-independence result was a British-created federation that consisted of three regions corresponding to the building blocks of colonial Nigeria: the North, with its capital at the new city of Kaduna and dominated by the Hausa-Fulani; the East, with its capital at Enugu and dominated by the Igbo; and the West, with its capital at Ibadan, dominated by the Yoruba. Lagos, the political and commercial capital, enjoyed a special status separate from the regions. Each region and Lagos enjoyed substantial autonomy.[8] This structure had the unintended consequence of ratifying the preeminence of the three big ethnic groups at the expense of the numerous minority tribes.[9] Specific regions, rather than the nation as a whole, became the theater of politics. In each of the three regions, postcolonial political leaders came from the largest ethnic group. Yet the three big ethnic groups that dominated politics constituted less than two-thirds of the federation's population.[10]

Because there was never European settlement in Nigeria, racism was less overt than in eastern or southern Africa, though it infused the colonial system as it did everywhere else in Africa. Even as late as 1960, few Nigerians had ever seen a white man or woman. That was a very different reality from their fellow Africans living in "settler" colonies such as Kenya or South Africa. National movements dated from the aftermath of World War I and strengthened after World War II, especially in the southern half of the country. Their leaders were mostly journalists or from the labor movement. But independence movements were never nationwide, nor were they genuinely mass movements such as the Indian National Congress. In the North, fear of domination by the more economically advanced and modern South contributed to a lack of enthusiasm for independence even at the end of the colonial period. There was never the violent agitation for independence comparable to, say, Kenya or even the Gold Coast (Ghana). [11]

After India and Pakistan became independent in 1947, Nigeria was by far the largest of Britain's overseas possessions. Oil and gas began to be exported commercially in the 1950s, and the potential size and importance of the oil and gas reserves was recognized by the colonial government.

Nevertheless, responding to winds of change inimical to colonialism and in the context of the Cold War, by 1960 the British government determined that the national interest would best be served by withdrawing from its African empire—less than fifty years after it had amalgamated Nigeria—rather than face challenges like those of France in Indochina or Algeria. That wider decision took little account of Nigeria specifically but was influenced by the rapid growth of independence agitation in the Gold Coast. [12]

Having reached the decision to shed its African empire, the Macmillan government pursued an independence process designed to generate maximum Nigerian goodwill and to protect British economic and security interests. Its goal was a government structure that took into account, and was acceptable to, both the Big Three and the myriad smaller ethnic groups. The final constitutional arrangements also recognized the profound cultural differences between the North and the rest of the country. For example, the legal and constitutional position of women in the North remained much inferior to their sisters in the rest of the country. As part of the horse-trading among Nigerian politicians leading to independence, the North abandoned sharia in the criminal domain.

The British-chaired pre-independence roundtables, conferences, and negotiations became the occasion for the emergence and articulation of the "Nigeria Project" (as the Nigerian elites called it). The vision was of a huge nation of numerous ethnic groups and religions united by democracy, pursuit of economic development, governance according to the rule of law, and the occupation of an important place on the world stage. The British and indigenous elites intended for a friendly Nigeria to provide Africans with a seat at the table with other great powers. After the 1967–70 civil war, with the dissolution of the three regions and their replacement with numerous states, a corollary emerged that Nigeria would be a federal entity providing equal access for all to educational opportunities and public-sector employment.

The concept expanded later to encompass high federal offices and the natural resources under government control, the greatest of which was oil. This corollary is now labeled "Federal Character." The hope and expectation was that the ideals of the Nigeria Project and Federal Character would become a focus for a common identity that would supersede ethnic or religious identification. Yet, despite these laudable aspirations, in the run-up to independence, day-to-day politics remained ethnically and regionally based, rather than national. [13]

INDEPENDENCE AND ITS AFTERMATH

On Independence Day, October 1, 1960, Nigeria's prospects looked good. In place was a Westminster system of government to be conducted according to the rule of law by political leaders of high quality, including Abubakar Tafawa Balewa, Ahmadu Bello, Obafemi Awolowo, and Nnamdi Azikiwe. Its federal system was designed to accommodate the country's many ethnic groups and its religious divisions. Nigeria was already the breadbasket of West Africa, and its nascent industries boded well for future economic development. Its level of material development was said to be on par with that of South Korea or Malaysia. And that was before the country began to exploit its immense oil and natural gas reserves. Many Nigerians today recall the late 1950s and the early 1960s as a golden age. In 1963, Nigeria became a republic, with Azikiwe as the first president.

Nigeria's prospects were promising, but by 1967 the country had danced over the brink and was in the midst of a civil war. The unraveling of the national dream was the result of unresolved ethnic rivalries combined with competition for spoils that the new system could not contain. Fractious politics and military coups destroyed parliamentary institutions and the rule of law. Assassinations eliminated some of the leadership that had guided Nigeria to independence. Those murdered in the first coup of 1966, conducted by army majors, included the federal prime minister, Sir Abubakar Tafawa Balewa; the premier of the Western Region, Chief Samuel Akintola; and the premier of the Northern Region, the sardauna of Sokoto. Four of the five ranking senior military officers from the North were also murdered. There was popular suspicion that the coup was an Igbo conspiracy. General J. T. U. Ironsi, who emerged as chief of state following the first coup, was an Igbo. A subsequent, Northern countercoup later in the same year resulted in the tit-for-tat murder of many prominent Igbos, including Ironsi. [14]

The coups unleashed widespread and bloody pogroms against Igbos and Christians who had settled in the North. They resulted in the mass flight of Igbos back to Igboland. Under the leadership of Chukwuemeka Ojukwu, hitherto an officer in the Nigerian army, the Igbos seceded from the federation and established the independent, predominately Christian state of Biafra. The Igbos faced a dilemma. Their new state included numerous tribal minorities reluctant to support Biafra. The ensuing war between the national government in Lagos and Biafra was a struggle between two military dictatorships: Nigeria, led by General Yakubu Gowon, chief of state after the successful coup against Ironsi, and Biafra, led by now-General Ojukwu.

Biafra received some support from France, Portugal, and South Africa and, allegedly, from some private oil interests. The United Kingdom and the United States supported a unified Nigerian state, as did the Soviet Union. All three "great powers" tried to minimize their official involvement. However, a vocal minority in the West supported Biafra, whose government made shrewd use of visual propaganda. The Biafra war was the first time that Western media portrayed the widespread starvation of African children. A visibly starving Igbo child became the Western image of the civil war. In the United States, especially among university students, the cause of Biafra was linked with opposition to the war in Vietnam and support for the domestic civil rights movement. The large number of Igbo students enrolled in American universities at that time ensured that Biafra remained an important campus cause.

Gowon reestablished Nigerian unity through the conquest of Biafra, completed in 1970. General Olusegun Obasanjo, subsequently twice chief of state (1976–79 and 1999–2007), received the surrender of the last surviving Biafra radio transmitter. Estimates of war dead, including combatants and civilians, range from five hundred thousand to one million.[15] There was no postwar pogrom against the Igbos, as had been widely feared, and Gowon promoted national reconciliation through his "no winners, no losers" campaign. Nevertheless, there was an unspoken consensus among the political class that no Igbo could ever be the chief of state. This was new; Azikiwe, the nation's first president, was an Igbo.

The preservation of national unity through dictatorship was costly in terms of governance. The Nigerian army grew temporarily from some 10,000 to 250,000, and the war made the military thereafter a major political player. The new primacy of the military promoted a "barrack culture," an essentially authoritarian approach to political issues that was inimical to political compromise and the rule of law. The war was also the occasion for the megacorruption, especially with respect to government contracts, that has so disfigured Nigeria ever since. Kleptocracy was new.

COUPS D'ÉTAT

After the Biafra war, military coup followed military coup. In 1975, Gowon was ousted by General Murtala Mohammed, who was subsequently murdered a few months later. His deputy, Obasanjo, ruled until 1979, when military-sponsored elections produced the civilian administration of President Shehu Shagari, which lasted until 1983.

Under a new constitution drafted by the military, the Shagari administration was characterized by violent, fractious politics and widespread corruption. Shagari was overthrown late in 1983 by General Muhammadu Buhari. Austere in personal manner, he had little tolerance for corruption by the political elites. Accordingly, Buhari was overthrown by General Ibrahim Babangida in 1985 with the elites' apparent approbation.

Babangida pursued economic and political reforms in an atmosphere of rampant corruption and growing repression. During his rule, Nigeria joined the Organization of the Islamic Conference and at the same time established diplomatic relations with the state of Israel. He organized Nigeria's best elections ever in 1993 as the cap to his political reforms. However, probably under military pressure not to accept Yoruba businessman Moshood K. O. Abiola's presidential electoral victory, he then annulled those elections. Already on course to leave office, he stepped aside for a caretaker, civilian administration headed by Ernest Shonekan. General Sani Abacha pushed out Shonekan a few weeks later and subsequently ruled in an increasingly brutal way until he died in 1998. During his administration, there were numerous human rights abuses, including the judicial murder of Ken Saro-Wiwa, a Niger Delta activist and writer. Nigeria became an international pariah. The Commonwealth expelled it, the Canadians closed their high commission in Lagos, and the United States reduced the size of its U.S. Agency for International Development (USAID) mission.[16]

Throughout the post–civil war period, the self-enrichment of individual military officers was made possible by immense oil revenues combined with weak institutions of governance little accountable to the public. Militarization and centralization of government authority went hand in hand. Power in Nigeria became much more centralized than its "federal" label would indicate.

Starting with Gowon, successive military governments attempted to manage ethnic and religious conflicts by creating an ever-increasing number of states: there are now thirty-six, plus the Federal Capital Territory, most of which depend for their funding on the federal government.[17] A specific ethnic group predominates in many of these states, with each of the Big Three dominating several of them. Paradoxically, this "morselization" has increased the power of the federal government because so many of the states are utterly dependent on it for nearly all of their revenue. Most state and local governments raise little revenue through taxation under their own authority. Few Nigerians pay direct taxes of any kind.

More positively for political stability, the proliferation of new states has provided additional arenas for elite competition and enrichment and has helped forestall Nigeria's splitting into multiple, antagonistic states, as nearly happened during the Biafra war.

The military, while portraying itself as a unified caste in comparison with chaotic civilian society, in reality became internally a cockpit of rivalry and intrigue. But the military dictators always paid at least lip service to the restoration of democracy and the return of the military to the barracks.

THE "MEN ON HORSEBACK" DEPART?

After Abacha's sudden and suspicious death in 1998, military government was exhausted and discredited at home and abroad, and international opinion strongly favored governance through ostensibly democratic institutions. A coterie of senior active duty and retired military officers with a few associated businessmen organized a transitional government. They established the current, ostensibly civilian Fourth Republic, in part because some of them feared a popular uprising or agitation for a new constitutional convention that they would not be able to control.[18] The military resuscitated the Second and Third Republic's constitution, based on Washington's presidential system.[19] (Westminster-style parliamentary governance, which had been adopted at independence, had lost credibility in the run-up to the civil war.)

This interim military government also resurrected a national, progressive-conservative party, now called the People's Democratic Party (PDP), as a vehicle for ending overt military rule on terms that would protect officer-specific interests. Within the PDP, the military interim caretakers and their civilian associates manipulated the selection of retired general Obasanjo as its presidential candidate. Although he had been a focus of Abacha's personal paranoia, jailed, and nearly murdered, Obasanjo was part of the military system. He was also a Yoruba, as Abiola had been, and a Christian alternative to the sequence of discredited Muslim military dictators. He had an excellent international reputation and was well placed to end Nigeria's pariah status. Obasanjo's primary presidential opponent, Olu Falae, was also a Yoruba Christian. But, though he had served in the Babangida government as minister of finance, he was a civilian.[20] Obasanjo was elected president in 1999, though the elections were so blatantly rigged by the military and its allies that former president Jimmy Carter left the country rather than endorse them in his capacity as the leader of the National Democratic Institute's election observation team. Others, while acknowledging the fraud, saw the elections as a step forward because they ended overt military rule.[21]

Since then, according to its constitution, the Nigerian Fourth Republic has been governed by theoretically equal executive, legislative, and judicial branches. The states and the 774 local government authorities (LGAs) have substantial powers and responsibilities and together receive just under half of the nation's oil and gas revenue under a complicated formula administered through the federal government's Federation Account in the spirit of Federal Character. Nevertheless, the states that produce the oil receive a special, additional allocation, with those having much larger budgets than the rest.

The military imposed the Fourth Republic's constitution and its institutions without any popular referendum. At the time, this lack of any democratic process occasioned little comment because the constitution closely followed its Second and Third Republic predecessors that had resulted from broad consultations within the political elites. However, by the time of the 2005–6 political crisis associated with President Obasanjo's efforts to retain power, members of the National Assembly were lamenting to me that the constitution's democratic credentials had not been strengthened by a popular referendum.

The transition of 1998–99 resulted in some, if limited, evolution in Nigeria's governance. Active duty military no longer occupied as by right cabinet positions, nor were the governorships their monopoly. The return of civilians to these positions widened the forums for elite competition within the traditional context of power sharing that dated from the transition to independence. The chief of state, no longer a serving army general, was an ostensibly civilian president who, in fact, only observed as convenient the forms of civilian government while he retained the substance and the command culture of military rule without its more flagrant human rights violations.

Abroad, in the heady days after Abacha's death, the Fourth Republic was welcomed by democratic, international opinion leaders largely uncritically as a fundamental break with the discredited military past. However, after more than a decade of the Fourth Republic, too much of Nigeria's governance has remained much the same as it had been under the military and, in certain aspects, the colonial period. It is true that the state-sponsored, egregious human rights violations of the Abacha period ended. However, politically motivated violence remained high. Most Nigerians remained powerless and voiceless, despite the efforts of civil society organizations, including the Anglican and Roman Catholic churches; intellectuals such as Wole Soyinka and Chinua Achebe; professional organizations such as the Nigeria Bar Association; and the mostly free print press and independent radio. As for the country's oil wealth, only a tiny elite benefited from it, and it did not lead to broad economic and social development. After fourteen years of civilian rule, many of the country's social statistics remained comparable with the worst in West Africa. And too many Nigerians, especially in the North, did not have enough to eat.

Chapter Two

If Nigeria Is So Rich, Why Are Nigerians So Poor?

Poverty is about people; statistics only attempt to measure it. Nevertheless, the standard social indicators used by international aid agencies confirm that most Nigerians are very poor. This reality can be obscured by rising national income statistics and rapid economic growth that have misled many American observers into thinking the country is richer and more developed than it really is. Under the Fourth Republic, this ghost prosperity has been mostly the result of high world oil prices and has had minimal impact on most of the people. Rising national income has not promoted the development of the country. To the contrary, the standard of living for many people has fallen, possibly below the levels that existed at Nigeria's independence in 1960. According to official statistics, from 2004 to 2010, those living on less than $1 a day grew by nearly 20 percent.[1]

In 2008, the National Population Commission (NPC) of Nigeria, in cooperation with relevant federal agencies and with funding and technical expertise from the U.S. Agency for International Development (USAID) and international consultants, carried out demographic, health, and education surveys. Despite the notorious unreliability of most Nigerian statistical surveys, these met USAID standards and provided the best overview of the Nigerian social reality.[2]

According to the NPC data, the national average for under-five mortality is about 157 deaths for every 1,000 live births. In comparison, the United States has an under-five infant mortality rate of 8 deaths per 1,000 births, and Liberia, until recently a war zone, has 133 deaths per 1,000 births. Moreover, a huge regional discrepancy exists in Nigeria, between a high of 222 deaths per 1,000 births in the Northeast and a low of 89 deaths per 1,000 births in the Southwest.

Nationwide, while there has been some improvement, the complete immunization of children sits at 22.7 percent. As with under-five mortality, the Nigerian nationwide statistics mask huge regional differences with a low of 6 percent in the Northwest to a high of 42.9 percent in the South.

The NPC study also reports that regional differences persist in the median age of first marriage of females, which has a relationship with fertility rates. Lower age of first marriages often means more children. Overall, the median age at first marriage of women is 18.3.[3] For rural women, it drops to 16.9 years. The Northwest has the lowest median age at first marriage of 15 years as opposed to the Southeast, which has a median age of about 23 years. The NPC also finds a positive relationship between female education and female age at first marriage. As educational attainment increases, so does the age of first marriage. For women with no education, the median age of marriage is about 15 years, but for the group with a secondary education, the age is 22.

Poverty is so pervasive throughout Nigeria, particularly in the North, that the researchers conducting the Nigeria Living Standards Survey (NLSS) in 2004 lowered their metric for poverty (poverty line) to a per capita income of 26,000 naira,[4] approximately $200, far below the international standard of less than $1 per day for measuring poverty in the developing world. The reduction was mandated by the Olusegun Obasanjo administration. Nevertheless, the figures were still bad. Over half of the population (54.2 percent) lived below the revised poverty line. In the Northeast and Northwest, a disturbing 72 percent of the population lived in poverty. Even in the comparatively prosperous South and Delta regions, 27 percent and 35 percent of people fell below the poverty line. Had the NLSS used a more realistic definition of poverty, some 90 percent of the population would likely have been counted as poor.[5] Contributing to these remarkable statistics has been the death of the middle class dating from the collapse of the last oil boom in the 1980s. It has largely been replaced by the so-called respectable poor: educated, white-collar Nigerians without the means to maintain a middle-class standard of living.[6] There is anecdotal evidence that a middle class is again emerging, especially in Lagos, with its roots in small enterprises, telecommunications, and information technology. It is often defined as including those with an income of $2 a day or higher. It remains a very small percentage of Nigeria's enormous population, even though it may number in the millions in absolute terms. Recent World Bank income statistics[7] show that Nigeria's gross domestic product (GDP) per capita not only is much lower than the average in sub-Saharan Africa but also has decreased below what it was 1970.

The concentration of Nigeria's vast oil wealth in the hands of a small group of wealthy Nigerians has made income distribution among the most unequal in the world. A knowledgeable executive from a New York bank commented to me that there were at least 115 Nigerian U.S.-dollar billionaires.

Nigeria's widespread poverty can clearly be seen in the faces of its children, and not just in the North. According to the NPC, many of Nigeria's children are stunted, meaning they have below average height to age ratios, indicative of chronic malnourishment. Access to medical treatment and quality of care is equally bad. Emergency care does not exist in many parts of the country. Shortages of pharmaceutical and medical supplies are endemic. In 2010, the chairman of the Pharmaceutical Society of Nigeria's Lagos branch complained that, according to UN statistics, the Nigeria health system ranked 187 out of 191 nations.[8]

In 2007, only one medical facility (South African owned) provided Western standards of care in Nigeria. Located in Lagos, it catered primarily to oil company expatriates. As a subscription enterprise rather than fee for service, the rates were too high even for the U.S. mission. Instead, its American employees and family members were evacuated to London or Johannesburg for any complicated or invasive treatments. While I was ambassador, the mission provided medical insurance for locally engaged staff, but it was sufficient only to cover the expenses of local medical services.[9]

I saw the social consequences of severe poverty during my August 2004 visit to Kano, the predominately Muslim state in the north of the country. Kano state is home to 9.38 million people and the city of the same name numbers just under 4 million according to the dubious 2006 census. Kano is one of the most ancient cities in Nigeria, surrounded by mud walls sporting wonderful gates and old quarters that look all but impenetrable. It had been the southern terminus of the trans-Sahara overland trade for a millennium and an important manufacturing center, especially for textiles and leather goods. Even as late as the 1980s, it had been a cosmopolitan city, home to large Lebanese and South Asian communities, and even a small number of Europeans and Americans.

Since then, however, there has been a significant exodus of these groups. Local community leaders confirmed that the Lebanese who remained or who had recently arrived were poorer than those who had departed.[10] There continues to be direct air links to Europe, Egypt, Lebanon, and the Gulf States, but a manager of a European airline told me in 2007 that the profit is no longer in passengers but rather in shipping Nigerian goat hides to the Italian shoe industry.

Compared with the Kano I knew well in the late 1980s, its appearance now is marred by litter, especially plastic bags and empty plastic bottles. Throngs of street children, dressed in rags, beg for change and food. Many of them appear to be five or six years of age, though some are perhaps older than their appearance suggests because of malnutrition. They swarm at Kano traffic lights, markets, and "go-slows" (traffic jams), and outside restaurants and gas stations. Muslim interlocutors told me that most are from rural areas: their parents send them to Kano to study Islam under a malam (Islamic teacher) from sunup to about 10:00 a.m. Thereafter, they beg, carrying small plastic bowls that look like Tupperware. The money they collect goes to the malam to pay tuition, but they keep the food they are given. For that reason, my staff and I would buy loaves of bread to give them rather than money.

Estimates of the number of students in the largely unregulated Islamic schools in the North run into the millions. Most children enrolled in these schools are focused on memorizing the Koran. Only a minority have a curriculum that includes modern science, mathematics, or English. Most graduates have no skills that prepare them to participate in a modern economy.

Those who are able to survive (a pediatrician in Kano in 2005 remarked to me that often they did not live long) band together into religio-criminal gangs, available for hire to sack churches or restaurants where alcohol is served. More recently, they have been recruited as foot soldiers for Boko Haram and other radical Islamic movements at war with the Nigerian political economy. In return for their services, these children receive between 50 and 150 naira each.[11] During the 2003 riots against the Miss World Beauty Pageant in which the name of the Prophet Mohammed allegedly had been defamed, "street urchins" in Kaduna received payment to take "to the streets killing, maiming, and destroying anything human or material which in their judgment constituted a clog on the wheels of Islam."[12] In Kano, as is usual in Nigeria, the identity of the "hidden hand" manipulating "urchins" for political purposes is unclear, but there is credible speculation that *ogas* use them against their rivals. In addition, some of my interlocutors expressed concern that they are also used by shadowy radical Islamic elements, including Boko Haram, outside the control of the city's traditional elites.

Members of the city's Islamic establishment expressed their uneasiness to me about the growing numbers of homeless children. Traditionally, children studied with an imam or malam in town during the season when there was little farmwork to be done in the countryside. The alms they collected in town to pay for their education represented, in effect, a transfer of resources from the richer urban areas to the poorer countryside. It relieved the parents of the burden of feeding their children at times when food was especially scarce.

Inequality between the rich and poor has increased significantly because of uneven access to oil wealth, exacerbated by a decline in agricultural productivity in the countryside. Poor, rural families are sending their children to urban areas in increasing numbers for longer periods to relieve the pressures of high birthrates and scarce food. Yet the decay of the city's industrial base has, at the same time, exacerbated urban unemployment and made it much more difficult to absorb rural poor.

OIL: THE BLESSING BECOMES A CURSE

Up until the 1970s, the North exported groundnuts and cotton, which were the basis of Kano's prosperity. With the arrival of the oil economy and during the decades of military government, investment in agricultural and transportation infrastructure fell. Hence, the export of agricultural products became more difficult. For example, groundnuts and cotton were then transported by railways, which have since deteriorated. Roads are also decaying. State commodity marketing boards destroyed their own industries by levying requirements beneficial to special interest groups. I was told that the cotton marketing board required that cotton be stored in plastic sacks—to the benefit of the plastic manufacturers. But the plastic bags deteriorated, and plastic fragments intermixed with the cotton fiber, reducing its value on the international market. Meanwhile, petroleum produced staggering wealth for a tiny elite. Nigeria became one of the earliest victims of the "resource curse."

A traditional ruler[13] was scathing in his criticism about the increasing poverty and shortcomings in agricultural investment, which could help relieve some of the growing tension. He blamed the failure of the agricultural sector on "oil and bad government." Rapacious and corrupt officials systematically robbed the poor by promoting self-aggrandizing economic policies. Agriculture and infrastructure were starved for investment in favor of the oil economy. In contrast, he recalled the days, not so long ago, when Nigeria was a breadbasket for the rest of West Africa.

The collapse of the region's energy production has also hurt Kano's industries' international competitiveness by forcing manufacturers to produce their own power with generators and expensive diesel fuel. In 2012, Nigeria's installed electricity capacity was about 4.35 gigawatts; by comparison, South Africa—with a population less than a third of Nigeria's—has a capacity of over 40 gigawatts. At the same time, Nigerians have literally been left in the dark. The country's net energy generation decreased from 23 billion KWh in 2004 to 18.8 billion KWh in 2009. Over the past decade the Nigerian government has spent about $16 billion to restructure the power sector, but most of the money has disappeared through corruption.[14]

An important consequence of this failure has been the actual deindustrialization of the country. Manufacturers told me that they were involved in two businesses—manufacturing and power generation. "Every time the generator comes on, the profits go off," I was frequently told. The reduced fuel subsidies of 2012 have made diesel fuel more expensive in real terms. All four of Nigeria's petroleum refineries are usually offline, and government efforts to privatize them have failed. An overvalued naira also priced Nigerian nonpetroleum exports out of the world market by making them too expensive abroad. As a result, the North's textile industry—which once employed hundreds of thousands—has become almost entirely defunct.

Dysfunctional government trade and investment policy, such as failure to invest in transportation infrastructure to bring goods to market and to supply the energy for manufacturing, has also made Nigerian industries vulnerable to international competition, especially from Chinese manufacturers.[15] "Traditional" Nigerian fabrics are now produced in China, smuggled into Nigeria too often with official connivance, and then sold more cheaply in the markets than those of local manufacture.

The government's seemingly unpredictable and arbitrary banning of certain imports has not only created a black market in many goods but also undermined foreign investor confidence in Nigeria. With the exception of Lagos where a middle class may be emerging, the growing impoverishment of most Nigerians has reduced their ability to purchase consumer goods. Many are too poor to buy even razor blades or shampoo. This lack of consumer demand further hinders the Nigerian economy's ability to provide jobs to slow the population's increasing impoverishment.

Another prevalent explanation is that the North had no oil. However, Federal Character mandates that the federal government redistribute oil revenue to the Northern states. Furthermore, many Northern businessmen have been involved in the oil and gas industry, especially in providing support and ancillary services, which helps to redistribute oil wealth from the Delta region to the Northern states. As many Southerners rebutted, the Northern-dominated military dictatorships ensured the flow of oil wealth to the North. The crushing poverty of the North reflected the drying up of those flows under the Obasanjo government, they said.

The World Bank viewed part of the problem as stemming from volatile and unpredictable sources of government revenue resulting from fluctuations from oil prices.[16] After the civil war and during the decades of military rule, a growing national debt negatively impacted government spending on investment and social services and frightened away foreign investors. Inflexible exchange rates undermined the competitiveness of Nigerian-produced goods in both domestic and international markets. In effect, Nigeria failed to respond to the volatility of oil prices. It spent too much when oil prices were high, cut back too slowly when oil dropped, and borrowed to make up the difference. To make matters worse, according to the World Bank, this spending was often conceived hastily, leading to waste and corruption.[17]

However, others I spoke with saw the problem as a result of not necessarily mismanagement and corruption but rather the lack of foreign investment flowing into the Nigerian economy. Reflecting the "statist" mind-set I often encountered, this was viewed as the fault of international governments and not of domestic economic mismanagement. Time and time again, business leaders, politicians, bureaucrats, and citizens alike asked me why the U.S. government did not "direct" American companies to invest in Nigeria. They argued such investment could support democracy and strengthen the country's leadership role in West Africa, all desirable U.S. policy objectives in the region. When I would reply that the U.S. government had no such power over American companies, their look was incredulous—nor did they like to hear that Nigeria was competing with the rest of the world for scarce capital and that American investors tended to place their money where they thought it would be safe and profitable.

Apart from the lack of infrastructure and power shortages, Nigeria's business climate is less than hospitable. According the World Bank's 2012 Doing Business survey, Nigeria landed in the bottom third at 131 out of 183 economies surveyed.[18] In each area discussed, Nigeria scored poorly and in many cases scored more poorly than it did in earlier surveys.[19] Furthermore, while Nigeria does have formal procedures for doing business, they are often bypassed in lieu of informal arrangements and corrupt practices. These realities mean that international businesses looking to operate in Nigeria must consider the implications of the U.S. Foreign Corrupt Practices Act, which includes antibribery provisions and mandates certain accounting procedures.

It is no surprise that, outside of oil and gas, American investment in Nigeria has been limited. In a December 2004 speech to the Lagos Chamber of Commerce, I cited as contributing causes the poor personal security environment because of violent crime, the failure of the courts to uphold contracts, and arbitrary trade and investment policies and practices. The deputy governor of Lagos state did not like what he heard. In rebuttal, he said that Nigeria was a "toddler," that it would take "fifty years for Nigeria to get its act together," that the West should not hold Nigeria to such a "high" standard, and that the U.S. government should "encourage" "big corporations" to invest in an "emerging democracy." His arguments were political and sentimental. Others in the Lagos business community gave my speech high marks for "telling us like it is."

Whether under the military or the civilians, the fundamental issue is bad governance. The federal government's economic policies reflect the special interests of those who control it. Accordingly, economic policy is focused on providing short-term benefits to the heads of the patronage networks that dominate Nigerian governance to the detriment of long-term economic development. This results in under-investment in agriculture and the infrastructure to move agricultural products to the market, an overvalued currency, a dearth of energy production for domestic consumption, and often irrational and inconsistent trade and investment policies; in short, bad governance, crony capitalism, and spectacular levels of corruption impoverish the country.

sible arguments for it. Obasanjo successfully persuaded United Kingdom prime minister Tony Blair to sponsor Nigerian debt relief in conjunction with his Labour government's "Year of Africa." Debt relief appealed to Labour's pro-developing world political base and provided a theme for the United Kingdom's G-8 presidency and European Union chairmanship.

The finance ministries of creditor nations, however, often viewed debt relief with skepticism. Nigeria did not meet the usual international criteria because of its oil revenue and because it was not subject to International Monetary Fund conditions that often accompanied it. There were also questions about the depth of the government's commitment to reform. Foreign ministries and the diplomatic community in Abuja led by the U.S. embassy,[20] on the other hand, were in favor of debt relief as a gesture of support for what was still seen as the post-1999 "democratic dispensation" and for Nigeria's peacekeeping role in West Africa. Americans held little Paris Club debt. But there was U.S. Treasury concern that debt relief for Nigeria could be cited as a precedent by other countries asking for relief where much of the debt was held by Americans. The principal Nigeria creditors were European, led by the British.

In the end, and despite rancorous disagreements among the involved agencies, the White House imposed an interagency policy in support of debt relief for Nigeria. Abuja spokespersons, from the president on down, assured foreign interlocutors that the money saved from interest payments would be used for socially responsible purposes.

There was, however, Nigerian domestic opposition to debt relief. Some, already suspicious that Obasanjo was seeking to remain in power indefinitely, wanted to deny him a domestic political victory. Other critics wanted Nigeria just to repudiate the parts of the debt they considered odious, which, after all, had mostly been acquired by discredited military governments. And still others were skeptical about what would happen to the money saved from interest payments. They feared it would end up in *oga* pockets or in political campaign chests, especially Obasanjo's, rather than being spent on infrastructure, health, and education. In the end, the creditors never extracted meaningful guarantees from the Nigerian government as to how the money saved from debt relief would be spent.

Despite such opposition, Obasanjo carried the day, at home and abroad, with the strong political support of Blair as well as from Washington and Paris, underpinned by the credible, technical arguments of Okonjo-Iweala. The final agreement negotiated was better than the alternative of default for creditors and good for Nigeria. Paris Club members received about $12.5 billion from Nigeria and forgave $18 billion. Nigeria rid itself of most of its external debt and gained access to international credit markets. Even the Nigerian people may have benefited. In 2007, a cabinet minister told me that

funding for women's literacy programs in the North came from funds released by the termination of Paris Club debt service payments.

Obasanjo and Okonjo-Iweala had sold debt relief not only on economic
arguments but also as a means to support democracy in Nigeria. So for many
of those who worked for debt relief for Nigeria, the rigged 2007 elections
were a betrayal. A year before those elections, in June 2006, Okonjo-Iweala
was demoted to foreign minister with no public explanation. Three months
later, she resigned (or was fired) and returned to the World Bank as manag-
ing director, a position more senior than the one she had left in 2003.

There is no clear answer as to why the president let go of his finance
minister who had been such a success. On the street, explanations ranged
from presidential pique at the international accolades she was receiving, to
anger that she had opposed his remaining in office for a third term, to veiled,
unsubstantiated accusations by her enemies that members of her extended
family were personally corrupt.[21] Nevertheless, until the end of the Obasanjo
administration, her economic reforms remained in place in broad outline, and
later President Umaru Yar'Adua gave numerous assurances to the international community that he would continue them. A World Bank policy research working paper noted with satisfaction that the formal economy had
improved because of the macroeconomic policies implemented by Okonjo-
Iweala. GDP per capita more than doubled between 2000 and 2005. Nigeria
accumulated foreign reserves valued at $28 billion at the end of 2005, up
from $5.5 billion in 1999, while external debt dropped from $35 billion to $5
billion because of the deal she cut with the Paris Club. Gross public debt fell
from 85 percent of GDP in 2000 to 31 percent of GDP in 2005, while net
public debt virtually disappeared. Nevertheless, the World Bank warned
there was evidence that too much of the government's foreign reserves were
being spent in 2005 and 2006, perhaps with an eye toward the 2007 elections.[22]

While these economic reforms improved the Obasanjo administration's
image abroad, there was little effort to explain to the population what the
reforms sought to accomplish. Given the high level of public distrust of
government, there was too much self-congratulation by Obasanjo's "dream
team," which further undermined the popular credibility of the program. By
the time she fell, Okonjo-Iweala was deeply unpopular with the Nigerian
public who blamed her for reducing fuel subsidies. With unusual candor,
Vice President Goodluck Jonathan publicly acknowledged these realities on
May 12, 2008:

> It is important to emphasize that the performance of the Nigerian economy in
> the past four or more years has been remarkable, with a stable macro-econom-
> ic environment and a growth rate averaging 6.3 percent. . . . However, it is
> obvious that the associated benefits of growth were yet to trickle down to a

large segment of our people. . . . The challenges of poverty, growing inequality, coupled with increasing graduate unemployment remain worrisome. . . . We cannot overflog the issue of infrastructural deficit that continues to becloud our investment climate.[23]

Nigeria's debt burden has grown during the Umaru Yar'Adua and Goodluck Jonathan presidential administrations, though it has not returned to Paris Club levels. But foreign reserve balances have risen and fallen dramatically for reasons that are obscure. By 2012, the country was once again borrowing abroad, and its domestic debt levels were high. Abraham Nwankwo, director general of the Central Bank's Debt Management Office, in October 2012 forecasted that Nigeria would owe around $16 billion to foreign creditors by 2015 and $8.44 billion domestically.[24] Much of the borrowing appears to make up for unanticipated revenue shortfalls. In fact, the fuel subsidy regime, riddled with corruption as it is, consumed about a quarter of the government's revenue in 2012. The government faced a serious security challenge in the North, and the 2012 budget provided $5 billion for containing the Boko Haram insurrection. In addition, the governor of the Central Bank complained that oil theft was costing the treasury more than $10 billion in lost revenue annually.[25] The Jonathan administration faced significant financial challenges that limited its options in dealing with security threats in the North or in carrying out an ambitious development agenda. President Umaru Yar'Adua appointed Lamido Sanusi, a son of a former permanent secretary at the Foreign Ministry and a grandson of the sultan of Sokoto, to be Charles Soludo's successor as governor of the Central Bank. He is a career banker and highly respected in the international community. As governor, he proceeded to reform the banking system by closing some banks, firing the management of others, and generally attacking corruption. The international financial community has applauded his efforts. He has continued in office under President Goodluck Jonathan.

President Jonathan recalled Ngozi Okonjo-Iweala from the World Bank again to be minister of finance in 2011. He expanded her duties and made her the head of his economic team. She sought to reduce the government's current expenditures, which consumed almost three-quarters of the budget. She also sought to expand public works to reduce unemployment. In 2013, she was in the process of establishing a fund in which oil revenue above a particular threshold would be deposited. Those funds would then be invested in the international capital markets as long-term assets. Opposition came particularly from the governors, who would see their states' revenue decrease. As of 2013, it remains to be seen whether she will be successful.

Sanusi and Okonjo-Iweala were popular among the international investment community, but much less so at home. Sanusi, a member of the Northern establishment, was not a part of the predominately Christian and Ijaw inner circle around Jonathan. His banking reforms directly challenged the interests of some of the patronage/clientage networks that dominate Nigeria. He displayed impatience at the National Assembly's efforts to call into question his reforms.

Unlike Sanusi, Okonjo-Iweala continued to lack a domestic power base, and, as was the case under Obasanjo, she was entirely dependent on the authority of the presidency and her own international prestige. The general public blamed her for President Jonathan's highly unpopular effort to remove the fuel subsidy in January 2012. Protests and strikes in support of the subsidies shut down the country for a week. Using a mixture of carrots and sticks, Jonathan eventually prevailed, at the cost of restoring half the subsidy. Though she bore the blame, there is anecdotal evidence that Jonathan did not consult her in advance when he moved to eliminate the subsidy over New Year's weekend. If true, this indicated that she had only limited influence with the Jonathan administration. Nevertheless, her and Sanusi's presence in the Nigerian government went a long way to reassure the investment community of Jonathan's commitment to genuine economic reform.

On the other hand, the Roman Catholic archbishop of Abuja, John Onaiyekan, a cardinal since 2012, observed that the fuel oil subsidy, so disliked by the international financial institutions as a distortion in the market, represented a tiny resource transfer to the mass of the Nigerian people. They otherwise received little or nothing from the current political economy. It was therefore morally justified, "no matter what the World Bank says." The cardinal, expressing a view I found to be widely held in Nigeria, was quoted in the *National Catholic Reporter* as saying, "if I were the Archbishop of New York, I would want to identify the Catholics working in the World Bank and the International Monetary Fund, and I would tell them what is happening in Africa. They may be very fine people, very generous as individuals, but they are operating a system that is iniquitous."[26]

Since 2009 there has been a grassroots, radical Islamic insurrection in the North against the Nigerian political economy called Boko Haram. In the Delta, there are signs of an imminent renewal of an insurgency rooted in popular resentment that the region benefits too little from the oil and gas it produces. In 2012, in particular, Boko Haram undermined the credibility of Jonathan's ability to govern in the North. In the past, a Delta insurgency led to dramatic declines in Nigeria's oil production, which directly impacts state revenue. These insurgencies could potentially slow or even stop Jonathan's reform agenda. Malaysia, Singapore, and Taiwan were at roughly the same level of development as Nigeria in 1960. Except for Malaysia, they had dramatically less than Nigeria in terms of natural resources but managed to break through the constraints of underdevelopment. Nigeria's enormous oil and gas reserves have the theoretical potential to transform Nigeria's economy. However, despite the actions of committed reformers such as Sanusi and

Okonjo-Iweala, that opportunity, so far, has been lost, and many or most Nigerians are as poor as they were at independence.

Chapter Three

Who Runs Nigeria?

The idea is essentially repulsive of a society held together only by the relations and feelings arising out of pecuniary interest. —John Stuart Mill [1]

A Nigerian Roman Catholic cleric commented to me early in 2005 that the same people had run Nigeria by the same kleptocratic rules since the end of the Biafra war, when enormous revenue from oil started seriously to distort traditional governance relationships. Nigerians and the international community, especially the United Kingdom and the United States, he continued, fooled themselves into believing that the return of civilian government in 1999 signaled a break with the past. But that transition did not mark an end to Nigeria's dysfunctional political culture and style of bad governance any more than had independence from the British in 1960. The civilian political class behaved as badly and in much the same way as its military predecessors. Nigerians, he said, had been "excessively patient." He wondered what would happen when that patience runs out, "as it must." Nigerians, he continued, retain the vision of the "Nigeria Project," and that was the baseline by which they found wanting Olusegun Obasanjo and the political system that was dominated by only a few hundred big men competing and cooperating among themselves when necessary for access to the country's petroleum wealth.

Though civilian government had been ostensibly restored, President Obasanjo's inner circle was initially mostly from the uniformed services, the military, the police, and the customs service. His chief of staff, General Abdullahi Mohammed, had been the director of military intelligence for the Nigerian army before Murtala Mohammed's 1975 coup. General Theophilus Danjuma, defense minister and a former chief of army staff, had his eye on the military. General Aliyu Mohammed Gusau, Obasanjo's national security advisor, was his link to the Northern establishment, especially former chief of state Ibrahim Babangida, and oversaw the security apparatus. His chief "fixer," Tony Anenih (who had performed the same function for Sani Abacha), was from the national police, while his vice president, Atiku Abubakar, had had a long career in the customs service.[2] All of them were also involved in private business.

Obasanjo also drew on civilians who had been perennials in military governments. Jerry Gana, who served as minister for information for Obasanjo's first term, held the same position in the Abacha regime. Ojo Maduekwe, minister of transport in Obasanjo's first administration and chairman of the People's Democratic Party (PDP) in his second, had also been a special advisor to Abacha.

Over time, Obasanjo's circle grew also to include a few civilians with no independent power base of their own and therefore particularly dependent on him. Notable were the brothers Andy and Chris Uba, who performed a wide range of staff duties. He also made use of technical experts, including finance minister Ngozi Okonjo-Iweala from the World Bank, and governor of the Central Bank Charles Soludo, an academic who had held posts in the United States. Vice President Atiku Abubakar, using his American connections, recruited a number of these technocrats to government service.

Umaru Yar'Adua's inauguration as president in 2007 marked the first time since the end of the civil war that a civilian succeeded another ostensible civilian as head of state. During his short presidency, he greatly reduced the military trappings. His successor, Goodluck Jonathan, is also a civilian. Hence a pattern of a civilian presidency is in the process of solidifying, with a diminishing of the military character of the presidency under Olusegun Obasanjo.

THE *OGAS,* "BIG MEN"

The power of the president and the federal government, military or civilian, is circumscribed by weak institutions of government in an enormous country fragmented by ethnic and religious divides. In most places, power is exercised through patron-client networks without much reference to the formal structures of governance or to the Nigerian people, to whom the political elite has never been accountable. Especially at local levels, there has been remarkable continuity in how and by whom Nigeria has been run since the end of the civil war.[3]

The wielding of power by oligarchs, "big men," *ogas*, or "kingmakers" is a West African tradition, and elsewhere it has not necessarily been associated with corruption. But the Nigerian style of *oga* domination fueled by corruption emerged from the confluence of the militarization of governance during the Biafra war and immense, sudden amounts of oil wealth. Elite maneuvering and bargaining have become nonstop to access ever-greater amounts of power based on oil wealth. Whoever is chief of state is the biggest *oga* of all.

Though *oga* is a Yoruba word meaning "master," it has entered common usage in Nigeria to describe the ruling oligarchs, and it is used with that meaning here. In most parts of the country, a client will address his patron to his face as *oga*. In the North, however, the word connotes being puffed up with pride or hot air and would never be used by a client to his patron.[4]

During the late colonial period, the Nigerian military was small and of little importance, though like any colonial force, it was probably disliked by the local people. At the time of independence, the Nigerian army's role was mostly ceremonial. Except among some Northern emirate families or a few exceptional individuals,[5] a military career was not the choice of the elite or those who aspired to join it.

None of the "giants" of the independence era—Ahmadu Bello, Obafemi Awolowo, and Nnamdi Azikiwe—were military men. The Ironsi and Gowon coups and the civil war changed that. By the end of a bloody, difficult war, the military viewed itself as having saved the state, and its former professionalism withered. Many officers used their contacts to go into business. It became a maxim that all senior military officers were first and foremost businessmen. Military officers became a major element in the emerging national political class.

During and after the civil war, officers could and did become very rich; a paymaster position was notorious (or celebrated) for providing a springboard to great private wealth. Some of their abuses recalled those of the eighteenth-century British Royal Navy. For example, paymasters might hold soldiers' pay, due on the first, until the end of the month, collecting personally the interest from the month's deposit.

Military officers were not quiet about their money. By the late 1980s, the most expensive parts of Lagos were peppered with outsized mansions built by colonels.[6] Public contracting procedures and government financial oversight were rudimentary or nonexistent. Officers and retired officers soon acquired business links, facilitated by the rapid growth of the petroleum industry, which expanded during the years of military dictatorship. With control over state revenue, the networks of officer *ogas* and their associates and friends developed their characteristic rapacious quality during the rule of Babangida, under Abacha, and finally (his critics claim) under the nominally civilian Obasanjo.[7]

The growing impoverishment of most Nigerians paradoxically strengthened the system because it cemented their reliance on patronage networks for survival. In return for support, officers provided oil money for *ogas* to distribute to "deserving" clients when there were diminishing alternative sources. Military officers, post–civil war and mostly retired, were joined by governors, former governors, chairmen of local government authorities, business leaders, and a few traditional rulers. As my Roman Catholic cleric observed, as a group they largely behaved with impunity, as had their military colleagues and predecessors.

Beyond a threshold negotiated by the federal government with the oil companies, more than 90 percent of the profits from oil go to the federal government. The legal principle of federal ownership and control of Nigeria's natural resources dates from the colonial period and was consolidated during the civil war when the oil fields were, literally, conquered territory. General Obasanjo confirmed federal ownership when he was military head of state.[8] Earlier, presidential allocation of oil revenue to the governors without requiring accountability started during the Gowon administration. Though it was part of General Yakubu Gowon's strategy of tying the states more closely to the federal government in the aftermath of the civil war, over time it greatly facilitated corruption.

Under the Fourth Republic's current revenue allocation formula, the federal government retains 58 percent of the oil revenue; about 30 percent goes to the states, and about 12 percent to the local government authorities. In addition, 13 percent of oil revenue off the top goes directly to the oil-producing states before the remainder is placed in the federation account for the wider, formulaic dispersal.[9] Increased revenue allocation to the states and the local government authorities opened up new opportunities and venues to fund patron-client networks.

During President Obasanjo's second presidential term (2003–7), and to the applause of the international financial community, Okonjo-Iweala, Soludo, and anticorruption expert Obi Ezekwesili introduced a new element of transparency and accountability with respect to federal funds. By contrast, as a practical matter, governors and local government area councils still are not accountable for how they spend the money. State legislatures, where such oversight authority rests, are too weak and undeveloped to perform this function, and many of their members are not independent but rather part of the patron-client network of the sitting governor. Access to oil money has made elective office at the state and local levels more lucrative than in the past. Competition for such offices among the *ogas* accordingly has intensified, sometimes involving the use of paid thugs or militias against their rivals' clients, thereby feeding the expanding culture of violence.

Coteries of patron-client networks are interconnected at every level of society and government. Even the Lagos "Area Boys," thugs involved in various extortion and protection rackets, have their *oga*. So, too, do the "ragpickers" working the Lagos refuse dumps. The system is based on mutual dependence and support. George Packer illustrates how this system worked at the microlevel in a Lagos neighborhood.[10]

Prior to the Jonathan administration, knowledgeable Nigerians readily identified persons, all retired generals, who were leaders at the national level around whom these networks often coalesced, the pinnacles, as it were, of patronage; their lists nearly always included Abdulsalami Abubakar, Danjuma, Babangida, and Obasanjo. Only Danjuma was not a former head of state. Three of the four were intimately involved in successful coups.[11] Their collaboration during the first years of the Fourth Republic was basic to political stability in the aftermath of Abacha. Subsequently, their unity fractured over Obasanjo's goal of retaining the presidency despite constitutionally mandated term limits and, at the national level, the Ijaw coterie that surrounds Jonathan has reduced their influence.

The 2011 end of power alternation between the North and the South with the presidency of Jonathan, a southern Christian, even though it was the North's turn, tested again patronage/clientage cohesion. It contributed to the instability in Nigerian politics and the seeming paralysis of the federal government. In 2011, both Goodluck Jonathan and General Muhammadu Buhari sought popular support by appealing to ethnic and religious identities outside traditional patronage networks.

There have been other patrons who were powerful at the regional, state, and local government area level, such as the former dictator of Biafra, General Chukwuemeka Ojukwu in Igboland, and a few of the traditional rulers, such as the ooni of Ife or the sultan of Sokoto, who headed networks of their subordinate traditional rulers. Some, such as Gusau, have powerful networks in their own right but from time to time subordinate themselves to others at the national level (Obasanjo in Gusau's case). Governors, too, have been successful in building formidable networks based in their own particular states. In the first six months of his presidency, Umaru Yar'Adua married off two of his daughters, one to the governor of Bauchi state, the other to the governor of Kebbi state. One governor was part of the president's PDP; the other, the most important opposition party. Many political families, such as the Igbinedions in Benin or the Sarakis in Kwara, also have an important big business connection.

Not all network leaders have been military officers or politicians. The Dangote family of Kano is at the pinnacle of the richest civilian network of them all. *Forbes* magazine in 2008 estimated the net worth of patriarch Aliko Dangote at $3.3 billion and ranked him the 334th-richest man in the world and the world's second-richest black person. (*Forbes* placed Dangote above Oprah Winfrey, who weighed in at $2.5 billion.)[12] Dangote's wealth is based on commodity trading, especially cement and sugar.[13] The Saraki and Dangote families were particularly close to Obasanjo and, later, Yar'Adua. The press widely reported that Dangote provided the jet for Yar'Adua's 2007 presidential campaign.[14]

Babangida, too, has alliances with big business. Alhajie Indimi, based in Maiduguri, is one of Nigeria's richest businessmen and the head of a significant civilian patronage network. He married his daughter to a Babangida son in July 2004. At a diplomatic dinner the following month, he boasted about his five thousand guests and the fifty-five private aircraft on the ground at the local airport for the festivities.

Ogas, whether from the military, politics, or business, seek to protect the parochial interests of their subordinates and clients to ensure their continued fealty. At times, this results in arbitrary and inconsistent government measures. For example, it was widely believed that President Obasanjo from time to time banned the importing of certain goods in contradiction to his general policy of economic reform in order to benefit his clients and himself. Obasanjo was the proprietor of a big chicken business, and, to nobody's surprise, he banned imported poultry, although ostensibly to control the spread of avian influenza.

Patronage networks are not immortal and can be fragile. Abacha destroyed those of Moshood K. O. Abiola, Shehu Yar'Adua, and, for a time, Obasanjo. However, with largely unfettered access to Nigeria's oil revenue as president and concurrently oil minister after 1999, Obasanjo during his first term rebuilt his network and thereby freed himself from being a client of the military coterie that had placed him in power in 1999. Instead of a patron-client relationship between the generals and Obasanjo, their relationship was transformed into an alliance of equals, with the advantage shifting to the president the longer he was chief of state.

THE ELITES: COOPERATING AND COMPETING

Intense politicking is characteristic of relations among top players. Typically, horse-trading is done at night—often, all night. *Ogas* will gather before midnight at an agreed meeting place, often an Abuja mansion, accompanied by large retinues. The *ogas* will go into a separate room, while their people will wait together in a hall. The retainers are often joined by outside supplicants who have learned through the grapevine about the opportunity to have a word with one of the big men, and there is usually a jostle of servants. Meetings can last until the first Islamic prayers of the following day.

The Arewa Consultative Forum, a Northern, multiethnic organization, sometimes serves as a venue where Northern networks develop a common position. Afenifere, a Yoruba religious and political organization, may serve the same purpose in Yorubaland. Igbos also have "cultural" organizations that can be the venue for political coordination. None of these cultural organizations has much power themselves. Rather, they provide a convenient venue for the *ogas* to use. They are especially useful if the *ogas* are seeking to rally broad support outside their charmed circle for a particular issue. For example, Afenifere and the Arewa Consultative Forum were two of the venues where the *ogas* coordinated their opposition to a third term for President Obasanjo.

There is an edge behind elite collegiality. Its facade cracks when a change of government looms because Nigeria's winner-takes-all political culture has not changed, and "winning" can be literally a matter of life and death, as Obasanjo said publicly in the run-up to the 2007 elections.

During such unsettled periods, patrons in parts of the country recruit groups of thugs for use against their political opponents and their clients. The line between criminal gangs and "youth unemployment schemes" can be thin. Human Rights Watch documented that President Yar'Adua, while governor of Katsina, maintained with state funds several hundred ruling PDP unemployed youth. Some of them were involved in the 2007 election violence.[15] Much of the violence in the Delta during Obasanjo's second term was perpetrated by gangs recruited by gubernatorial candidates in the 2003 elections. When the elections were over and the victorious governors no longer needed them, the gangs turned to entrepreneurial crime or went to work for others. Some observers posit that Boko Haram, the radical Islamic insurgency in the North against the Abuja government, is protected and supported by local *ogas* disaffected by the end of power alternation between North and South.

The patron-client system appears to have rules. A paramount one is that there is to be no president for life. Another is that patrons at the pinnacle of the networks are never killed by their rivals, though their clients are fair game. A third is that money accumulated by a political figure in office is sacrosanct.

Individual *oga* grabs for excessive power have led to network realignments that can bring down suddenly a Nigerian head of state. That was the fate of Abacha. Similarly, Obasanjo's efforts for a third term dangerously destabilized the political system. He risked a coup or other irregular change of government until his ambitions were defeated in the National Assembly. Defeat reflected a nationwide *oga* consensus against a third term. The consequences of Jonathan's 2011 election, even though it was the North's turn, are still working themselves out.

Rival patrons, however, ensure the personal and financial survival of an ex-chief of state. Those who aspire to the highest office in the land or to control that office through surrogates want no precedent of presidential accountability by legislative oversight—nor do they want a presidential killing that could someday be a precedent applied to them, hence the durability of national political figures such as Gowon, Buhari, Babangida, Obasanjo, Danjuma, and Ojukwu, despite the pervasive violence of Nigerian politics. They rose to prominence during the civil war forty years ago, have held power, lost power, and lived to play again.[16]

At the time of his death, Abacha was in the process of transforming himself into a civilian president who would thereby be able to retain power indefinitely through rigged elections. He was breaking the rule against presidents for life. In addition, he imprisoned Obasanjo, Shehu Yar'Adua, and Abiola in the mid-1990s. On the street, it is widely believed he also had Shehu Yar'Adua killed, thereby breaking the rule against the killing of rival elite leaders.[17]

Officially, Abacha died of a heart attack. The story endlessly repeated on the street, however, is that he died from an overdose of Viagra while cavorting with three Indian prostitutes procured by a Lebanese businessman at the behest of his colleagues. Others, from the security services, allegedly "in the know," say he was poisoned with strychnine injected into an apple with which he was teased by those same Indian prostitutes.[18] However he was dispatched, Abacha had forfeited the protection accorded by the informal rules that govern patron behavior. He also forfeited the inviolability of his money. After Abacha's death, Obasanjo as president led a partially successful effort to recover state assets that his predecessor had looted.

I found most of the *ogas* to be articulate, charming, and shrewd political operators. They saw Nigeria's continued survival as very much in their personal pecuniary interest. A few had a sophisticated knowledge of the United States, to which some sent their children for schooling, though more went to the United Kingdom. Even those of military origin were anxious that "the military boys" not come back because of the likely negative impact on their personal position and on Nigeria's international image. Their stance was essentially defensive. They wanted to preserve what they had now, and they wanted the United States to help in areas such as education or public health, so long as their own authority and perquisites remained untouched. Viscerally, they distrusted participation in Nigeria's government by the people, whom they often characterized to me as "not yet ready." The resulting Nigerian political system has been characterized by Human Rights Watch as "criminal politics."[19]

Among rich *ogas*, there is little tradition of philanthropy, as opposed to the religiously motivated distribution of alms to the crowds of beggars at the gate. There is little philanthropic infrastructure and no particular tax advantages to its practice. However, there are notable exceptions. Danjuma established a foundation that is involved in a range of philanthropic activities. Ex-chief of state Gowon established a foundation that worked closely with the Carter Center on the elimination of certain diseases, notably guinea worm. General Mohammed Buba Marwa, former military governor of two states and an early presidential candidate in 2007, supported African studies at an American university.[20] Another Nigerian philanthropist is Atiku Abubakar, the former vice president. He established a secular, American-style university in Yola, the capital of his native Adamawa state. President-elect Abiola, another major Nigeria philanthropist among other activities, had endowed a lecture series for the African Studies Association in the United States before he was arrested by Abacha, and former senate president Ken Nnamani founded the Ken Nnamani Centre for Leadership and Development in Abuja.

THE GLUE THAT HOLDS IT TOGETHER

As early as Shehu Shagari's 1979–83 administration, corruption was already deeply embedded in the political culture and the formal and informal economy. It infected even the universities and religious establishments. Following his coup against the Shagari administration, Buhari attempted to suppress corruption, with only very limited success. Nevertheless, his initiative threatened to disrupt the relationships through which Nigeria was ruled and contributed to *oga* support for Buhari's overthrow by General Babangida.

President Obasanjo's anticorruption rhetoric, his participation in the founding of Transparency International, his fiscal and economic reforms, as well as his occasional anticorruption show trials masked for foreign observers the pervasiveness of corruption. They encouraged an unrealistic hope outside Nigeria that President Obasanjo, and subsequently, President Yar'Adua and President Goodluck Jonathan, would have the political power and will to move against corruption. But Obasanjo himself is both a product and a perpetrator of the politics of patronage, and Yar'Adua and Jonathan are prime beneficiaries—it gave all three of them in turn the presidency. To do what Nigerian reformers and the international community want would compromise or destroy the system of which they are a part. Obasanjo, Yar'Adua, and Jonathan were probably sincere in their advocacy of measures promoting transparency and against corruption, but as an aspiration for the future rather than as a practical political agenda for now. Certainly Obasanjo, Yar'Adua, and Jonathan would understand St. Augustine's prayer, "Lord, make me chaste, but not yet."

Fiscal transparency would undermine patron-client networks. This is widely recognized in Nigeria. Obasanjo established the Independent Corrupt Practices Commission (ICPC) and the Economic and Financial Crimes Commission (EFCC). Both received technical assistance from the United States. The EFCC is capable of excellent police work. A U.S. Federal Bureau of Investigations expert told me it was the most professional law enforcement body in West Africa. It was compromised, however, because it almost exclusively proceeded against Obasanjo's political rivals and personal enemies while he was chief of state. Nevertheless, the EFCC was widely seen as a step in the right direction, and if its targets of prosecution appeared politically selected, few doubted their guilt. Its first executive chairman, Nuhu Riba-du,[21] behaved increasingly independently of Obasanjo and his circle. As early as 2004, Obasanjo's close associates were expressing concern about his political reliability.[22]

In December 2007, Yar'Adua's attorney general abruptly transferred Ribadu from the EFCC, ostensibly for training. This occurred at a time when there were escalating calls for the EFCC to investigate former president Obasanjo and his family for alleged corruption. EFCC investigations were also under way against powerful former governors, some of whom were close to Obasanjo or Yar'Adua or both. President Yar'Adua's unwillingness to intervene raised questions at home and abroad about how far he would (or could) go in the fight against corruption. Subsequently, Ribadu was demoted, then fired from the police and threatened with legal prosecution for alleged corruption. His successor at the EFCC was Farida Waziri, a retired police assistant inspector general and head of the antifraud unit. There was skepticism in Nigeria and abroad that she had the necessary energy and commitment to move the EFCC forward.

Ubiquitous patronage and corrupt behavior fueled by oil money is a root cause of Nigeria's political and economic sclerosis. Nevertheless, dysfunctional though it is, it holds together the Nigerian political elites and, by extension, the state. The cost may be high for ordinary Nigerians, but there has been no repeat of the civil war.

However, should the patrons and their networks start to devour each other, to violate with impunity the rules that have governed their behavior up to now, the resulting elite instability might open up space for a possible military coup or even violent social upheaval, such as Nigerians believe happened in Ghana following flight lieutenant Jerry Rawlings's 1981 coup. From that perspective, the periods from late 2005 to May 2006 and from the illness of Yar'Adua in 2009 to the present, including the election season of 2011, were particularly dangerous. In the case of the former, Obasanjo (or people around him) tried to manipulate the political system so he could remain in power indefinitely. His personal enemies (and he had many) would likely have taken things into their own hands with popular support if these efforts had succeeded. This Armageddon was avoided when the National Assembly, reflecting an elite consensus in the face of nationwide popular anger at Obasanjo, refused to approve the necessary constitutional changes. In 2009, a military coup was avoided by the expedient of making Jonathan an "acting president" until Yar'Adua's death. His subsequent election as president in 2011 in violation of the power-sharing alternation between North and South alienated parts of the Northern patronage/clientage networks and created space for the expanded activities of Boko Haram.

REFORM? REVOLUTION?

A riff makes the rounds in Lagos:

Question: Why is Ghana so much better off than Nigeria when it has no oil?
Answer: Flight Lieutenant Rawlings and stakes on the beach.

Rawlings staged a successful military coup in 1981 and then murdered much of the traditional Ghanaian establishment. He then, so the story goes, rebuilt an uncorrupt, democratic Ghana from the ground up. In fact, Rawlings murdered only a handful of leading political figures, but his victims did include three former heads of state.[23] In a country as huge as Nigeria, a Rawlings-style assault on the elites is all but impossible. The significance of the Rawlings riff, however, is that at least some who have a stake in the present system conclude that meaningful reform is possible only if the elites are eliminated. They see no other way out. On a popular level, this also appears to be part of the motivation of Boko Haram.

The unsuccessful 1990 coup by midlevel Christian army officers against Babangida seemed to foreshadow the possibility of a bloody, populist assault on the system. In addition to expelling the Muslim North from the federation, the coup plotters allegedly planned to murder any Nigerian with a "white Mercedes." They were prepared to kill indiscriminately anybody who fit their fanciful template of corruption.

Yet there are signs of political resilience and institutional growth that could over time bring about fundamental change without Armageddon. President Yar'Adua, ostensibly elected president in April 2007, lacked his own personal ties to the military, though his murdered elder brother was an army general. After more than a year as chief of state, Yar'Adua finally imposed his own choices on the top of the military's leadership. The junior Yar'Adua showed the potential to establish a civilian style for Nigeria's executive that it had hitherto lacked. Those working at Aso Villa, often holdovers from the previous administration, commented with surprise and pleasure on the new president's personal courtesy and his willingness to listen to different points of view, in contrast to what they said were his predecessor's barked orders and temper tantrums. Yar'Adua sought much better relations with the National Assembly than his predecessor, and, beginning in 2007, he ordered the immediate implementation of Supreme Court decisions that were awkward for the government, in contrast to his predecessor who simply ignored those he did not like.

Yar'Adua's presidency effectively ended in November 2009, when he was hospitalized in Saudi Arabia. Though he returned to Nigeria in February 2010, nobody beyond his wife and two or three others was able to see him. In March, Yar'Adua received two groups of handpicked religious leaders. In

April, he was seen by a few staffers. It was clear, however, that though the president was still living, he could not exercise his functions. Yet he could not, or would not, surrender his duties to the vice president, as provided for by the constitution.

The National Assembly's designation of the vice president as the acting president ended the stalemate. Even if extra-legal, the National Assembly acted as a part of a political process, rather than as the result of overt military intervention, a positive development in a country long plagued by military coups. It was a response to strong elite views that the stalemate in presidential authority must end, and, apparently, it was orchestrated by David Mark, the president of the Senate and a retired general, possibly to forestall more direct military intervention.

Even more than Yar'Adua, Jonathan has no personal links to the military. It remains to be seen whether he has the will or the means to move against the other, more substantive obstacles to genuine civilian governance in Nigeria and whether the challenges of Boko Haram will allow him to do so.

The two other branches of the federal government—the judiciary and the legislature—are potential venues for positive transformation of Nigeria's political culture. The judiciary, especially the election tribunals, the Court of Appeals, and the Supreme Court, is acting with greater independence from the executive; at least on occasion. Following the 2007 elections, the judicial system invalidated numerous Independent National Electoral Commission (INEC)–announced results. Yar'Adua publicly said he would abide by its decision and that, if the presidential elections were invalidated, he would not run again.

Late in 2008, the Supreme Court upheld Yar'Adua's election on technical grounds, though in the case brought by Buhari by a majority of only four to three. Nigerian democratic reformers were encouraged by the close vote and the court's acknowledgment of the shortcomings of the elections. Paradoxically, Yar'Adua's immediate enforcement of court decisions, which was consistently done, strengthened not only the judiciary but also the president himself by burnishing his reputation as an advocate for the rule of law.[24]

As shown by its defeat of Obasanjo's efforts for a third term as president in May 2006, the National Assembly has also shown signs of greater assertiveness and independence. In 2007, an informal group called Integrity forced the resignation of the speaker of the house, an Obasanjo ally, for corruption. Another group, G-21, sought to democratize the inner workings of the PDP. Nevertheless, efforts by the National Assembly to hold the president fiscally accountable have consistently failed, in large part because it lacks control of the disbursement process or the ability to provide meaningful budget oversight. Members of the National Assembly have no staffs; there is no functioning equivalent of the U.S. Congressional Budget Office or the U.S. General Accounting Office. Perhaps of even greater importance, members are mostly the clients of powerful patrons, especially the governors of the states they represent. The undignified behavior of individuals on the floor of the National Assembly, including fistfights and shouting matches, do not help its image among the general public. Meanwhile, when President Obasanjo saw the need, he apparently drew on oil revenue without reference to any formal budgetary process. It is widely suspected that Jonathan drew on oil revenue to meet the enormous expenses of his 2011 election. For a president, there was little distinction between public and private purposes of expenditure.

Since 1999, Nigeria has been haunted by the ghost of returned military dictatorship. After he became a civilian head of state, Obasanjo sought to establish control over the military. He forcibly retired officers who had served in political positions under Abacha. Nevertheless, the military is still top-heavy in its ranks. The navy has many more admirals than seaworthy vessels, and the air force has more generals than flight-ready aircrafts. During his first term, Obasanjo's minister of defense was the powerful Danjuma. For his second term, however, he appointed as minister of defense a defeated governor who showed little interest in military matters. The president became the de facto minister. Yar'Adua's initial minister of defense was Mahmud Y. Ahmed, a career civil servant without apparent military background or ties. There was speculation that Obasanjo, from his perch as chairman of the Board of Trustees of the ruling PDP, wanted to continue as de facto minister. Subsequently, however, in July 2009, Yar'Adua made Godwin O. Abbe minister of defense, perhaps a sign of Obasanjo's then-waning influence. A retired general and a veteran of the civil war, Abbe had served as a military governor in two states under Babangida. His appointment as minister of defense was credible. At the same time, Ahmed was made secretary to the government, the traditional head of the civil service.

Obasanjo as president personally involved himself with officer promotions and assignments in a way typical of a traditional patron. But Obasanjo did not have it entirely his own way. Other "big" patrons, such as Babangida and Danjuma, also had strong lines into the officer corps. Smaller patrons at various levels were active duty or retired officers with a military following. All of them looked after their clients within the military and in turn received loyalty from them. Obasanjo, Yar'Adua, and Jonathan could not and cannot count on the unconditional loyalty of the military, especially if perceived as violating the rules, such as the one against presidents for life. Despite Obasanjo's efforts to corral the military, soldiers still have guns, and there remain disgruntled midlevel and junior officers, especially against the background of continued military failure to bring Boko Haram to heel. There has been enough speculation about a military coup to keep an *oga* awake at night.

In 2009, the Yar'Adua administration faced an escalating insurrection in the Delta and a revolt by Boko Haram that spread rapidly to other Northern cities. When the police failed to control the outbreaks in both cases, the military responded seemingly without civil direction. Indeed, as the paralysis of the Yar'Adua administration advanced, the military appeared to be moving into the resulting power vacuum. Something approaching the restoration of military rule within a civilian structure may have been under way. However, no dominant military personality challenged directly the Yar'Adua presidency or the subsequent Jonathan presidency. Nevertheless, Jonathan's closest early advisors as acting president and president were all retired generals such as Obasanjo, Danjuma, Gusau, and Andrew Azazi. Now, however, his inner circle appears to be mostly Ijaw and Christian and without the power bases of the retired generals.

Like the federal government, state governments are institutionally weak and increasingly irrelevant to the Nigerians in the street. They are, however, of importance as a venue for elite competition for the oil revenue distributed through the Federation Account. Nigerians commonly regard corruption as worse at the state level than at the federal. Governors, usually at the pinnacle of their own networks, dominate their state legislatures and have a large voice in determining who represents their state in the National Assembly and in the president's cabinet.[25] They often have a patron-client relationship with the chairmen of the local government authorities in their state.

ABUJA

In part because control of the government means access to wealth, the elites who run Nigeria live in Abuja for a part or most of the year, and the lobby and bars of the Transcorp Hilton (sub-Saharan Africa's largest hotel, among the most profitable in the Hilton chain worldwide, and owned by Nigerian business interests within Obasanjo's network) are an important center of Nigerian political life. All of the state governors have official lodges in the capital, and many of them have private houses as well. Abuja has the unintended consequence of further separating the *ogas* from the people they govern.

Nevertheless, except for enormous and grandiose houses, there are few shrines of conspicuous consumption, unlike in the Persian Gulf: there is no Pucci or Gucci emporium, no Rolls-Royce or Jaguar dealership (though Mercedes-Benz is present). But, in general, the Nigerian elite shop elsewhere, typically in London or Dubai.

A visitor to Nigeria's new, modern federal capital will find eerie similarities to Washington, DC. Both are planned cities built where there had been nothing. Much of what is now the Federal Capital Territory of Abuja had been infested with the river blindness parasite, so people avoided living there. The site was selected primarily because of its central location and because it was not associated with a particular ethnic group.

Like Washington in the nineteenth century, Abuja today may be described as a city of "magnificent intentions" with grandiose buildings standing often isolated in the bush and connected by an incomplete freeway network. There are few markets or shops for a city of its size. Like Washington, Abuja is an expensive city to live in—the cost of living allowance for U.S. embassy employees was as high as 42 percent while I was serving there. This means, roughly, that it cost Americans about 42 percent more to maintain the same standard of living in Abuja as they had enjoyed in Washington, itself one of the most expensive of American cities. [26]

In Abuja, constitutional separation of powers is symbolized by the elaborate buildings housing the presidency (Aso Villa), the National Assembly, and the Supreme Court. Indeed, the organizational chart of the Nigerian federal government mirrors that of the U.S. federal government. That apparent resemblance, like that between Nigerian chiefs of state and American presidents, is ersatz. Regulatory agencies, especially, exist mostly as aspiration.

Unlike Washington, there is a ring of squatter and other informal settlements around Abuja, which then minister of the Federal Capital Territory Malam Nasir el-Rufai estimated has a population of some 7 million. He also told me that Abuja was the fastest-growing city in Africa and had already far outgrown its planned infrastructure. Electricity and water are erratic; the *ogas* have generators. The *ogas* and the diplomatic community usually buy clean water from private suppliers, who deliver it to residential storage tanks.

Living conditions in the capital for most people are bad. Abuja is popularly regarded as worse than Lagos because of the shortage of housing. Civil servants of all ethnic groups with homes in the former capital have long resisted being transferred away. Government employees with some education who wear ties to work often live in townships without paved roads, water, or electricity. While the water in the reservoir (built and managed by the Israelis) is pure, the piping system is compromised, with the mixing of brown and blue water, requiring extensive in-home purification to make it potable.

The Nigerian government has never assumed responsibility for affordable housing. Indeed, David Mark, current president of the Senate and a retired general, publicly remarked when he was minister of the Federal Capital Territory during the Babangida dictatorship that "Abuja is not for poor people." Moreover, following British colonial practice, until the end of the second Obasanjo administration, the government provided housing for the most senior of officials and members of the legislature.

The servants' quarters of these and other establishments are sought after by midlevel civil servants as a place for them to stay; most keep their families elsewhere. More junior civil servants and the displaced domestic servants end up in the shanty towns. In his last years in office, Obasanjo privatized much of this official housing stock by selling it at fire-sale prices to members of his administration.

In many parts of Nigeria, Abuja has come to be viewed as a symbol of arrogance and the parasitic character of Nigerian elite politics, rather than as the focus of national unity as intended by its founders. I frequently heard Delta residents say, "in the Delta we have water everywhere but no bridges, while in Abuja there is no water but there are bridges (highway overpasses) everywhere." As might be predicted, levels of violent crime are very high. Both Lagos and Abuja were rated by the Department of State as "critical threat for crime posts." This is the highest (worst) designation outside an active war zone. Unlike Lagos, Abuja is also the venue for periodic attacks by Boko Haram.

Regardless of the shortcomings of Abuja, denizens of the Villa used to tell me that it had the singular advantage of being a difficult venue from which to stage a coup. The Presidential Brigade of Guards is barracked in Abuja, but there is no large base such as Dodan Barracks in Lagos or the Headquarters of the First Mechanized Division in Kaduna to provide the fodder for a coup attempt, they would say. [27] This presupposes a coup similar to those earlier in Nigeria's history, especially the overthrow of Shagari. More recently, however, Ernest Shonekan's government collapsed when he was simply told by Abacha and other generals that he had to go, without the need for troops in the streets.

Nigeria's governance as described here has been challenged by intellectuals such as Wole Soyinka and Chinua Achebe and by journalists writing for the country's mostly free press. The legal profession, through the Nigeria Bar Association led by Olisa Agbakoba and his successors, as well as a host of human rights lawyers, has been a forceful advocate for the rule of law, and religious leaders—notably the Anglican primate, Peter Akinola; [28] the Roman Catholic cardinal of Lagos, Anthony Okogie; and the Roman Catholic archbishop of Abuja, John Onaiyekan—regularly and publicly denounce Nigeria's corruption that pays too little mind to the welfare of the mass of the people. These critics make no excuses. Their standard of judgment is Western democratic practice. They do not accept that "African values" or the "legacy of colonialism" justify bad governance.

Many others within Nigerian civil society, including members of the professions, academics, church leaders, journalists, and those self-employed in the modern economy, are looking for a way out of patron-client politics and for the realization of the "Nigeria Project." Using the terminology of prerevolutionary Russia, these critics are "modernizers" or technocrats. They espouse democratic values and see a direct relationship between Nigeria's growing impoverishment and the failure of governance. Though they lack a power base, they are politically sophisticated and know how to use the judiciary and the legislature to advance their agenda. However, they are not revolutionaries.

Nevertheless, if such civil society elements continue to strengthen, they may be able to support the establishment of a multiparty system that, in turn, could change over time Nigeria's system of governance. That would require future opposition political leaders to demonstrate exceptional political skill. Nigeria is the home to extraordinarily talented people, and such leaders can be found. All bets are off, however, if oil prices settle at a low level with a deleterious impact on government revenue causing the *ogas* to circle their wagons or if Boko Haram succeeds in destroying the Northern elite and brings down the Jonathan government. Meanwhile, the regime of *oga* patronage with a veneer of democratic federalism inadequately addresses Nigeria's profound challenges. The people of Nigeria distance themselves from government as much as they can. There is the risk that many of them will distance themselves from the United States if they perceive Washington to be an uncritical supporter of the Abuja status quo.

Chapter Four

Faith

On December 25, 2009, a young Muslim from Northern Nigeria, Umar Farouk Abdulmutallab, tried to destroy Northwest Flight 253 as it approached Detroit. He was foiled only by luck and the quick thinking of his fellow passengers, not by the elaborate, intrusive, and expensive security procedures the United States put in place after the 9/11 attacks. If he had succeeded, it would have resulted in the greatest loss of life from a terrorist attack on American soil since 9/11.

Initially, Nigerian politicians and other commentators insisted that Abdulmutallab had been radicalized in the United Kingdom and joined al-Qaeda in Yemen. For them, the crimes of this son of a rich Nigerian businessman had little to do with Nigeria. Why Abdulmutallab became a terrorist prepared to murder hundreds of innocent people may never be known. Nevertheless, for this pious, even fanatical Muslim, the discontinuity between revivalist Islamic preaching and the worldly practices of the nominally Muslim Northern establishment that included his own family is likely to have been a factor in his radicalization.[1]

Abdulmutallab's story provides a convincing reason for Americans to understand Islam in Nigeria. So, too, does Boko Haram, which directly threatens the Nigerian state, and some suspect it has links to anti-American jihadist movements. What happens there can affect us here. And what is happening is the concurrent revival of both Islam and Christianity, refracted through an African prism, which is reshaping the country that hosts them. Faith matters. Many Nigerians note proudly that they live in the "world's most religious country, and the happiest," despite its crushing poverty. The first proposition is likely to be true, and the second might have been before Boko Haram.

Islam and Christianity meet in the Middle Belt of Nigeria. The fault line runs from east to west across the country roughly at the level of Jos and recalls similar fault lines in Sudan and Côte d'Ivoire. Broadly speaking, the South-South and the Southeast are Christian, the Middle Belt and the South-west are mixed, and the North is Muslim. But as an exception to this tidy picture, there is now a substantial Christian minority in the North and a smaller Muslim minority in the East.

In accordance with President Bush's policy direction, while I was ambassador to Nigeria, the U.S. embassy made outreach to Islamic communities in the North and the Middle Belt a priority, with a particular focus on practical assistance: digging boreholes, building seed storage facilities, and repairing schools. Bridging the gap between Nigerian Muslims and the United States, however, was a daunting task. Nigerian Christians are well disposed toward the United States because of the myriad ties between the churches that are common to both countries. Nigerian Muslims, on the other hand, are mostly unfamiliar with the large and vibrant American Muslim community, and vice versa.

On my watch, for the first time the Department of State assigned to the embassy an American diplomat who was both a competent Hausa-Fulani speaker and a practicing Muslim. She played an invaluable role in shaping our Northern and Islamic outreach. The embassy expanded exchanges between American and Nigerian imams, professors, journalists, and students and conducted a multifaceted strategy to make better known in Nigeria the American Muslim community. The embassy, in association with the Library of Congress and the relevant Nigerian institutions, led an effort to preserve and catalog ancient Islamic manuscripts found in the North, building on previous work by academic institutions. The embassy also expanded nation-wide its network of reading rooms, called American Corners.[2] Nevertheless, the embassy had limited resources and Nigeria is huge. Our impact was less than we liked to think.

In November 2007, polling data indicated worldwide Muslim dislike and distrust of the United States was at an all-time high. An exception to this bleak picture was West Africa, though Nigeria was not as exceptional as I would have hoped. Indeed, the 2006 Pew Global Attitudes Project found that 62 percent of Nigerians had a favorable view of the United States. However, the data showed a big discrepancy between Christians and Muslims. Eighty-nine percent of the former viewed the United States favorably, while only 32 percent of the latter did. Worse, Pew data showed that the gap between Christian and Muslim perceptions of the United States had grown since 2003.[3]

The negative Pew Muslim polling data may have reflected Northern hostility to President Olusegun Obasanjo, whom the United States uncritically supported until he sought to remain in power indefinitely in 2006. More recently, Goodluck Jonathan has gone out of his way to identify himself with President Obama. His 2011–12 approach to Boko Haram indicates that he saw it as a security problem rather than a political one, thereby further alienating many Northern Muslims. For many Muslims, the United States was identified with Obasanjo, Jonathan, Christianity, and secularism, all anathemas. Nigerian opposition to U.S. action and policy with respect to Iraq, Afghanistan, Palestine, and Iran exacerbated this animosity and was grist for anti-American Friday sermons in mosques. Suspicion of U.S. motives in the Gulf of Guinea also played a role.

RELIGION AND RELIGIOSITY

From an American perspective, Nigerians, both Christian and Muslim, are highly religious. Almost everybody, in what Americans would regard as secular circumstances, uses faith vocabulary. Almost all public events are opened and closed with prayer. Causation of events, big or small, public or private, is routinely ascribed to divine intervention or the willful lack thereof. Christians and Muslims in Nigeria share a rejection of the Western concept of a separation of the religious and secular spheres of life. Each religion seeks to find in the other evidence of deviation from the literal interpretation of sacred texts. Each tries to outdo the other in opposition to "moral laxity," often reflecting traditional West African social and behavioral norms as much as religious teaching. For example, both are homophobic, and adherents of both faiths favor government sanctions against homosexuality. Leaders of both religions bitterly criticize American integration of gays and lesbians into the national mainstream, and they often cite it as evidence of Western degeneracy.[4]

Despite their many similarities, each faith is also suspicious of the other. Christians see Muslims as profoundly backward and enjoying a demographic advantage because of polygamy, overlooking the fact that informal polygamy is also widespread among Christians. Muslims routinely say that Christians are aggressive, are addicted to sharp business practices, and lack integrity. Each believes that the other receives massive financial assistance from abroad. Muslims fear Christians are bankrolled by American evangelicals, and Christians cite Saudi and, more recently, Iranian money allegedly flowing to Muslim foundations and charities. The Nigerian media, mostly headquartered in the South, is routinely insensitive and simplistic in its reportage about Northern Nigeria. And it is the Nigerian media that colors the too-often superficial Western view of the North.

Over the past fifteen years, Muslims appear to have become more "Islamic" in the Saudi Arabian sense. Long major centers of Islamic thought and practice, Kano and Maiduguri have become centers of the current wave of reform that seeks to purify Islam of perceived Western values and residual African influence and practice. Reformers seek to purge Nigerian Islam of the cult of saints, of the use of charms and other magical elements, and of various forms of mysticism, which often derive from pre-Islamic African religion. They advocate a much closer adherence to the Islamic practices of the Middle East as well as the reimposition of sharia, the code of Islamic law, in the criminal domain. And they have enjoyed some success.[5]

In Kano, most women are now covered, though not veiled, and, unlike in the late 1980s, no Muslim woman would shake hands with me. Pork has disappeared from restaurant menus, and alcohol is available at only a few venues that have a Lebanese character or ownership. I saw praises of Osama bin Laden stenciled on walls. After the police went home at 6:00 p.m., traffic was directed by Muslim militia, the Hisba.

The Christian quarter, the Sabon Gari, resembled an Igbo armed camp, though with the prostitutes, alcohol, and pork that appeared largely absent from the rest of the city. Nevertheless, the two faiths do coexist, if uneasily. Much radical Islamic rhetoric is directed toward the ruling Muslim establishment's non-Islamic behavior, such as that of Abdulmutallab's father's lending money at interest, rather than toward Christians. Indeed, many Christians left Kano when sharia was reintroduced in 2000 but came back when its regime proved milder than they had anticipated.

Conflict between groups accurately or inaccurately characterized as Christian or Muslim, however, has resulted in horrific violence. For what they are worth, official Nigerian government statistics ascribe 1.2 million internally displaced people to religious and ethnic conflict, a statistic that does not take into account post-2009 Boko Haram activity. Then there is the widely accepted estimate of at least 13,500 deaths from religious or ethnic conflicts since the ostensible restoration of civilian rule in 1999.[6] To cite only a few examples: Mobs burned some forty churches in Maiduguri in February 2006, ostensibly because of outrage over the "Danish cartoons" allegedly disrespectful of the Prophet.[7] Many Christians were killed, and a Catholic priest's legs were broken so he could not escape before he was "necklaced"—a common form of vigilante murder where a tire is placed around the victim's neck, filled with gasoline, and ignited. According to witnesses, the police stood by and did nothing. When the bodies of Christian victims arrived for burial in the Southern and predominately Christian city of Onitsha about a week later, there was a rampage against local Hausa-Fulani Muslims. Observers estimated that at least one hundred of them were hacked to death as they tried to flee across the Niger River Bridge.

While it is tempting to ascribe many of Nigeria's ills to religious conflict, and to its close associate, ethnic rivalry, doing so oversimplifies or obscures the root causes. Too often, conflicts between newcomers and local groups over land or water or between groups struggling for local power are assigned religious labels that commentators and headline writers seize upon, overemphasizing the religious dimension. Moreover, elites will use religious and ethnic rivalries to advance their particular agendas. Shared religious identity, especially Christian, can be a means of forging political alliances among the numerous small ethnic groups in the Middle Belt and the North.

Even as religious enthusiasm may promote sharp elbows between Christians and Muslims, interfaith cooperation also exists. It is, in fact, the norm in Yorubaland, less so in the Middle Belt and the North, though by no means absent. To cite one example, the sultan of Sokoto and the then president of the Christian Association of Nigeria, the Anglican primate, jointly called for peaceful elections shortly before the April 2007 polling. Then, in 2007, the newly enthroned sultan of Sokoto, Muhammadu Sa'adu Abubakar, took the lead in reviving the Nigerian Inter-Religious Council, jointly chaired by himself and the chairman of the Christian Association of Nigeria. Its purpose is to build bridges between the two communities and to provide a mechanism for resolving conflicts.[8] The current sultan has continued to be involved in numerous other efforts to mitigate religious conflict. At the community level, one successful project deploys teams of Muslim and Christian clergy into neighborhoods and villages to defuse potential crises that might acquire a religious coloration. This effort, led by a Pentecostal pastor and an imam, has become institutionalized and now receives international funding. Numerous other peace and reconciliation nongovernmental organizations operate all over the country, many of which receive small amounts of funding from international donor agencies.

ISLAM

Despite the growing influence of Saudi-style Islam, multiple traditions exist in Nigeria, often colored by the faith's African experience. Preeminent since the early nineteenth century has been the Sokoto caliphate, one of West Africa's most recent precolonial empires. Founded in 1804 by Usman Dan Fodio, the British preserved most of its institutions after they defeated it in 1903. Under the leadership of Lord Frederick Lugard, the British insulated it from Christian missionaries and their modernizing schools and hospitals, condemning the region to economic and social backwardness in comparison with the rest of the federation that persists to this day. Dan Fodio's direct, biological successors remain the sultans of Sokoto, and today the office is generally regarded as the premier among Muslim traditional rulers in Nigeria.[9]

The urban-based, pre-independence Sokoto caliphate included among its core followers imams, teachers, merchants (including slave traders), craftspeople, and government officials. Its lingua franca remains Hausa, and the largest ethnic group is still the Fulani, though a large number of minority tribes historically subordinate to the Hausa-Fulani live in the region. In the caliphate, Muslim culture is highly developed and rooted in the millennium-long presence of Islam in West Africa. However, its impact in the rural areas is often superficial. The emirs found in most major towns in Northwest Nigeria, along with some in the Middle Belt, owe allegiance to the sultan but exercise substantial local autonomy.

Second in historical importance to the Sokoto caliphate is the sultanate of Borno, led by the shehu, based in Maiduguri on the edge of the Sahara. Its Islamic tradition is generally regarded as the most ancient in West Africa. Dan Fodio failed to conquer Borno, which means it has remained outside the current Sokoto emirate system, though the shehu functions in many ways parallel to the sultan, although on a much smaller scale. Like the sultan, the shehu's subordinate emirs and chiefs owe him obedience but enjoy considerable autonomy. The dominant ethnic group and language in Borno is Kanuri, though as in the lands of the Sokoto caliphate, there are many minority ethnic groups.

Despite the shehu's moderate form of Islam, Borno's close proximity to the Sahara makes it open to more radical influences from Sudan and Chad. Boundaries are porous, and legitimate trade and smuggling are the economic lifeblood of the region. Borno imams and malams (Islamic teachers) may train in Khartoum and move back and forth with ease. The Mahdi tradition of radical, eschatological Islam associated with Sudan is also found in Borno. The so-called Nigerian Taliban began its operations there and seems to draw on some Mahdi and other Sahelian indigenous traditions, rather than on Middle Eastern or South Asian influences. Despite its name, it appears to have no connection with the Afghan Taliban. Maiduguri was also the headquarters of Boko Haram and is the home of preachers who regularly denounce the United States.[10]

Historically, Sokoto and Borno have been rivals, traces of which persist today. During the colonial period, British policy was concerned with balancing the two. Since their military defeat by the British, the authority of the two sultanates has been gradually whittled away by the state. Now, state governors play a major role in selecting the sultan of Sokoto and the shehu of Borno, albeit within the parameters of traditional rules of succession. At the local level, Islamic traditional rulers subordinate to the sultan and the shehu remain highly influential. They continue to provide justice and arbitrate disputes outside the formal justice system. Together, the courts of the sultan and the shehu are as close to a mainstream Islamic establishment as there is in Nigeria. They emphasize improving Islamic education and the traditional political process as a means of mitigating the appalling social conditions in the North. Both were bitterly opposed to Obasanjo's efforts to retain power by manipulating the constitution and the political process, and both were disenchanted with the United States and the United Kingdom because of their support for Obasanjo. They also remain suspicious of American intentions in the Gulf of Guinea and are viscerally opposed to any Western military presence in Nigeria or in West Africa. Nevertheless, they remain friendly toward the West. Their leadership is accessible to outsiders and the current sultan frequently travels abroad. The current sultan of Sokoto supported Jonathan's candidacy in 2011.

Islamic institutions in Yorubaland and the Middle Belt have a tradition of distancing themselves from the authority of Sokoto. In Yorubaland, there are no emirs, with the exception of the emirate of Ilorin, which was conquered by the caliphate but remained Yoruba rather than Hausa-Fulani in population. In the Middle Belt, unlike in the North and Yorubaland, minority ethnic groups are the majority and no single one dominates. If Islam in the caliphate and Borno is institutionalized, in Yorubaland it is characterized by individual affiliation,[11] with no single paramount Yoruba ruler. Traditional, indigenous Yoruba religion is well organized, sophisticated, and very powerful, both as a stand-alone but also as an underlying system of faith among those nominally Christian or Muslim. Yoruba families routinely include both Christians and Muslims. Adherents of both may celebrate each other's holidays, but they also participate together in traditional Yoruba rites, which bridge and subordinate the differences between Christianity and Islam. President Obasanjo, a Yoruba Christian, has a Muslim sister to whose faith he publicly referred, and as president, he let it be known that he fasted during both Ramadan and Lent. Sharia has never had the recognition it enjoys in the North and parts of the Middle Belt, and at present it has no official standing in the states of the Yoruba-dominated Southwest or in the Middle Belt.[12]

Yoruba Muslims, based in the cosmopolitan cities of Lagos and Ibadan, tend to be the most outward looking of Nigeria's Muslims. They follow developments in Iraq, Afghanistan, Iran, and Palestine, and many are highly critical of U.S. policy in the Middle East. While the current Islamic revival appears less strong in the West than in the North, some Yorubas are rejecting their historic syncretistic approach to Islam in favor of greater strictness.

The fourth division of Islam, as identified by the distinguished American scholar of Nigerian Islam John Paden,[13] is the Middle Belt.[14] Like the domains of the sultan and the shehu, the Middle Belt was originally part of the old Northern Region of colonial Nigeria. But in this part of Nigeria, minority ethnic groups dominate, and, as in Yorubaland, Christianity and Islam are roughly equal in size. Its Islam tends to be tolerant, though Jos is a center of Izala, a reform movement that advocates social justice as defined by Islam, a radical challenge to the status quo. For reasons specific to Jos, the city is also the center of repeated violence between Muslims and Christians. Historically, Jos was the center of a Christian tribe, the Baroum. However, over the past eighty years, Muslim Hausa-Fulani have migrated to the area from the

North and prospered, relative to the indigenous population. This growing economic inequality has promoted conflict that is occasionally exacerbated by local political leaders competing among themselves for power. As in Yorubaland, there is no tradition of an overarching polity, such as in the caliphate or the domains of the shehu of Borno. However, there are emirs in some parts of the region who are subordinate to the sultan of Sokoto.

The Middle Belt is the location of the national capital, Abuja. Military chiefs of state of Middle Belt origin have governed Nigeria for long periods and by example have promoted an atmosphere of tolerance and respect between the two religious traditions and the avoidance of sectarian triumphalism. General Yakubu Gowon, a Christian from a Middle Belt minority tribe, ruled from 1966 to 1975, and General Ibrahim Babangida, a Muslim from another minority tribe, ruled from 1985 to 1993. In addition, General Sani Abacha, a Muslim Kanuri, ruled from 1993 to 1998. All were reluctant to be photographed entering or leaving their respective houses of worship. [15]

The Nigeria Supreme Council for Islamic Affairs often plays the role of a unified political voice representing the various Islamic traditions, with the sultan as president and the shehu as vice president. Its most recent secretary was a Yoruba layman and Lagos-based lawyer, Lateef Adegbite, until his death in September 2012. The three were friendly toward the West, especially the United States. However, the establishment strain of Islam that they represent is now challenged both by Christian expansion into traditionally Muslim parts of the country and from within, by various Islamic reform movements, often with links via the Internet to the Persian Gulf and South Asia.

The new [16] wave of reform buffeting Northern Islam generally seeks to restore Koranic rigor and eliminate indigenous African elements as well as Western influence. Boko Haram is rooted in these reforms. Some of its practitioners are attracted to violence; others simply withdraw from mainstream society. But both manifestations are antithetical in style to the sophisticated, compromise-based governance of the sultan and the other traditional rulers. To a greater or lesser extent, they tend to be hostile to the United States, but the primary focus of their opposition is the secular government in Abuja. While still clearly a minority movement, precision is impossible about how rapidly it is gaining ground.

The sultan told American audiences in November 2007 that incidents attributed to al-Qaeda in Northern Nigeria were the handiwork of "a few disgruntled extremists who probably did not understand the Arabic translation of the words 'Taliban' or 'al-Qaeda.'" [17] He observed that the local worthies that owe him allegiance, including ward heads, village heads, district heads, and emirs, know the people at the grassroots level. They would know if al-Qaeda or Taliban were present. Through this network he had received no warnings or complaints about alleged exploits by either. Federal prosecutors and the security services sometimes have a different view. Nevertheless, new currents in Nigerian Islam appear to be overwhelmingly indigenous, rather than foreign.

CHRISTIANITY

If the diversity of Islamic thought in Nigeria is subtle to outsiders, that of Christianity is quite obvious, with multitudinous denominations, including those of European origin, the "African churches," the Aladura (or "praying" churches), the "health and wealth" churches, and so forth. Denominational identification in a particular area often reflects the national origin of the European missionaries who initially worked there. The East's Catholicism owes much to Irish missionaries. However, some Igbo villages were converted by Scots Presbyterians or English Anglicans and have adopted their respective denominations. Parts of Yorubaland were converted by Anglican missionaries from Sierra Leone as well as England. Other parts were converted by Baptist missionaries, as was President Obasanjo's home village. The European missionaries have long since departed but the denominational variety remains. Nigerians train their own clergy and now even export them to the developed world. The largest Roman Catholic seminary in the world is Bigard Memorial in Enugu. The seminary has about one thousand students. By comparison, the largest U.S. Catholic seminary enrolls 200.[18]

The divisions among the Christian churches may be less profound than the multitude of denominational labels implies. Past differences among the mainstream churches and with the African churches, primarily over the extent to which Christianity could accommodate African practices such as polygamy, have become less salient in practice, as have the more conventional differences between Protestants and Catholics. Instead, denominational differences have been subordinated by the rapid spread of Pentecostal and evangelical patterns of thinking and styles of worship characterized by emotional, "spirit-filled" expression. The spontaneity and emotionalism associated with Pentecostal worship in the West is increasingly characteristic of all denominations, including the Roman Catholics. Clergy is often charismatic and frequently authoritarian. From a Western perspective, they are fundamentalist in theology, with an emphasis on rules of behavior that are based on a literal reading of the Bible. Reflecting their high rate of growth, Christians are increasingly self-confident about their position in Africa and vis-à-vis the Christian churches in the developed world, of which they are often highly critical.[19]

Especially visible in the Southwest are megachurches with tens of thousands of adherents. The Mountain of Fire and Miracles Ministries, also known as "Prayer City," in a rural area abutting the Lagos-Ibadan expressway, conducts services regularly attended by up to two hundred thousand worshippers at a time and has branches worldwide, including in twenty-two U.S. states. Its congregation claims to be the largest in Africa. It occupies a huge campus, consisting mostly of open-air pavilions, and its members frequently camp there through the weekend, encouraged to stay put by the night banditry that plagues the Lagos-Ibadan expressway. Its charismatic general overseer, Daniel Kolawol Olukoya, has a degree in microbiology from the University of Lagos and a PhD in molecular genetics from the University of Reading in the United Kingdom. The fact that some of its members have automobiles (the full parking lot is visible from the expressway) is a sign that at least some of its membership comes from the remnants of the middle class in Lagos and Ibadan. But the bulk of its worshippers appear to consist of the Lagos and Ibadan working poor.

The Christian Association of Nigeria (CAN), an umbrella group that until 2013 when the Roman Catholics "suspended" their membership at the national level because of "leadership issues," included almost all of the churches. It functions as a mechanism to coordinate their positions on political and other secular matters. The media ascribes to the president of CAN the role of national spokesman for all the churches. Some of the most powerful, mainstream clerical political figures in the country have held this office: Methodist archbishop of Lagos Sunday Mbang, Cardinal Anthony Okogie, Anglican primate archbishop Peter Akinola, and the Roman Catholic archbishop of Abuja, John Onaiyekan. More recently its president has come from the Pentecostal tradition and its vice president from the "African" tradition (a branch of Christianity that in the past incorporated certain "African" norms, especially toleration of multiple wives). Not least because its language is English rather than Hausa-Fulani, CAN is better known to the Western and Nigerian media than the Supreme Council of Islamic Affairs, which it superficially resembles.

Christian leaders, like their Muslim counterparts, do not hesitate to cultivate political links to their advantage, and vice versa. The Aso Villa chaplain was a prominent Obasanjo sycophant and Third Term cheerleader. President Obasanjo constructed an exquisite chapel at Aso Villa and led the fundraising efforts to complete the Christian National Ecumenical Center in Abuja, where construction had stopped for nearly a generation.[20]

Some speculate that Christianity has, in fact, spread to the point of becoming the majority religion across the country—and many Muslims fear they are right. In fact, precise data is lacking on the percentage of the population that adheres to one or the other of the two religions. A notable scholar of African Christianity cites statistics showing Christians in 2000 at 46 percent of the population with Muslims at 44 percent. He finds credible that, while Islam has grown from 26 percent of Nigeria's population in 1900 to 44 percent in 2000, Christians have increased from 1 percent to nearly 50 percent of the population in the same time frame.[21] Others, however, put the figures at nearer 46 percent Christian and 52 percent Muslim.[22] Whichever is correct, for Muslims, who long regarded West Africa as their own neighborhood, Christian growth is disquieting.[23]

Christian rhetoric is often triumphalist and appears consistently to highball Christian numbers. For example, the Anglican primate regularly claimed that his flock approached 20 million faithful, making it the second largest after the Church of England in the Anglican Communion. He enjoyed observing that American Episcopalians numbered only a little more than 2 million. Nigerian Catholics repeatedly told me that the Church's sheer numbers in Nigeria made Nigerian cardinal Francis Arinze, resident in Rome since 1985, papable. Arinze has long been involved in Christian-Muslim dialogue. But no Nigerian ever mentioned that to me as one of his qualifications for the papacy.[24]

A Northern Muslim governor told me he estimated that 40 percent of the North's population was now Christian. Certainly, on the outskirts of traditionally Muslim cities such as Kano or Maiduguri, I saw literally dozens of signboards advertising Christian churches, many of them simply a circle of chairs beneath a tree. But others had substantial buildings.

Why Nigerians have chosen to abandon their traditional religions for Christianity and Islam is beyond the scope of this book, but a likely factor is that both faiths are commonly associated with modernity. In fact, with the exception of the Yoruba, educated Nigerians generally disdain traditional religion and are often embarrassed by its persistence. Fela Ransome-Kuti, the celebrated Yoruba musician, was an exception. The son of an Anglican priest, he rejected Christianity because it was "foreign" and "imperial" and reverted to the Yoruba gods, at least in public. But for nearly all of his countrymen, Christianity or Islam is a step forward from "paganism."

Northern Muslims are highly sensitive to claims of Christian conversions from Islam. In fact, they are likely rare. Some of the North's growing Christian population is the result of Igbo and Yoruba migrating into the region in search of economic opportunity. Conversions to Christianity do take place among minority tribes living in rural areas in the North that formerly were animist. A senior Roman Catholic cleric suggested to me that, once Christianity emerged as a viable alternative, it was more attractive to at least some of the latter than the religion of the "slave-catchers," the dominant, Muslim Hausa-Fulani.

Expanded activities of Christian institutions, especially the provision of renewed rudimentary educational and medical services, may make Christianity attractive to the non-Islamic indigenous population.[25] Christian denominations of all stripes are aggressive proselytizers. As an otherwise gentle Anglican bishop once said to me, "we will roll back Lord Lugard," in reference to the first British royal governor of consolidated Nigeria who forbade missionary activities in the caliphate. With the progressive impoverishment of most people over the past twenty years, and the accelerating decline of political institutions, the church can be compelling as the center of secular as well as spiritual life.

RADICALS

Despite growing Christian influence in the North, the region's formal politics were still overwhelmingly dominated by Muslim elites until the Boko Haram insurgency undermined most traditional institutions from 2009 onward. Until then, like their counterparts across the country, Muslim elites benefited from oil wealth at the expense of regional development. Some have houses abroad, as did Abdulmutallab's father in London. Theirs is the form of Nigerian Islam best known by Western scholars, diplomats, and businessmen and held by outsiders to be authoritative. At the same time, the Northern elite has been weakened at the national level. It lost control of the federal government under President Obasanjo until the May 2007 inauguration of the Muslim president Yar'Adua. But Yar'Adua did little for the North, and his death in May 2010 resulted in the subsequent presidency of the Christian Goodluck Jonathan. The North lost its previous dominant position in the military when Obasanjo purged the officers, mostly Northern Muslims, who had held civil office during the Abacha era. The decline of the traditional Northern elite opened the door for the emergence of not only younger potential leaders in the traditional mode but also indigenous Islamic protest or revolutionary movements. The activities of a few of these groups—the so-called Shiites, Taliban, and even more obscure sects—worried the traditional elite as well as the security services, until Boko Haram essentially upstaged them. Like the Taliban, the "Shiites" of Northern Nigeria share little with Middle Eastern Shia; "Shiite" instead refers to "radical" and may imply the receipt of funding from Iran.

West African Islam has seen indigenous radical reform movements before. Dan Fodio's 1804 jihad was initially a movement to purify Islam of the malpractices of the then-current establishment. The Maitatsine riots of 1980 in Kano and other Northern cities were, among other things, a social protest against the ostensibly Muslim elites, who were seen as rich, abusive, and corrupt, hence non-Islamic. Maitatsine left more than five thousand dead before it was suppressed by the Nigerian army. Contrary to Dan Fodio, there was also no state-building dimension to its rebellion. Indeed, the Maitatsine appeared hostile to any constituted authority, and its followers murdered policemen when they could.[26] Though it is tempting to see the Maitatsine as a forerunner of Boko Haram, the two movements are radically different. The Maitatsine incorporated many elements of traditional African religion into their belief systems, while Boko Haram is rigidly orthodox and fundamentalist.

Starting in 2000, in the aftermath of the Abacha military dictatorship, twelve Northern states officially adopted sharia in the criminal domain with significant popular support. The governor of Zamfara state, Ahmad Sani, started the process, apparently for short-term political gain. But he unleashed a popular movement that the Northern Islamic establishment could not stop, even if it had wanted to. Many people saw the restoration of sharia as the answer to the pervasive corruption and injustice. When the reintroduction of sharia was marked at the stadium in Kano in 2000,[27] claims circulated that more than a million people attended. However, implementation of sharia has varied considerably across the states that adopted it.[28] A few spectacular sharia trials have attracted Western media attention, notably that of Amina Lawal, an illiterate woman accused of adultery, mostly because of the prospect of barbaric punishments such as amputation and stoning. However, no stoning and only a few amputations have been carried out because sharia has within it legal safeguards that led to the convictions being overturned on appeal, or the governors have refused to approve such punishments. (Lawal ultimately was acquitted by a sharia court.)

More importantly, sharia has had no visible impact on corruption. While its advocates argue that sharia has never actually been implemented in practice, the fire has largely gone out for its earlier supporters and no additional states have adopted it since the first wave. Boko Haram denounces the implementation of sharia in the Northern states as "political" and advancing the interests of the rich rather than the poor. It advocates a strict sharia that would apply equally to all.

In 2003, Osama bin Laden singled out Nigerian Muslims and urged them to "incite and mobilize the Islamic nation . . . to break free from the slavery of those regimes who are slaves of America." He characterized Nigeria as among the "unjust and infidel" regimes, along with Jordan, Morocco, Pakistan, Saudi Arabia, and Yemen. Bin Laden's message failed to resonate among the Islamic establishment.[29] Lateef Adegbite, secretary-general of the Supreme Council for Islamic Affairs, utterly rejected bin Laden's call. He responded to the press, "we the Muslims are for peaceful co-existence. We don't want war against anybody."[30]

In fact, violent, radical opposition to Nigeria's traditional Islamic establishment and the federal government existed before Boko Haram. Groups such as the so-called Shiites, Taliban, and now Boko Haram tend to be radical and utopian. They also have overlapping supporters. They appear to be indigenous to Nigeria. Some of them may draw on the radical tradition of the Mahdists of Sudanese origin. With the exception of the "Shiite" malam Ibrahim Zakzaki, who has become a public figure and a preacher of note, its

THE LIMITS OF ECONOMIC REFORM

When Olusegun Obansanjo was elected president in 1999, there was hope that he would institute meaningful economic reforms. And he did make the attempt. My sense was that President Obasanjo approached economics in general and debt in particular the way the soldier he was would approach personal consumer debt. From his perspective, all debt was bad. Nigeria's was especially bad because much of it had been acquired by previous governments for frivolous purposes or because of corruption. Obasanjo concluded that debt was a major cause of Nigeria's failure to develop. He directed Ngozi Okonjo-Iweala as minister of finance to address it and other issues hindering development. She was joined and supported by an economic reform "dream team" that included Charles Soludo, the governor of the Central Bank; Obi Ezekwesili, the anticorruption czarina; and Malam Nasir el-Rufai, the minister of the Federal Capital Territory, the largest single federal bureaucracy in Nigeria.

As finance minister, Okonjo-Iweala delinked government expenditure from volatile oil revenues. She based the federal budget on a conservative estimate of the future price of oil. Any resulting surplus was placed aside in a special account. This helped reduce the threat of inflation and insulated the government against drops in the price of oil. She accordingly built up foreign reserves and successfully brought inflation down from around 26 percent to about 11 percent.

In 2005, she negotiated a settlement of most of the country's foreign debt with the Paris Club, an informal group of nineteen government lenders. This allowed Nigeria in 2006 to become the first African nation to fully pay off its debt to the group. The Paris Club settlement freed Nigeria from debt service of some $1 billion per year. With Ezekwesili, Okonjo-Iweala also overhauled contracting procedures and introduced a degree of transparency in government expenditure without precedence in Nigeria's history. In return for her relative success, she became the toast of the international financial community, as did Obasanjo, so long as he supported her.

Despite Okonjo-Iweala's international popularity, as an Igbo who had lived for more than twenty years in the United States as a World Bank vice president, she was outside the contemporary *oga* networks and depended on Obasanjo for her political survival. Accordingly, at a diplomatic dinner in 2004, she made a spirited defense of Obasanjo's trade bans and other retrograde trade and investment policies even though they ran counter to the spirit of her own reform efforts. She also reminded her audience that Nigeria took its debt seriously and had not tried to repudiate the obligations run up by the Abacha dictatorship. Debt relief, she continued, was a major foreign policy priority for Obasanjo, and she believed in it too—passionately. In capitals and at international conferences, Okonjo-Iweala marshaled the plau-

leadership is obscure and fractured, and its goals appear to be millenarian rather than those of practical politics.

Boko Haram, led by Mohammed Yusuf, was part of the "Taliban" tradition. Based at a mosque in Maiduguri,[31] Boko Haram opposed Western education of any sort as well as the secular government of Nigeria. His movement appears to have enjoyed some support from influential people in Borno state. In July 2009, Yusuf led a bloody insurrection against the Abuja government that started in Maiduguri and spread to other cities in the North. Numerous police, low-level government officials, and Christian clergy were murdered until the Nigerian army, with great difficulty, suppressed it and handed Yusuf over to the police who murdered him while in custody. Its followers melted back into the population. Boko Haram appears to have been an entirely indigenous movement without links to al-Qaeda or Iran. Its followers' collective ability to melt back into the population may indicate that it already enjoyed a measure of popular support.

Before Islamic society in the North suffered the hammer blows of Boko Haram after 2009, not all Muslims influenced by new currents of Islam resorted to violence; instead, some communities, often led by charismatic imams, chose to distance themselves from mainstream society. Their approach was quietist and pietistic. While we know remarkably little about these groups, anecdotal evidence suggests they were mostly urban, based especially in Kano and Maiduguri. Some communities appeared to number in the several thousands. We do not have evidence that these groups were politically active. However, there is anecdotal evidence that these groups could function as a way station to violent radicalism. Boko Haram is an example of the "wilderness" to insurrection trajectory.

The Kaduna *Weekly Trust* and the Lagos *Vanguard* reported another example. A group from Maiduguri, identified as "Hijrah," withdrew to the bush around Kannamma in Yobe state to distance themselves from mainstream society. There, they pursued religious studies and farming. Suddenly, for reasons unknown to outsiders, in January 2004, the group turned violent. It attacked the police station, killing police and stealing arms and ammunition. They then moved to another police station and stole more weapons and vehicles. They distributed leaflets announcing their plans to create a special Islamic state in Nigeria, ostensibly under its spiritual leader "Mullah Umar" (recalling the Afghan Taliban leader), and saying they would kill any "unbeliever in uniform," presumably a reference to the police. They also called on Muslims throughout the country to "jihad" against the establishment. The Nigerian army claimed subsequently to have killed or captured more than fifty of the radicals, including their leader. However, many of the radicals appeared, once again, to have successfully melted into the bush.[32]

In September 2004, *This Day*, a Lagos newspaper citing Nigerian police sources, reported further "Taliban" attacks on police stations. The police claimed they killed fourteen "Taliban" as they were escaping into the bush and captured their leader, Abubakar Aliyu Abubakar. Two weeks later, *Vanguard* reported that "Islamist rebels" attacked police stations and took hostages in Borno state, near the Cameroonian border.[33] These groups appear to be part of the mix out of which Boko Haram evolved.

The "Shiites" are similar in background and appear to be particularly detested by the North's Islamic establishment, not least because of their ability to stir up popular urban unrest. There have been several "Sunni-Shiite" clashes in Northern Nigerian cities. Influenced and possibly funded by Iran, Zakzaki has been their most prominent leader, with his headquarters in Zaria. He denounces the corruption of Nigeria's military and civilian governments, which he characterizes as non-Islamic, and has been jailed numerous times for these activities. His followers refer to themselves as "brothers" and number, he claims, some 3 million (certainly an exaggeration), organized into the "Islamic Movement in Nigeria." Publicly, however, Zakzaki renounces the use of violence.[34]

In Sokoto, Malam Umaru Dan Maishiyya was murdered in July 2007 as he left his mosque, having just delivered a fiery sermon. The "Shiites" were popularly held to be responsible for his murder, and at least one was lynched on the spot. The authorities arrested the local "Shiite" leader, Malam Kasimu Umar, and more than a hundred of his followers. A year later, a sharia court sentenced Umar and 112 followers to eight-year jail terms on charges of unlawful assembly, inciting the public, and constituting a public nuisance—but not murder. At their sentencing, those convicted continued to insist on their innocence. The municipal authorities bulldozed the "Shiite" Sokoto compound and Umar's family house. According to the press, the Sokoto governor's spokesman said the demolition was done to "prevent chaos and insecurity in the metropolis" and to "prevent further outbreak of violence in the state." "Shiites" claim that Malam Umaru was murdered by the security services to provide a pretext for the local authorities to move against them.[35]

At least a few of the Northern elite have long recognized the potential threats from a relatively small but radicalized group of discontents. In 1995, Maitama Sule, one of the founding fathers of the Nigerian federation and a kingpin of the Kano elite, expressed his concern about the rise of militant Islam to Karl Maier: "If we do not nip this thing in the bud now, we may end up with a revolution which is not just religious, but may be political, social and economic. Symptoms of revolt look large on the horizon today."[36] At a dinner I hosted for the Kano elite nine years later, Sule remained extravagantly pro-American in his formal remarks, while quietly warning of the dangers of Islamic radicalism once again.

The 2003 suspension by Northern state governments of a joint World Health Organization (WHO) and Nigerian federal government campaign to

eliminate polio through vaccination illustrates the growing authority of some
of these radical currents in Islam.[37]

In June of that year, an obscure pharmacist at a Northern university
claimed to have discovered minute, harmless traces of estrogen in the polio
vaccine. Radical Islamic preachers, long suspicious of Western health campaigns in Northern Nigeria, especially those undertaken in partnership with
the "Christian" government in Abuja, thereupon condemned the polio vaccination campaign as a diabolical Christian plot to reduce the Muslim birthrate.
An emir introduced these fears at a meeting of the Jama'atu Nasril Islam, an
umbrella group of Muslim organizations, in July 2003. The Supreme Council
for Sharia in Nigeria (SCSN) then took up the antivaccination cause. At a
news conference, its president, Dr. Ibrahim Datti Ahmed, called on the federal government to suspend the use of oral polio vaccine based on allegations
that it contained antifertility agents. Such was the strength of the resulting
popular outcry that the governor of Kano state, and eventually other Northern
governors, suspended the vaccination campaign.

The consequences of the yearlong suspension were devastating. Polio
reemerged in Nigerian states where it had been eliminated and spread as far
as Indonesia. At the embassy, we were deeply concerned that polio of Nigerian origin would spread to the United States, and the State Department engaged the highest level of the Nigerian government to urge the restart of the
campaign. The Nigerian federal government, however, was largely powerless to do so. Health issues, such as vaccination, are predominately (if not
exclusively) the province of the states rather than the federal government,
and suspension of the polio vaccination was a popular movement in the
North.[38]

Jama'atu Nasril Islam and the SCSN are not radical organizations, and
their call for suspension received some establishment support. For example,
the emir of Dutse acknowledged in a press interview that he was deeply
suspicious of President Obasanjo and the Nigerian government for trying to
limit the growth of the North's population and using vaccination as a means
to do so.[39] The emir of Kazaure urged that polio immunization be suspended
pending a thorough investigation of the vaccine. Repeating a common theme,
the emir expressed dismay as to why the promoters of polio vaccination,
especially the United States and the WHO, did not focus their attention
instead on other deadly diseases like measles that annually kill millions more
Nigerian children than does polio.[40]

The federal government sought to mobilize Northern Islamic establishment opinion in favor of the vaccination campaign. Vice President Atiku
Abubakar, a Northern Muslim and not yet the president's bitter enemy, in
July 2003 urged eight Northern governors to take leadership and responsibility for polio eradication efforts. He urged them to win the support of traditional and religious leaders as well as opinion leaders.[41] These efforts en-

joyed some brief success. The following month, the district head of Kangama assured the WHO representative of the support of the traditional rulers for polio vaccination.[42] And there were hints that the Nigeria Medical Association had started the process to expel Dr. Datti Ahmed for advocating suspension of the vaccination campaign.[43]

However, opposition to vaccination had been simmering at the grassroots level for a long time, apparently sustained by Islamic preachers outside the control of the traditional authorities. In an August 2003 editorial, the *Weekly Trust* (Kaduna) noted long-standing, popular suspicion of "polio immunization as a systematic depopulation program by the United States of America, the World Health Organization, and the Nigerian governments at state and federal levels." The editorial also linked polio immunization to HIV/AIDS.[44]

The popular support reflected a deep hostility to the government of President Obasanjo and probably indicated a decline in the influence of the previous sultan and his emirs. The upper reaches of the Northern Islamic establishment understood the damage caused by suspension but recognized that it lacked the power to compel the Northern population to submit their children to vaccination against their will.[45]

The Northern governors did not feel strong enough to resume the vaccination campaign until after international Islamic opinion had been marshaled in their support, especially through the Organization of the Islamic Conference, and until the vaccine could henceforth be procured by "Islamic" sources in Malaysia. Hints from the Saudis that they might require proof of vaccination for hajj participants finally helped turn the tide. We similarly raised the possibility of the same requirement for a U.S. visitor's visa.

The polio debacle resulted from the confluence of factors: the memories of pharmaceutical trials carried out in the region in the past by a Western company that allegedly lacked proper controls,[46] deep suspicion of Obasanjo's "Christian" government, and widespread belief that he intended to remain in office indefinitely. That the United States was seen as an uncritical supporter of the president added to suspicions about U.S. involvement in the vaccine program.

In 2012, with a resurgent Boko Haram increasingly dominating the Northeast, once again the polio vaccination campaign appears to be failing. While there is no direct evidence that Boko Haram is behind it, the campaign's association with Abuja and the West makes it likely that Boko Haram's affiliated field preachers are rallying opposition to it.

AL-QAEDA?

Despite the seemingly indigenous roots of these new currents, a number of Nigerian prosecutors and the security services believe that a small number of individuals affiliated with al-Qaeda have been present in Northern Nigeria from time to time since 9/11. Unlike the domestic focus of most indigenous movements, the security services believe that these individuals aim to undermine both the Nigerian federal government and U.S. interests in the region. Mostly, they are not of Nigerian origin, or they have lived abroad for long periods.

In 2001, the press reported that the State Security Service (SSS) arrested seven Pakistanis in Ogun state in Yorubaland as suspected members of al-Qaeda and deported them. In 2002, immigration officers arrested an Algerian, alleging he was a member of al-Qaeda. [47]

In January 2007, *Vanguard* (Lagos) reported the arraignment of a director of the *Daily Trust* (Abuja), Muhammed Bello Damagum, on three counts of having received $300,000 from al-Qaeda to recruit and train Nigerians in Mauritania in terrorism. He pled not guilty and was granted bail. In October 2007, the Nigerian press reported that the SSS had arrested two men in Kano who had traveled to Algeria to al-Qaeda training camps for terrorists. [48] In November 2007, the SSS arraigned five people in the Abuja Federal High Court. The specific charges related to terrorism, conspiring to attack government facilities, and promoting insurrection. The deputy director of public prosecutions said they had been trained at a terrorist camp in Algeria run by the Salafist Group for Preaching and Combat, an al-Qaeda franchise.

Prosecutors of another terror suspect, Muhammed Ashafa, a Nigerian national, argued the Pakistani security services had arrested him on "reasonable suspicion" because he associated with two known al-Qaeda operatives. When Pakistan deported Ashafa in 2004, he was taken into custody by the SSS. The federal government subsequently charged that he was an al-Qaeda trainee in Pakistan, and the SSS claimed he had received $1,500 from an al-Qaeda group in Pakistan to plan attacks on American interests in Nigeria. He was also charged with receiving and decoding messages from an al-Qaeda cell in Pakistan for a Nigerian "terror group" with the intention of orchestrating an attack. In his bail application, however, Ashafa said that he gave over twenty statements confessing he was an al-Qaeda trainee, but only after he was seriously tortured by the SSS. Bail was granted on medical grounds. [49]

Over almost a decade, and in a country as large as Nigeria, the number of these cases is very small, and few, if any, have resulted in conviction. The SSS may have dealt with other al-Qaeda cases that never reached the courts, and, as we have seen, summary justice in Nigeria is not unknown.

In May 2008, a Lagos newspaper reported, and officials subsequently confirmed, that the Nigeria police had deployed antiterrorist squads in Lagos, Abuja, Port Harcourt, and Kano. The Lagos squad numbered eighty, and the commander had received U.S. training on the detection of weapons of mass destruction. Assigned to the Lagos squad were "two, newly procured modern armored personnel carriers." According to "one top security source," the deployment resulted from threats by al-Qaeda to "bomb some parts of Nigeria."[50]

In response, the Federation of Ahlus-Sunnah Organizations of Nigeria, an umbrella group of thirty Islamic groups, warned inspector general of police Mike Okiro against a "massive clampdown on Muslims" in his "current war" against al-Qaeda. The vice president of the SCSN and other Islamic scholars also issued similar warnings.[51] Their statements remind the federal government that it must balance its response to real or imagined threats from international terrorism with domestic Muslim sensitivities. Unfortunately, however, the Nigerian police are not known for their subtlety, and the potential remains for moves against real or imagined al-Qaeda threats to alienate parts of the Islamic community.

UNKNOWNS

This problem is compounded by that fact that the internal dynamics of Northern Nigerian religion remain obscure to not only outsiders but also the Nigerian elites, whether Christian or Muslim. To cite an example, on Friday, April 13, 2007, the day before nationwide gubernatorial elections, unknown gunmen murdered Sheik Ja'afar Mahmud Adam and two other followers as he led the dawn prayers at his Kano mosque, built by the London-based Saudi charity Al Muntada Al Islami.[52] That same day, I met with a cabinet minister, a Muslim. I opened the meeting by expressing my condolences on the sheik's death and said that the embassy was issuing a press statement deploring violence anytime and under any circumstances, especially the day before elections.[53] The minister responded by saying, "heart attacks often happen if you don't exercise." When I said that the sheik had been shot, he appeared genuinely astonished, and commented, "it will be hot in Kano." His lack of knowledge about this high-profile murder several hours after it happened seemed indicative to me of the disconnect between the ruling clique and what was happening in Northern Nigeria.

Sheik Ja'afar Mahmud Adam, educated in Saudi Arabia and often characterized by the Southern press as "hard line," was popularly venerated for his personal holiness, including by some of my local embassy staff. In 2003, the sheik had been active in presidential politics, supporting Obasanjo's chief rival for the presidency, General Muhammadu Buhari. Following those discredited elections, he "withdrew" from the world, organizing a community numbering in the thousands that sought to distance itself from mainstream society. Two of my local staff later told me that he was to give instructions to his followers on the day of his murder as to how to vote in the upcoming elections.

The following week, an unknown group in Kano, estimated by the press to number in the hundreds, killed nine police officers and the wife of one. They then barricaded themselves in a nearby water storage facility. The army spent a week dislodging them, apparently with considerable casualties. The perpetrators who survived again simply melted into the general population.

The days following the sheik's murder, different rumors emerged as to who was responsible: Boko Haram or, alternatively, some part of the official security apparatus. The sheik had attacked Boko Haram leader Yusuf's rejection of modern education. At the same time, he had bitterly criticized all twelve governors of sharia states for being too slow in implementing the full rigors of sharia. He was also harshly critical of Nigerian Muslims for practicing what he regarded as an Islam degraded by African and Western influences. At the time, most commentators believed the murder and the waterworks occupation were related to the upcoming elections. In light of the subsequent Boko Haram insurrection of 2009, that link is no longer so certain and instead may have been the result of rivalries among radical groups without reference to national politics. No satisfactory explanation has emerged as to what happened at the mosque and the water storage facility, and there is little indication that the Muslim establishment or the federal or state governments understood the dynamics or rival belief systems at play.

It is questionable whether the Northern elites can adapt sufficiently to respond to a society no longer monolithically Islamic and to the challenges posed by a younger generation hungry for power as well as increasingly militant groups that draw support from the impoverished population. A cabinet minister was uninformed about the murder of Sheik Adam. If the shehu of Borno had previous knowledge of Boko Haram, he declined to act before the insurrection. And no one was prepared for Abdulmutallab's al-Qaeda-sponsored plot. The Northern establishment's weakness in the face of new currents in Islam is shown by its inability to overcome popular resistance to polio vaccination, despite the international opprobrium.

U.S. OUTREACH

The complexity and diversity of Nigerian Islam poses challenges for the Obama administration's outreach efforts. The Obama administration has declined to designate Boko Haram a terrorist organization in terms of U.S. law. However, it has so designated certain individuals who are part of the movement. In any event, Boko Haram terrorist acts make it difficult, if not impossible, for American embassy personnel to travel in the North. Even if they could, they would most likely have an impact on the mainstream led by the traditional Northern elites rather than the radicals. Even in the face of that reality, it is well worth doing. The tolerant, Sufi mainstream remains by far the largest current within Nigerian Islam. But mainstream Islamic opinion could easily turn against the United States on the presumption that the war on terror is, in fact, a war on Islam, that we are irrevocably committed to the Christians, and that we have designs on Nigeria's oil wealth that we will use our military to secure. And, in fact, the Northern elite came perilously close to this view because of President Obasanjo's Third Term ambitions and the United States' perceived support of his administration. There is again a real danger that because of the close identification of the Obama administration with Goodluck Jonathan, moderate Islamic opinion will turn against the United States. The shortcomings in the administration of the U.S. visa regime, in which numerous Nigerians with Muslim names appear on various watch lists and thereby become subject to intensive inspection and delay, also undercuts U.S. outreach efforts, especially among the Islamic elite. The U.S. practice of "full body scans" of Nigerian Muslim women is particularly offensive.

Under these circumstances, our gestures toward the Northern elites, for example our work in preserving Islamic manuscripts, are critical. This brings us into direct contact with professors and other intellectuals at Northern universities who are at risk of being co-opted by an intellectualized, radical Islam.

The impoverished North, with its rivalry between Muslims and Christians and its new, indigenous forms of radical Islam, has become increasingly alienated from the government in Abuja. The 2011 elections, where a Christian president again took the helm, reinforced this alienation. The elections were not seen as credible by many in the North. In a period of strong Islamic religious revival, people like Abdulmutallab may act in response to the perceived dissonance between Islamic teachings and Northern reality. Most likely, their violence will continue to be directed against the Nigerian state. But al-Qaeda may be able to find fertile ground to recruit Nigerian operatives outside of Nigeria. Abdulmutallab's willingness to commit suicide is evidence that Northern Nigerian immunity to Middle Eastern tactics is eroding; so, too, is Boko Haram's beheading of three Pentecostal clergy during its July 2009 insurrection.

Unless Abuja moves to counter this alienation, the North has the potential to provide a major impetus toward state failure, particularly if religious, tribal, ethnic, political, and economic tensions continue to escalate. President Yar'Adua, a member of the Northern Muslim elite, did little to address this growing alienation. Jonathan's new administration is likely to be sympathetic to increasing the Delta region's share of oil revenue, which will mean less for the North, resulting in yet more impoverishment and social discontent. Hence, the North and the Delta are in a sense weights tied together that risk sinking the state, at least in its present form. The prognosis is not encouraging for Nigeria's continuing strategic partnership with the United States.

Chapter Five

The Niger Delta

The Niger Delta, about the size of Portugal, is a vast swamp, similar to the Mississippi River Delta south of New Orleans or Vietnam's Mekong Delta. In fact, it is one of the largest wetlands in the world. It is also Nigeria's richest ecological region, with over 850 tree species and 248 fish species, the largest mangrove ecozone in Africa, and the last intact lowland rainforest in the country. It is also where Nigeria's oil comes from.

Like its ecology, its people are also diverse. The Delta covers 9 states and is home to 33 million people dispersed among 5,000 to 6,000 communities. It is one of Africa's most densely populated regions. At least 40 ethnic groups speaking some 250 dialects live there. Ijaws are the largest, numbering 14 million. Although they have become the fourth-largest ethnic group in Nigeria, they have never enjoyed the recognition or the informal power accorded the Hausa-Fulani, the Yoruba, or even the Igbo within the federation.

Companies have drilled for oil in the Delta since the 1950s, and petroleum had become a viable industry by 1970. In some ways, it was the successor industry to palm oil, which, in turn, succeeded the trans-Atlantic slave trade.[1] The slave trade was inherently violent and decentralized—as was the palm oil trade, if less so. This pattern has persisted with petroleum. The civil (Biafra) war, centered in the region, broke out only six years after independence, leaving perhaps half a million dead before it ended in 1970. Since then, smaller-scale violence has persisted, including the Ogoni uprising of the 1990s, murder and kidnapping in Delta state until 2003, and Rivers and Bayelsa states until 2009. In 2012, there were signs that the cycle of violence was about to begin again.

The region has sustained significant environmental degradation related to oil extraction and population pressure. The World Wildlife Federation in 2006 calculated that up to 1.5 million tons of oil have been spilled in the

Delta over the previous fifty years.[2] The ubiquitous flaring of natural gas, despite the federal government's goal to eliminate the practice, is a significant contributor to global warming.

Yet oil has become the glue that holds Nigeria together. It motivates the *ogas* to preserve the federation and generates most government revenue and nearly all of Nigeria's foreign exchange. It allows Nigeria to be a major world player.

Foreign oil companies operating in a joint venture or under joint production contracts with the Nigeria National Petroleum Corporation extract most of the oil and natural gas. Shell, ExxonMobil, Chevron, Total, and Agip are the largest producers. Most of their employees are Nigerian; expatriates are few in number and are often technical experts who work thirty-day shifts alternating with long leaves outside the country.

Residents of the Delta have benefited little from the oil industry. Most of the population is poor, if not the poorest in the federation. The region is a byword for misgovernment and corruption at all levels. Residents have long complained that Abuja is tone deaf to their particular concerns, including the demarcation of the boundaries of local government authorities. Alienation from the federal government is widespread. In effect, little polling took place in the Niger Delta in the 2003 elections and almost none in 2007. The national and local *ogas* simply rigged themselves into office. Accordingly, an insurrection took hold, with attacks on oil installations that have, in some instances, reduced actual production to as low as 800,000 barrels per day (bpd), far below its estimated 3 million bpd production capacity.[3] Militants often argue that their attacks on the oil companies and expatriate hostage taking were intended to bring international pressure on Abuja for political change. The federal government, in turn, was largely unsuccessful in controlling the violence before it extended amnesty to the militants in 2009 and paid off their leaders.

Under President Olusegun Obasanjo, federal and state government spokespersons usually denied that the Delta insurrection had political goals and showed remarkably little sense of urgency about it. They claimed that the violence, which they acknowledged but usually downplayed, was the result of "criminals," "underdevelopment," and, occasionally, "ethnic strife." It was not until his first visit to the Delta of his presidency, a full year after taking office in 2007, that Umaru Yar'Adua even acknowledged it publicly. In 2009, militant activity spiked and thereby provoked a largely successful military crackdown. In the aftermath, Yar'Adua declared an amnesty, which thousands of militants accepted.

As in other parts of Nigeria, the Delta is characterized by legions of unemployed youth, many of whom turned to militant activity in their alienation. The amnesty was supposed to be accompanied by job training programs and other steps to reintegrate these fighters back into society. However, these provisions were largely a dead letter until President Goodluck Jonathan re-energized the amnesty program. Training then proceeded, but reintegration of militants back into their communities was less successful, and no political process was in place to address fundamental Delta grievances.

In 2007, a fellow ambassador in Abuja, an African, who was himself a veteran of an insurrection that lasted many years, made an incognito visit to the Delta. Upon his return, he told me he had no doubt that an insurrection was under way and that it enjoyed significant popular support, even though it was highly decentralized with its political goals muddled by gang warfare, ethnic strife, and criminal opportunism. His meetings with militants and community representatives as well as a number of trips into the swamps led him to conclude that it would be impossible for the federal government to militarily suppress the insurrection. The only solution, he said, was to address politically the region's deep-seated grievances and restore popular confidence in government.

As my ambassadorial colleague affirmed, militant political goals tend to be diffuse, ranging from outright independence (advocated by only a small minority) to much more modest political and economic reforms. A commonly cited militant demand is that the federal government should allocate a greater percentage of the oil revenue to the Delta states, local governments, and the communities that host the industry. Other militant spokespeople, often better educated, advocate shifting control of the petroleum industry from the federal government to the "local communities."

Nevertheless, most militants say they want the "liberation" of the Delta people from the "tyranny" of the current Nigerian state system, even if they do not advocate independence. Militants often have murdered, apparently gratuitously, soldiers and police because of their connection to the federal government.

Revenue distribution is a zero-sum game. If the Delta were allocated a larger percentage of the oil revenue, the other states or the federal government would receive less. And if Delta residents are poor, many residents of other states are even poorer. Critics of reallocation point out that the Delta state and local governments have failed to make use of their already huge revenues in a socially responsible way. Nevertheless, a revision upward of the share of the revenue going to the Delta would be more palatable to the *ogas* in other parts of the country than the federal government losing control of the petroleum industry altogether.

A number of politically motivated organizations formed and radicalized during the oppressive Abacha military dictatorship in the 1990s and provide the context for today's insurgency. The Movement for the Survival of the Ogoni People (MOSOP),[4] the Movement for the Survival of Ijaw Ethnic Nationality (MOSIEN), and the Ijaw Youth Council (IYC) date from those years, and they continue to provide a voice opposing the federal government.

The IYC's Kaiama Declaration (December 1998) called for democracy and respect for the region's indigenous people's rights and the environment. It demanded Ijaw control of the Delta's energy resources. The declaration resonated widely among the Ijaw, and by 2001 more than five hundred communities had at least nominally signed on to it. Among a highly diverse population, it represented something of a common manifesto of Ijaw grievances and aspirations.

Gang warfare, sometimes sponsored by *ogas* from all levels of government, overlaps with insurgency. For example, in July and August 2007, militias headed by rival *ogas* Ateke Tom and Soboma George fought each other openly in the streets of Port Harcourt and then elsewhere in the Delta. Neither was able to dominate the other. Many civilians were killed. Human Rights Watch in March 2008 published an analysis of this episode: "The clashes between the groups primarily represented a violent competition for access to illegal patronage doled out by public officials in the state government."[5] The report goes on to note that, although the Nigerian army eventually restored order, nobody was held accountable for the violence because state-level politicians and their national patrons were directly involved. *This Day* (Lagos) quoted a Port Harcourt resident as saying, "government never wants to do anything because they are involved. They are in power and could stop it if they wanted to."[6]

Overlaying the insurgency and gang warfare is tribal strife, particularly between the Ijaw and Itsekiri ethnic groups. Environmental degradation—popularly blamed on oil spills but also the result of overfishing and population pressure—has partially destroyed the local fishing industry, the main source of income for the region's residents.[7] As a result, more and more rural people have moved to urban areas in search of employment, especially Warri, traditionally the preserve of the Itsekiri. According to many of my Delta contacts, when rural people move into an urban, multiethnic environment such as Warri, their sense of ethnic identification increases, as elsewhere in Africa where there is significant rural-to-urban migration. The Itsekiris in Warri, in turn, resent the arrival of large numbers of different ethnic groups. This sets the stage for inter-ethnic strife, often connected with struggles among rival *ogas*. The subsequent killings, hostage taking, and sabotage are normally carried out by gangs or "cults," too often with the approval of their respective larger communities.

The federal and state governments, in turn, were unable or unwilling to control the violence. The militants and the criminals, with their access to sophisticated weapons and, allegedly, training by foreigners,[8] often outgunned the Nigerian military and police. And the gangs were often thoroughly enmeshed in the national *oga* patronage systems. For Delta residents, the government's complicity has discredited it.

For their part, the militants, gangs, and cults change their spots with impunity. One day, they are freedom fighters. The next, they are the muscle for disgruntled politicians. The day after that, they are a syndicate that exists primarily to enrich its members. These multiple roles have in common a war on the duly constituted authority of the Nigerian state. Militants see little or no contradiction among the different roles they play.

During the three years I served as ambassador, international donors supported small-scale, indigenous nongovernmental organizations for peace and reconciliation and some humanitarian projects that enjoyed limited success. However, federal and state government initiatives made little progress.

President Obasanjo's and President Yar'Adua's responses to the Delta witch's brew were peace conferences, summits, and "stakeholder" meetings, where government officials and a few militants negotiated "cease-fires" and "amnesties." All initiatives have been undermined by the federal and state governments' lack of political will to genuinely address Delta grievances. Either the government has failed to include all the armed groups in its dialogue or it has not kept its promises. For example, Yar'Adua's 2009 amnesty was viewed more favorably abroad than it was at home. There is deep-seated Delta cynicism about Abuja's initiatives: contacts told me the essential element of the amnesty was government payoffs of militant leaders.

Jonathan, acting president from February 2010 and fully constitutional president from May, is an Ijaw from Bayelsa state. He is under pressure from the Delta to bring about fundamental reforms. At the same time, however, he is constrained by demands from other parts of the country that their share of oil revenue not be reduced. As Nigeria's first Ijaw chief of state, he is between a rock and a hard place.

In 2008, a government-sponsored technical committee reviewed the best thinking over the past half-century on how to address Delta issues. It highlighted the Niger Delta Master Plan, itself the result of stakeholder consultations over a six-year period. At the heart of the master plan was a sustainable development strategy for youth training. Though it had promised to do so, neither the Yar'Adua nor the Jonathan governments issued a white paper based on the technical committee's report, which would be the next step.

In an attempt to influence public opinion, the federal government will periodically announce with fanfare the arrest of a militant leader, only to be followed by his subsequent release or escape. For example, in 2007, police arrested George, a militant leader allegedly affiliated with both the Movement for the Emancipation of the Niger Delta (MEND) and a Port Harcourt street gang, the Icelanders, for a traffic violation on a Sunday morning as he was going to his Anglican parish church. By midafternoon, sixty of his heavily armed men stormed through the city streets, defying attempts by both the police and the army to stop them, and broke him out of jail. A police officer later noted to a BBC journalist that, had they known who he was, they would not have arrested George.[9] Similarly, Abuja's announcement of an impending crackdown on the militants is followed too often by the latter's successful and humiliating operation against the security forces, often with significant government casualties.

The militants have also demonstrated that they can attack anywhere in the coastal region, including the outskirts of Lagos, largely with impunity. In October 2007, for the first time militants struck at an oil installation outside the Delta, in the far eastern part of the country, causing significant damage. They also embarrassed Abuja by attacking Cameroonian troops in the Bakassi Peninsula, which President Obasanjo had ceded to Cameroon against local wishes in response to an international legal judgment. Even offshore oil platforms, sometimes over sixty miles out to sea, have fallen prey to the militants. In June 2008, militants attacked Shell's Bonga Platform, sixty-five miles offshore, demonstrating their range.

Apart from attacking oil installations, ransoms from kidnapping oil industry employees also have long been profitable for militants. Company employees described to me on-the-ground efforts to "resolve" whatever the problem might be. In the past, that might include small payments to secure the release of an employee "held hostage," who on occasion might be found with his "captors" at the local bar.

Starting in late 2005, however, hostage taking changed. Whole groups of expatriate oil workers were captured and kept for long periods at camps isolated in the swamps. Their release was often tied to political demands, and the ransoms were much larger. Obasanjo tried to force state and local governments to stop paying ransom, and oil company spokesmen always insisted publicly that ransom was not paid. However, the president clearly was unsuccessful. The Lagos *Daily Champion* in May 2007 reported, "In the past three years, over one billion naira has been doled out to effect the release of some of the expatriate oil workers kidnapped by militants"; it had become so lucrative that "even prominent people" were now involved.

Victims tended to be employees of smaller oil service contractors, as opposed to those of the majors—Shell, ExxonMobil, Chevron, Conoco-Phillips, Total, or Agip—who house their employees in well-guarded compounds. However, the majors' employees were not immune. For example, militants killed the child of a Shell employee during a kidnap attempt in Port Harcourt.[10] Militants have also expanded kidnapping to expatriate children, the elderly, and even wealthy locals. In one incident, the aged father of the deputy governor of Bayelsa state, King Simon Ebebi, was taken hostage and released after seventy-two hours of captivity. It is highly likely that the Bayelsa state government paid the ransom. In another incident, the father of former Central Bank head Charles Soludo was also kidnapped and ransomed.[11]

Expatriate kidnappings often provoked indignation among Western governments and the Western media. The Italian press was especially shrill in its demands that Rome "do something" following a 2006 round of kidnapping of Italian expatriate oil workers. But the extreme fragmentation of the Delta militants combined with the Abuja government's inability or lack of will to act resulted in little being done at the federal level. One nongovernmental organization estimated that there were more than twenty militant groups in Bayelsa state alone. Each one in turn included numerous smaller groups, called "cults," overseen by an *oga* or master to whom members owed their allegiance. Mujahid Dokubo-Asari, a militant leader from the eastern Delta, claimed to the *Guardian* (Lagos) there were 312 separate Ijaw warlords in the entire Delta region, each with his own band and dedicated, he asserted, to bringing the Nigerian state "to its knees."[12] Despite this claimed unity of cause, Ijaw groups lacked an overall leader, nor was there an Ijaw "politburo" to coordinate the groups. Militant activities in the eastern and western parts of the Delta were separate and uncoordinated and seemed to respond to different leaders.

CORRUPTION—AGAIN

The level of state government corruption in the Delta is high. Diepriye Alamieyeseigha, the former governor of Bayelsa state, is illustrative. He was elected twice as governor, in 1999 and 2003, running as the candidate of the ruling People's Democratic Party (PDP). However, his victory was only possible because of fraudulent elections and a heavy reliance on violence and intimidation against the opposition. He then used his powerful position to loot the state treasury.

In September 2005, British police arrested Alamieyeseigha while transiting London (following cosmetic surgery in Germany) for allegedly laundering £1.8 million. The police also found £1 million—in cash—at one of his several London houses. Following various declarations of innocence and a failed attempt to invoke his Nigerian immunity as a state governor from British prosecution, Alamieyeseigha jumped his £1.25 million bail and fled to Nigeria. The Nigerian press reported he disguised himself as a woman, which he has indignantly denied. (One daily even published a front-page mock-up of his supposed appearance as a woman.) The press revealed that Alamieyeseigha's surgery in Germany had been for a "tummy tuck" and merrily reminded readers that the governor was "obese" (as he is).

Instead of turning him over to the British police, the PDP suspended Alamieyeseigha's party membership. The Bayelsa legislature then impeached and removed him from office under heavy pressure from the party's national leadership, using questionable procedures, including illegally preventing his supporters from voting. Once impeached, he no longer enjoyed governor's immunity in Nigeria, and the federal government jailed him, again using questionable legal procedures. In 2007, Alamieyeseigha pled guilty to various corruption charges in a Nigerian court and received a short sentence. President Yar'Adua released him in July 2007 "for time served" as a goodwill gesture to the Ijaw.

The irony of Alamieyeseigha's story is that despite his thuggish methods and blatant corruption, after his arrest many of his fellow Ijaws viewed him as a tribal hero and symbolic of regional grievances against the federal government. Demands for his release became a popular cause that fueled support for militants. [13]

The elected deputy governor, Jonathan, an Ijaw zoologist, replaced him as state governor. Although considered relatively uncorrupt, Jonathan had disclosed assets of $2.4 million, and the Economic and Financial Crimes Commission (EFCC), Nigeria's antigraft agency, seized $13.5 million in September 2006 from his wife, Patience, pending the outcome of corruption allegations. However, as far as I can tell, the results of the EFCC investigation were never made public. [14] And in December 2006, President Obasanjo handpicked Jonathan to be Yar'Adua's vice presidential running mate, apparently as a gesture to the Ijaw and because of his perceived lack of corruption, at least in comparison with his other fellow Delta governors. However, my impression at the time was that his vetting was hasty and sloppy because Obasanjo had expected to tap Rivers state governor Sir Peter Odili, his close personal and political ally, until the latter was publicly accused of corruption by Nuhu Ribadu, the head of the EFCC.

Many Ijaws held Jonathan in contempt because of his association first with Obasanjo and the federal government and subsequently with the Yar'Adua government. In the run-up to the April 2007 elections, militants burned part of his private house in Yenagoa. However, in 2010, with Yar'Adua's hospitalization, Northern threats to exclude Jonathan from the presidential succession converted him into an Ijaw hero reminiscent of Alamieyeseigha's similar transformation. Subsequently, the Ijaw have strongly supported him.

MILITANTS

Until President Umaru Yar'Adua's amnesty for Delta militants, ostensibly MEND led the political struggle against the federal government. [15] Its Joint Revolutionary Council (JRC) appeared to be the closest entity to a coordinating body for militant groups in the Delta. [16] It issued press releases with demands that tended to focus on the release of one or another particular imprisoned Delta leader. However, it did not speak for all groups. In one instance, the JRC announced a cease-fire when the Abuja government released Delta militant leader Dokubo-Asari from prison in July 2007 in an attempt to pacify Ijaw anger at the federal government. But within twenty-four hours, militants had kidnapped two Indian national oil workers.

Cynthia Whyte, apparently a man despite the feminine first name, was another militant spokesperson. He never appeared in public or on television, so far as I know, leading to speculation about whether he is a real person. In a December 2007 press interview, he referred to the Rivers state government as a "Bantustan," contemptuously associating it with South Africa's apartheid regime.[17] Another is Jomo Gbomo, who regularly claimed MEND involvement in militant events.

MEND's very existence has been questioned, and Delta governor Emmanuel Uduaghan, among others, has suggested that it exists only in cyberspace. At the very least, however, MEND was successful in creating the illusion of a broad-based insurgency. MEND may well have controlled few, if any, actual fighters. On the other hand, shortly after Uduaghan publicly characterized MEND as a "media creation," MEND apparently in retaliation bombed a peace-building conference sponsored and organized by a major Lagos newspaper.[18]

Government Ekpemupolo, commonly known as Tom Polo, claimed to be the commander of MEND in the struggle against the federal government. He first came to wide notice in 1997 during fighting in Warri between Ijaws and the Itsekiris, when he acquired a reputation for ruthlessness that he continues to exploit. He is accused of magic and sorcery, and he is personally feared by many of his followers. He has revived the worship of Egbesu, an Ijaw god of war, and some of his followers believe themselves immune to the bullets of their enemies. It is alleged that governors in Delta and Bayelsa states have hired him for "political enforcement" from time to time. Despite his fearsome, magical persona, there is little evidence that he has ever had broad authority over other militant leaders.

Two of the other larger militant networks, the Niger Delta Volunteer Force (NDVF), lead by Dokubo-Asari, and Ateke Tom's Niger Delta Vigilantes (NDV), owed their creation to politicians who used them to intimidate or destroy political opponents in the 2003 elections and then abandoned them once ensconced in office. Both groups then began providing their thuggish services to the highest bidders and expanded into criminal enterprises such as oil theft.[19] However, none of these groups is monolithic. Their members regularly shift alliances between various groups and political and criminal activities.

Among the Ijaw, perhaps the most recognized face of resistance to Abuja is Dokubo-Asari. He organized the NDVF in 2003, claiming its purpose was to achieve through force the demands outlined in the Kaiama Declaration of 1998, especially regional control of the petroleum industry. In September

2004, the NDVF declared "all-out war" against the Nigerian state, targeting police and the army. With it, Dokubo-Asari also fought rival gangs, siphoned oil and gas from pipelines, and destroyed energy infrastructure. Many local people appeared to support Dokubo-Asari's activities, particularly his oil theft, because the petroleum "belongs" to the people of the Delta, and he was using it on their behalf. Arrested for treason in September 2005 following his call for the dissolution of the Nigerian state, Dokubo-Asari continued to communicate with his followers from prison, apparently by cell phone. (Why the jail authorities allowed him to keep his cell phone is yet another Delta mystery.) He became a popular symbol of Ijaw rebellion against the federal government, and his detention was usually listed by Ijaw armed groups as one of their core grievances against the Nigerian state.

Dokubo-Asari was born Dokubo Melford Goodhead Junior to a Christian family in Rivers state in 1964. His father was a high court judge. A university dropout, he says that his conversion to Islam was a result of his growing political and social activism. He claims to have received military and political training in Libya and lists himself as an admirer of Osama bin Laden. The *Guardian* (Lagos) quotes him as saying, "I only admire, and I repeat, I admire Osama bin Laden. My last son is named after him. I admire him because he is confronting Western arrogance, the same way we are confronting the arrogance of the Nigerian state. So there is similarity in our struggle."[20] However, he also maintains that personal religious identification is not an issue in the Delta because Muslims make up less than 1 percent of the Ijaw population.

Prior to the NDVF, Dokubo-Asari helped found the IYC, a politically active organization with the goal of advancing Ijaws' interests in the Delta. The IYC has largely been led by university-educated activists. During this period, Dokubo-Asari claimed that he and the IYC worked for Rivers state governor Odili, assisting with voter fraud and intimidation in return for a largely free rein to "bunker" (steal) oil. However, Dokubo-Asari broke with Odili, and in a newspaper advertisement following the 2003 elections, he accused the governor of election fraud and of arming rival gangs.

In response, Odili allegedly hired another well-known Delta militant, Ateke Tom, and his NDV to move against Dokubo-Asari and the NDVF. Ateke Tom is less polished than Dokubo-Asari, and much less is known about his background. He appears to have little formal education. He emerged from one of the cults active in the state of Rivers. His followers believe that he possesses supernatural powers and they address him as "Godfather." From 1999 to the 2003 elections, he worked for the ruling PDP and was allied with Dokubo-Asari, according to the Lagos press.[21] Following the elections, the two organizations have fought regularly over territory and opportunities to steal oil. However, being opportunistic organizations, they have also joined forces from time to time for mutual profit.[22]

Another influential Delta militant is gunrunner Henry Okah. Much of his business appears to be based in South Africa, though his primary sales focus is the Delta. Arrested in Angola at the request of the Abuja authorities, Okah has been indicted in a Nigerian court on some forty-seven charges, including treason. He was to be tried in secret. His lawyer, Femi Falana, the president of the West African Bar Association and a noted human rights advocate, denounced the secret trial as the prelude to Okah's judicial murder by the Yar'Adua government. The fact that Okah was to be tried in secret fed suspicion that he had collaborators in the upper reaches of the government who wanted to shut him up. However, Yar'Adua released Okah in 2009 to avoid making him a martyr in Delta eyes and as part of the peace initiative that included his amnesty for militants. Okah then cooperated with the Abuja government and has subsequently been denounced by many of his former compatriots.

Smaller organizations, or cults, participate in various networks such as the NDVF or the NDV but are also independent criminal enterprises. They have names like the "Icelanders," "Greenlanders," "KKK," "Germans," "Mafia Lords," and "Vultures." Many were originally formed in the 1990s as university fraternities but later evolved into criminal gangs. [23] Far from having a collegiate background, members now tend to come from the bottom of local society, use narcotics, and practice sorcery. Some cultists even invoke the protection of the Ijaw deity Egbesu for immunity from enemy bullets. [24]

Like Dokubo-Asari or Ateke Tom's much larger networks, some cults were also initially used to influence electoral outcomes, especially by the ruling PDP. In the elections of 1999 and 2003, political candidates hired them to intimidate and fight their political opponents. Other cult employers include sophisticated industrial-scale oil theft organizations, as opposed to the smaller mom-and-pop operations. These groups appear to be parts of networks that include high-level politicians, military leaders, and employees of the oil companies. Their operations involve not only physically stealing the actual oil but also falsifying production and shipping documents. The magnitude of their theft varies; estimates range from 30,000 bpd to up to 300,000 bpd—more than 10 percent of Nigeria's total production—on a good day. [25] By 2012, the governor of the Central Bank, Lamido Sanusi, was estimating that bunkering exceeded 400,000 bpd. Profits fund the purchase of weapons used by cult members. Militant activity in the Delta provides good cover for these corporate oil thieves—so long as it does not get too far out of hand. Because corporate theft likely involves political figures at the highest reaches of the Nigerian government, this may contribute to the apparent lack of political will at the national level to address Delta issues before the administration of Umaru Yar'Adua. But too much militant activity can lead to a significant decline in oil production and in the availability of oil to be stolen. That results in lower profits for *ogas* all over the country, which is inherently destabilizing. However, much of time, high world prices made up for lost profits caused by militant violence and escalating bunkering.

Nigerian elite involvement in these criminal enterprises created strong incentives to oppose Western military or police intervention in the Delta, which would risk exposing its complicity. On the other hand, political activists, including some militant groups, do want Western involvement. From their perspective, the United States and the United Kingdom have the necessary leverage to extract political concessions from Abuja. However, little agreement exists among them as to what those specific concessions might be.

The Nigerian government responded militarily to the mayhem in the Delta by establishing a large military presence, the Joint Task Force (JTF). But the military and police were challenged by the swampy topography and the significant support or acquiescence the militants received from the local people. There are also whispers that the individual officers and men are complicit in oil theft themselves. To avoid pushing more residents into the militant camps, Abuja has usually avoided military operations that could lead to civilian deaths. So, during 2007 and 2008, the JTF largely stayed in their barracks. In 2009, the JTF attacked Ijaw villages suspected of harboring militants, causing significant loss of life, and threatened to carry out more attacks. If this represents a shift in military strategy toward the Delta, the consequences for further radicalization of the population remain to be seen. In the short term, however, the JTF's teeth encouraged at least some militants to accept Yar'Adua's amnesty and payoffs.

Starting under President Yar'Adua, and expanding under President Jonathan, certain militant leaders moved into the political establishment, living in Abuja and gravitating toward President Jonathan's Ijaw inner circle. The *Wall Street Journal* in 2012 quoted a national oil company official as saying that it paid $3.8 million each to "Boyloaf" Victor Ben and "Gen." Ateke Tom for their men to guard Delta pipelines. He said that "Government Tompolo" has a contract worth $22.9 million a year to do the same. The state oil company awarded Dokubo-Asari contracts worth $9 million a year to pay 4,000 former militants to protect pipelines. According to the 2012 national budget, Nigeria spends about $450 million on the amnesty program. This covers living allowances for former militants as well as the costs of retraining.[26] However, as the political position of the Jonathan government eroded under the onslaught of Boko Haram in 2012, some of the former militants seemed to be distancing themselves from the administration. Dokubo-Asari, once a Jonathan apologist, called for a sovereign national convention to remake the Nigerian federation. Delta kidnapping was on the upswing. First, it was mostly Nigerians who were the victims. By autumn of 2012, kidnappers were turning to expatriates. Former militant foot soldiers were complaining about the lack of work, despite their retraining. There were all the appearances that the cycle of violence in the Delta was about to start again.

BIG OIL

The major oil companies have responded to unrest in the Delta, in part, by fostering intimate relationships with both the federal and state governments. For example, much of their security is provided by off-duty officers from the Nigeria Police Force.[27] In addition, they have developed and cultivated excellent tactical intelligence networks. Until 2005 or so, the oil companies tended to keep their distance from their respective embassies and settled "labor disputes" or other issues informally, presumably often without the knowledge of their home offices in Nigeria or abroad. This changed as security in the Delta has deteriorated, and cooperation among the oil majors and the Western embassies on consular issues such as kidnapping became close.

In an attempt to win support from the regional communities, the oil companies have assumed those responsibilities the federal government has forgone such as building schools and hospitals. This approach has proven to be a two-edged sword. The companies become the focus of community ire when services are perceived as inadequate. The oil companies have pursued a variety of development strategies over the years, none of which has been particularly successful. They have provided much of the funding for the Niger Delta Development Commission (NDDC) and its multiple predecessors. The NDDC is the government-sponsored agency charged with sustainable development in the Delta. It has been largely unsuccessful because of a lack of national and regional political will. It has little visible presence in the Delta beyond its huge Port Harcourt office building. Given its lack of transparency and absent contrary evidence, there is suspicion that NDDC's revenue has been largely dissipated by corruption.

Oil companies make "customary and statutory payments" to host communities or to those who ostensibly hold the land and fishing grounds where oil exploration or drilling might take place. However, in the past, this often promoted intercommunal conflict between these "host communities" and their immediate neighbors. Furthermore, the oil companies typically negotiate these agreements and payments with traditional rulers who may—or may not—command the respect of local people and who may—or may not— share the proceeds with their subjects. Oil company lump-sum payments have had the consequence of increasing the power of traditional rulers and making those positions the focus of intensive and sometimes bloody competition.

In addition to these payments, at least 90 percent of the profits from oil above a certain threshold go directly to the Nigerian state.[28] Almost all oil company activities on land are joint ventures or production-sharing contracts with the government-owned Nigeria National Petroleum Corporation (NNPC). In joint ventures, NNPC is responsible for supplying its share of capital for the oil production. Offshore operations, which were growing ra idly through 2010, are usually managed through production-sharing contracts between a private oil company and NNPC. Under this arrangement, the oil companies carry all of the costs of exploitation and production. Once they have recovered their costs, production profits are shared with the NNPC. Under both arrangements, the oil companies pay royalties and taxes. An oil company executive told me that the profit margin from their operations in the Gulf of Mexico is far higher than from the Gulf of Guinea. In the latter, operating costs are high because of the difficulty of the natural environment and the ongoing security problems. Yet even in the face of the massive security problems since late 2005, the oil companies have not only stayed but also prepared to expand their operations. The oil reserves in Nigeria are simply huge, and the amount of existing investment makes it not feasible economically for them to walk away. However, this may change if security continues to deteriorate. [29] Shell, which pumps about half of Nigeria's oil, has raised publicly the possibility of reducing its Nigerian operations. Shell's production facilities, mostly located on land, are particularly vulnerable to militant attacks. Shell has also been active in the Delta for more than half a century, plenty of time for local grievances to accumulate. The Ijaw complain bitterly that Shell, as part of its effort to give its operations a Nigerian face, promoted President Obasanjo's fellow Yorubas rather than Delta indigenous people, especially the Ijaw. Under Jonathan, an Ijaw, these complaints have subsided.

As a senior executive of one of the international oil companies observed to me, it would be relatively simple to shut down the entire oil and gas industry in Nigeria. Coordinated sabotage of the ports and only a few of the key oil installations would be sufficient to do it. But this has not happened. It looks as though it is in the interests of all parties to maintain some fraction of oil production, especially when oil values per barrel are high.

The federal government continues to receive the lion's share of the profits from oil, transmitted by the oil companies that have largely assumed responsibility for the security of their own operations and on the sufferance of the militants. So long as this continues, and so long as it is not overtly challenged elsewhere, the Abuja government should be able to fund its operations in other parts of the country. For a long time, traditional Abuja international activism disguised the steady deteriorating of government authority at home. But Abuja's international role, especially fielding UN peacekeepers, is, like all other government activities, dependent on the oil revenues. If that dries up, so will Nigerian international peacekeeping.

President Yar'Adua's petroleum minister, Rilwanu Lukman, sought to restructure the petroleum industry in Nigeria. His goal included transforming the NNPC into an entity resembling the state-owned oil companies in Brazil or Malaysia. Goals included increasing the local content of the industry, providing NNPC access to capital markets, and increasing government revenue. He introduced his Petroleum Industry Bill (PIB) designed to accomplish these goals into the National Assembly in 2009. However, it also opened the question of the oil revenue distribution among the three tiers of government and among the states. Oil companies objected that Lukman's consultations with them had been superficial and that an unintended consequence of the legislation would be lower profits for them, thereby inhibiting future investment. Jonathan removed Lukman from the oil portfolio after he became acting president. Most observers expected little movement of petroleum reform until after the elections of 2011.

Jonathan made Diezani Alison-Madueke, a veteran of Shell, the petroleum minister and the head of NNPC in 2010. She worked for more oil industry contracts to go to local companies. However, she had made little progress in advancing the PIB, which was intended to, among other things, reform the relationship between the independent oil companies and the Nigerian state. By 2012, the bill was rapidly becoming part of the larger question of how oil revenue should be allocated in Nigeria. The North was concerned that any change would reduce their share, especially under a Christian administration. With the federal government increasingly distracted by the Boko Haram insurgency, the PIB remained far from passage. But because the legislation was on the table, and because its various drafts were riddled with contraction and inconsistencies, foreign oil companies were increasingly reluctant to make the necessary investments to expand production.

A dramatic fall in oil prices would result in diminished revenue flow. If this happens in tandem with a decrease in production from militant violence, the conflict could escalate to unsustainable levels. Alternatively, Abuja could seek again to placate the Delta with political concessions or payoffs. The decline in oil prices in 2008–9 was the backdrop to President Yar'Adua's Delta amnesty and to Abuja's "buyouts" to prominent militants.

Up till now, the United States has purchased about half of Nigeria's oil production. However, with new American shale-based oil production, U.S. dependency on imported petroleum may fall. As of 2012, American imports of Nigerian petroleum were down substantially in volume. Doubtlessly Nigeria can find other markets if necessary. The continued development of the African continent could well result in a much greater African demand for petroleum. Nevertheless, it remains to be seen what the consequences will be of a shift in the world petroleum market. The current Delta actors, criminal as well as legitimate producers, could find themselves squeezed out by violent, ideologically motivated operators. And international terrorism could likely focus international attention on the Gulf of Guinea.

Thus far, violence in the Delta appears to have few links to the religious and ethnic conflicts in the Middle Belt or with the Boko Haram insurgency in the North. However, in March 2010, the international press reported that Muslim militia leaders from Jos were trying to buy arms in the Delta. [30]

Future and as yet undocumented links cannot be ruled out. Delta Christian leaders have threatened mayhem against local Muslims if Boko Haram attacks on churches in the North continue.[31]

Arguably, the Nigerian state has been at best irrelevant to governance in the Delta. Before Jonathan, the federal government commanded little or no legitimacy in that region. But, with an Ijaw president in office and the amnesty payouts, Delta hostility to Abuja looks reduced for the time being. Once Jonathan leaves office, that could change. There was hope, more abroad than in the Delta, that free, fair, and credible elections in April 2007 would set the stage for the Nigerian state to regain the confidence of the Delta's residents. That did not happen. In 2009, President Yar'Adua's amnesty again seemed to open the prospect of reconciliation. Much is expected of President Jonathan, a Christian Ijaw. Yet without fundamental changes in Nigerian governance and politics, the dreary prospect is a resumption of violence, particularly as competition heats up for the elections of 2015.

Chapter Six

A President for Life?

Nigeria's experience of regime change has not been happy. From 1966 to 1999, changes in Nigerian presidential regimes usually resulted from coups, the threat of coups, or other extra-legal arrangements orchestrated by the military, not from elections. The one exception was 1979, when Olusegun Obasanjo's military government gave way to Shehu Shagari's civilian administration following credible elections. The only other credible presidential election Nigeria experienced occurred in 1993, the culmination of Ibrahim Babangida's reform program. That election, subsequently annulled by Babangida, was won by a Muslim Yoruba businessman, Moshood K. O. Abiola.[1] As for the other presidential elections, in 1983, 1999, 2003, and 2007, each was successively less credible than its predecessor. The polling in 2011 was better than previously, but the incumbent's reelection was still ensured by irregularities and led to the bifurcation of the country along religious lines. However, the sequence of elections in 1999, 2003, 2007, and 2011 may have established the principle that the regime now changes through rigged elections rather than by military coup. By and large, the Bush administration chose to downplay or ignore Nigeria's pattern of electoral fraud, undermining its moral authority with many of Nigeria's democratic reformers. By contrast, the Obama administration has taken a stronger line. When he made his only Africa trip in 2009, President Obama deliberately chose Ghana, a country that has had credible elections, over Nigeria. On her several trips to Nigeria, Secretary of State Hillary Clinton was forthright about the importance of democracy and credible elections to economic development.

In the run-up to the 2007 elections, Obasanjo faced the prospect of being a lame duck in his last year in office; the constitution limited a presidency to two terms. There was the potential that as a former president he might be held accountable for his actions as a chief of state by a subsequent government that he did not control. He would no longer enjoy the protection conferred on a sitting president of constitutional immunity from civil and criminal prosecution. And President Obasanjo's entourage at Aso Villa would certainly be out in the cold. These were new challenges for the Nigerian body politic and were the context in which "Plan A" and "Plan B" emerged.

Plan A, by which Obasanjo would remain president by running for rigged reelection after amending the constitution to abolish term limits, was the preferred solution for Villa denizens and probably for the chief of state himself. (Nigerians sometimes called it "the Mugabe option.") However, as we have seen, a long-standing, if unwritten rule of the Nigerian oligarchy is "no presidents for life." The longer Obasanjo remained in office, and with growing doubt about his intention to depart, the more unpopular he became. His car was stoned several times in 2005 and 2006. Among the political elite a consensus emerged against Third Term shaped by fear of the public's growing anger. On May 16, 2006, the Senate tabled, thereby defeating, the constitutional amendments necessary for Obasanjo to run again for the presidency. After that setback, he pursued Plan B, by which as ex-president he would wield power from a position within the ruling People's Democratic Party (PDP). However, his continued exercise of political power from a PDP perch carried substantial personal risks in an environment of ubiquitous violence.[2]

Obasanjo's efforts to retain the presidency and, when that failed, some of the substance of presidential power exercised from a party position distorted the political process and played a primary role in the failure of the elections of 2007. It influenced the election of 2011 as well. It was Obasanjo who handpicked Goodluck Jonathan as vice presidential candidate in 2007, which meant that Jonathan became president in 2010 when President Yar'Adua died. He then ran for the presidency in 2011, resulting in the alienation of much of the North and the electoral bifurcation of the country.

By April 2007, to many, perhaps most, politically aware Nigerians, it was more important to get Obasanjo out and a Northerner into the presidency than to have free, fair, and credible elections. No matter how poor the preparations for the elections were, on no account were they to be delayed, thereby allowing Obasanjo to remain in office.[3]

OBASANJO

Obasanjo is physically imposing, authoritarian in manner, and short tempered. He is capable of physical and intellectual courage. While in prison under Sani Abacha, he did not break. As president, he denounced the popular stigmatizing of HIV/AIDS victims, and he publicly donated his blood as part of a "Safe Blood" campaign. Increasingly authoritarian at home, Obasanjo, outside Nigeria, remained a staunch opponent of military coups and worked for regional peace and security, and he was a reliable partner of the Bush administration on African regional issues. He was internationally celebrated for overseeing the transition to a civilian government in 1979. As a civilian chief of state after Abacha's death, he established the principle that one civilian succeeds another—no more regime change through military coups. And he presided over economic reforms. Had he followed the example of Nelson Mandela and withdrawn from power at the end of his second term, his reputation would be that of Africa's most celebrated statesman. Instead, he tried to retain the presidency indefinitely and, when that failed, the substance of power through his office in the ruling party.

Obasanjo's early career is an example of how military service provided an opportunity for a poor boy to get ahead in a late colonial African country and end up first as dictator and subsequently as president. His parents are sometimes described as "middle class," a meaningless designation given Nigeria's level of economic development at that time. His home, Abeokuta, was a center of Baptist missionary activity, and his parents became Baptists. His family sent him to the Boys Baptist High School in Abeokuta, which provided him with a Western secondary education. After graduation, he taught briefly before enlisting in 1958 in the pre-independence army still run by the British. Shortly thereafter, he was sent to Aldershot in the UK for officer training. (The British also sent Abacha to Aldershot at about the same time.) According to one of his biographers, Obasanjo disliked Aldershot for reasons ranging from the weather to the alleged English obsession with class and race. But it led to his jump from the enlisted ranks to the officer corps. [4] For Obasanjo, his family's Christianity made a Western secondary school education possible, and that in turn led to Aldershot and then to an officer's billet. The rest, as it were, is history. [5]

Obasanjo's military career included a peacekeeping stint in Congo, but it really took off during the civil war. As a colonel, he commanded the federal division that took the last Biafra radio station in Owerri, ending the war. (This is the basis of claims by his sycophants that Obasanjo "won" the Biafra war.)

The bloody coups that preceded the civil war had opened the political space for the military, which promptly took advantage of the opportunity. A circle of army personalities dominated Nigeria's governance until the political crisis that started in 2010 with President Yar'Adua's fatal illness: Abdulsalami Abubakar, Abacha, Babangida, Muhammadu Buhari, Theophilus Danjuma, Yakubu Gowon, Murtala Mohammed, Obasanjo, and Shehu Yar'Adua (Obasanjo's deputy when he was military chief of state and the elder brother of President Umaru Yar'Adua). All but Danjuma and Shehu Yar'Adua have been heads of state at one time or another. All are close to the same age and were adults at independence in 1960.[6] There has been no true generational change in Nigeria's senior leadership since civilian government was destroyed by coups and the civil war, though the younger President Yar'Adua might have constituted one, if his health had not failed. Jonathan, a generation younger, and with his close political associates may constitute one.

While Obasanjo did not participate in Murtala's successful coup against Gowon, he supported it. Murtala in return made him his chief of staff, in effect his deputy. After Murtala was killed in the Dimka coup in early 1976, Obasanjo and Danjuma escaped, rallied resistance, and put down the coup. The Supreme Military Council[7] then made Obasanjo chief of state, which he served as from February 13, 1976, to October 1, 1979. The centerpiece of Murtala's political agenda had been the restoration of civilian, democratic governance. Obasanjo retained that platform and oversaw the writing of a constitution, the reconstitution of the political parties, and, finally, the elections that resulted in the civilian presidency of Shagari. Obasanjo received international accolades for being the first major African military ruler to relinquish office voluntarily to a duly elected civilian government.[8]

Or so it is said. Persons in a position to know have told me repeatedly that Obasanjo did not relinquish power voluntarily. In fact, they say, the other generals who were a part of his government forced him to do so; at one point, a general is said to have held a pistol to Obasanjo's head to ensure that he allowed the transition process to go forward.

Whether true or not, the story that Obasanjo voluntarily handed over power to a democratically elected civilian government has suited most of the political actors ever since and has become part of the larger national myth. It is congruent with the idea that the military is the guarantor of the Nigerian state, that it takes power only at the request of the people, and that it hands power back to the civilians as soon as it has cleaned up the mess, regardless of what the current mess may be. However, some *ogas* today believe that Obasanjo sought to stay in power in 1979, relinquished office only to save his skin, and would still do whatever was necessary to retain political power. This view, reflecting and reinforcing a pervasive distrust and dislike of Obasanjo, played a role in the coalescing of the patronage networks that blocked a third presidential term in 2006.

After Obasanjo ceased being military chief of state in 1979, he served as an international elder statesman. He was active in Commonwealth affairs, and he helped found Transparency International. As a member of the Commonwealth Eminent Persons Group, he played a positive, if minor, role in facilitating South Africa's transition to nonracial democracy. He apparently had no role in the Buhari coup that brought down the Shagari government, or in the Babangida coup, which ended Buhari's rule, or that of Abacha. He lived modestly. I visited his Ota chicken farm with Ambassador Princeton N.

Lyman in 1989 for lunch. The house was not large, and Obasanjo was affable and unpretentious. He spent much of the time discoursing, lying on the floor, his head propped up with one hand.

As the human rights abuses of the Abacha regime piled up, Obasanjo was courageous in speaking out against them. In consequence, Abacha had him arrested and charged with treason. Convicted by a kangaroo court, he was sentenced to life imprisonment, later reduced by Abacha to fifteen years in response to the international outcry over the obvious injustice of the proceedings.[9] Abacha probably had Shehu Yar'Adua murdered while similarly imprisoned, and Obasanjo believes he too would have been killed had former president Jimmy Carter not focused international attention on his plight. Years later, he told many people that God had preserved his life and that while in prison he became born again.

By the time of Abacha's sudden and suspicious death in June 1998, Nigeria had become an international pariah. The judicial murder of Ogoni author and Delta activist Ken Saro-Wiwa was the occasion of Nigeria's suspension from the Commonwealth. Relations with the United States were poor, and the U.S. Agency for International Development (USAID) reduced its mission to little more than a skeleton.[10] Within the country, opposition to military rule intensified. The military's claim that it held power only to facilitate a transition to civilian democracy was seen as a sham. Numerous of my contacts told me that Nigeria was close to a popular uprising at the time of Abacha's death.

With Abacha out of the way and soon to be followed by Abiola, who conveniently died of a "heart attack" just before he was to be released from jail,[11] the Nigerian military and political class turned to rehabilitating Nigeria's international standing and to reducing the political temperature inside the country while also preserving what it could of its position. To do that best required the quick restoration of civilian, ostensibly democratic governance. The military promulgated a new constitution, a modest revision of that of the Second Republic and broadly based on American principles. There was to be a federal system with formal separation of powers at the national level, and states and local government authorities were to enjoy significant powers. The military facilitated the creation of new political parties, which, however, in the Nigerian tradition could not have a confessional or geographic focus. Like their predecessors, these new political parties were solely machines for winning elections, not for articulating or advocating a national vision. The *oga* networks still called the shots but now through emerging civilian rather than military entities.

The PDP, godfathered by the transition leadership, was established before Obasanjo was able again to become politically active. It soon enjoyed the support of many of the *ogas*, especially in the North and in the military. But, like the other parties that emerged at the same time, it was not popularly identified with policies of either the right or the left. A consensus in favor of Obasanjo as the PDP presidential candidate emerged early within the party, fostered by those such as interim chief of state General Abdulsalami Abubakar, ex-chief of state Babangida, and General Aliyu Mohammed Gusau, subsequently Obasanjo's national security advisor for seven years, as well as some rich businessmen. They ensured that Obasanjo and Atiku Abubakar, a Northern Muslim businessman from Adamawa who had been in exile under Abacha, were respectively elected president and vice president in the rigged elections of 1999.[12]

The military and civilian *ogas* determined that the presidency should go to a Yoruba as a form of compensation to that ethnic group for Abiola's exclusion from the presidency. Because all of Nigeria's military dictators since the overthrow of Shagari at the end of 1983 had been Muslim, they also thought the presidency should go to a Christian. Obasanjo filled both of these requirements and had an excellent international reputation to boot. For the military leadership, Obasanjo must have appeared to be low risk. He was a part of the military system that had ruled Nigeria for so long, notwithstanding Abacha's paranoid hatred of him. In 1972, for example, Obasanjo had actively participated in the military effort to convince a skeptical public that having the military remain in power was essential to Nigerian state building and economic development, albeit as part of a permanent transition program to civilian democracy.[13] And he had served as a military chief of state.

POWER ALTERNATION OR "ZONING"

Nigerians who were engaged in that transition have all told me essentially the same story: the understanding in 1998–99 was that henceforth the presidency would alternate between the North and the South, between Christian and Muslim; its rotation would be a manifestation of Federal Character. After one term, Obasanjo would step aside for his vice president, Atiku Abubakar.

Obasanjo spent much of his first presidential term rebuilding his own patron-client network and restoring Nigeria's international standing. With both he was remarkably successful. His efforts on behalf of international peacekeeping and conflict resolution burnished his already high international reputation, while he purged the military and the security services of Abacha's "political appointees," who were mostly Northern Muslims, replacing them with those who became part of his own network. On the other hand, his relations with the National Assembly were bad in large part because he was insensitive to its prerogatives, and the latter made repeated, unsuccessful attempts to impeach him. Other than lip service, he did little or nothing about corruption, and, despite substantial oil revenues, he did not address Nigeria's fundamental domestic problems, ranging from disaffection in the Delta and the North to the growth of poverty.

During his administration, Obasanjo became increasingly unpopular at home, as much because of his military and autocratic style as his unwillingness or, more often, inability to address difficult domestic matters.[14] In a society that expects "big men" to personally distribute largesse to their servants and supporters, his stinginess with his own money was notorious and was regularly contrasted with Vice President Atiku Abubakar's liberality.

In 2003, rather than stepping aside in favor of Atiku, Obasanjo sought the presidency a second time. In the North, there was a widespread view that he was reneging on the understood agreement that the presidency would rotate. His relationship with Atiku Abubakar was also deteriorating, though the final break did not occur until near the end of his second term. Nevertheless, there was the strength of his resurrected patron-client network and his international support and prestige; he finally secured the PDP 2003 presidential renomination, though with difficulty and only with the last-minute help of Atiku Abubakar who sought to avoid a full-blown succession crisis. In return for his support in 2003, the vice president asked for, and apparently received, Obasanjo's assurances that he would support the former's candidacy for the presidency in 2007. But, already, some political operatives were concerned that Obasanjo intended to remain president for life.

Obasanjo's presidential opposition in 2003 was Muhammadu Buhari, also a former military dictator. Buhari is austere, and his image is that he is incorruptible. His house in Kaduna is modest; when I would call on him, he would answer the door himself, and the legion of servants and retainers that usually surround *ogas* was absent. While he was chief of state following his 1983 coup against Shagari, he waged a famous "war against indiscipline" that included high-profile measures to improve the notorious lack of sanitation in Lagos. He was popularly associated with "Sanitation Saturdays" in which vehicular movement was prohibited for several hours and the population was required to clean up the trash and garbage. (In modified form, Sanitation Saturday still exists.) As a result, the notorious multistoried garbage piles disappeared from the streets, though the sanitation problem in Lagos remained far from solved. (Babatunde Fashola, governor of Lagos since 2007, building on the achievements of his predecessor, Bola Tinubu, has made remarkable strides in rehabilitating the city's infrastructure, including sanitation.)

In its fight against corruption, Buhari's military regime was prepared to ride roughshod over what it regarded as legal niceties that blocked the administration of justice but to others was the essence of the rule of law. It was during his time as chief of state that Umaru Dikko, a former minister of transport in the Shagari government who had fled abroad to avoid prosecution for corruption, was found in a packing crate at London's Stansted Airport. The crate was labeled "diplomatic baggage" and addressed to a ministry in Lagos. Dikko was the victim of an apparently officially sanctioned kidnap attempt. The episode damaged Buhari's international reputation, especially in the United Kingdom.

Yet Buhari's reputation at home was that he, almost alone among the rulers of Nigeria, tried to address the problems of the country. The popular view was, and largely remains, that Buhari's anticorruption campaign was waged against the *oga* networks on behalf of the "everyman." Certainly the *oga* networks seemed to welcome Babangida's successful coup against him. Buhari is a sincere Muslim, which makes him an object of suspicion in parts of the Christian South. Nevertheless, at present, Buhari is probably the only national political figure with genuine popularity, at least in the North. His presidential campaigns in 2003, 2007, and 2011 were characterized by apparently modest levels of expenditure. For those who have benefited from Nigeria's current political economy, Buhari is high risk.

Accordingly, Obasanjo defeated Buhari for the presidency in the rigged 2003 elections. Domestic and outside observers thought the polling was worse than it had been in 1999. As he had in 1999, and as they would do again in 2007, Obasanjo's surrogates sought to stifle domestic and international criticism by raising the specter of another military coup if the political process were discredited by foreign and domestic critics.

As they were to do after the similarly rigged elections in 2007, international opinion led by the United States urged Buhari and others aggrieved not to take to the streets but rather to appeal for redress to the courts. In 2003, Buhari agreed reluctantly, having little alternative other than bloodshed.

The judiciary moved glacially, with the Supreme Court finally upholding the 2003 election results only in July 2005 in a decision that was inconsistent with findings of lower courts and that commanded little public respect.[15] Stories of varying plausibility circulated of Villa pressure on individual Supreme Court justices, mostly involving threats to make public instances of their own personal corruption. By then, however, less than two years away from the 2007 elections, many *ogas* viewed 2003 as history, if not ancient history. And Obasanjo remained firmly in charge of the party and the security services.

OBASANJO'S SECOND TERM

On the basis of its first year or so, Obasanjo's second term seemed more successful than his first. His relations with the National Assembly improved, if marginally, in part because he ensured that his own candidates replaced those in the PDP who had opposed him during his first term. His economic "dream team" put in place important reforms and achieved forgiveness of most of Nigeria's foreign debt. The activities of the Independent Corrupt Practices Commission and the Economic and Financial Crimes Commission (EFCC) seemed to be promising, and under the leadership of Obi Ezekwesili, the government contracting processes became more transparent. The president lent his full encouragement and support to the Nigerian and U.S. effort against the spread of HIV/AIDS and to treat and care for the victims of the disease. And he did what he could to support polio immunization.

But Obasanjo was unable to address the progressive impoverishment of the Nigerian people, despite soaring international oil prices. Most of the petroleum products used domestically had to be imported, because Nigeria's refineries were rarely operational, largely because of mismanagement and under-investment. It was widely said that people close to the Villa benefited from the export of oil and then benefited again when refined petroleum products were imported back into the country. As the gurus of the international economic community recommended, the Obasanjo administration removed some of the subsidies from gasoline and kerosene. Accordingly, prices went up, increasing popular misery and outraging those who regarded themselves as the tribunes of the people. The availability of electric power continued to decline. This reality accelerated the deindustrialization of the economy. Obasanjo launched a number of initiatives to construct new power plants, but by the time he left office, none were as yet on line.

A program to privatize state assets became bogged down and appeared to enrich Obasanjo's cronies. The federal government and its boosters in the international community lauded the spread of cellular communication: they said there were 11 million (sometimes up to an exaggerated 30 million; by 2012 the estimate was 90 million) cell phones in Nigeria. But only a minority of the population could afford them, and there was much anecdotal evidence that people reduced their already inadequate caloric intake so they could purchase phone cards.

Statistics about crime are unreliable in Nigeria, but the sense of the expatriate community was that levels dramatically increased, starting in 2005. Highly unusual, it was accompanied by an epidemic of rape, especially of passengers traveling on luxury buses,[16] in which gangs robbed and then raped every female passenger. At a diplomatic dinner I attended in February 2005, several members of the National Assembly present made an explicit link between popular anger at those who ran Nigeria and the increasing brutality of armed robbers. They commented that Nigeria would likely not break up into separate states; there would be no future Biafra. Instead, it would go the way of Congo, breaking down into small units dominated by warlord heads of local patronage networks with the federal and even state governments largely becoming irrelevant to most Nigerians.[17] One observed that this had already happened in the Delta. In a different context, former chief of state Abdulsalami Abubakar, in January 2008, expressed the same fears about the morselization of Nigeria. [18]

In 2005–6, there was a series of major plane crashes with no survivors, in each instance with official explanations of little or no credibility. The U.S. embassy was directly involved in the first of this grim series because it resulted in the death of the mission's chief of its Office of Overseas Defense Cooperation. [19] In that tragedy, it took some twenty-four hours to find the crash site—which turned out to be close to the end of the runway of Murtala Mohammed Airport in Lagos. Until the crash site was found, various official Nigerian spokesmen were announcing that, not only were there survivors, but also many had been transported by bus to a local hospital. This is but one example of the lack of transparency—even resorting to fiction—that so undermined confidence in Obasanjo's government. A subsequent crash killed more than a dozen senior military figures, mostly from the North, and yet another claimed the lives of the sultan of Sokoto, his son, and other members of the Northern elite. Then, more than seventy children were killed in a crash at Port Harcourt; that flight was bringing the children home for the Christmas holidays from a Catholic boarding school outside Abuja. In a different category, there was the nonfatal Air France flight that crashed into a herd of cows that had wandered onto the Port Harcourt Airport's unfenced runway.

Within hours of the first of this series of civil aviation disasters, Obasanjo lost his first lady, Stella Obasanjo. Her death was the result of complications from cosmetic surgery in Marbella, Spain. Popularly suspected of corruption, it was common to hear that she had died as the result of a "hidden hand," but without any accompanying credible evidence. [20]

The federal government either ignored or mishandled the escalating crisis in the Delta, which became significantly worse beginning in December 2005, with growing numbers of police and military casualties and a boom in expatriate kidnapping—nor did Obasanjo address growing Northern disaffection, especially with his government. In 2005, the press carried stories of military operations in the North against the "Taliban," a radical Muslim group that attacked police stations and that now appears linked to Boko Haram. By then, Northern opinion had become viscerally hostile to Obasanjo. Many in the Northern establishment believed he was seeking to hold office indefinitely and that he could not be trusted.

It was not only Stella Obasanjo's death that led to public speculation about a "hidden hand." The chaotic response and lack of transparency by the federal government to the civil aviation disasters certainly lent credence to views of a cover-up—of anything and everything. The unwillingness or inability to address the insurrection in the Delta led to speculation that "big men" in Abuja "close to the president" were somehow benefiting. Many of our contacts said that Obasanjo was seeking to create an atmosphere of chaos so he could stay in power indefinitely by declaring a state of emergency.

There were serious calls to rethink the constitution of the federation. There was agitation in the National Assembly and the press in favor of a "sovereign national convention," an extra-legal body somehow chosen by the people that would rebuild Nigeria's governance from the ground up and write a new constitution. Ojo Maduekwe, then secretary-general of the PDP, later foreign minister from 2007 to 2010, observed that such a convention would be a definitive sign that the Nigerian state had failed because its convening would mean that regular institutions of governance no longer functioned.[21]

A sovereign national convention would likely reduce presidential power by reaffirming term limits and abolishing existing presidential immunity from civil and criminal prosecution. To forestall convening it, Obasanjo established in early 2005 a National Political Reform Conference, essentially an advisory body that would make recommendations on possible constitutional changes but respect current legal structures. In effect, his administration selected most of its members, who collectively never commanded much popular confidence. It was chaired by Justice Niki Tobi, a Supreme Court justice. It debated a wide range of issues, including federalism, regionalism, and resource control. On the crucial issue of oil revenue allocation, the Delta delegations blocked any consensus, insisting that up to 50 percent of the revenue should go to the region that produced the oil. The conference limped along for several months and had no long-term, concrete achievements. However, it was the venue for tabling proposals for constitutional amendments—more than one hundred—that were eventually combined and transmuted into a bill before the National Assembly. Most of the amendments were noncontroversial, indisputable improvements on the current text. However, one would have eliminated office term limits.

PLAN A

Worries over the presidential succession were a leitmotif that ran through other issues. A Villa denizen close to Obasanjo told me that the president worried about his potential lame-duck status and that he was anxious that the "dream team" economic reforms be maintained. A cabinet minister repeated to me the shibboleth that only the president could keep the "army boys" out. A party official commented that Obasanjo frankly enjoyed the attention he received because of the uncertainty about his future plans. Obasanjo's enemies openly speculated that he held on to power because he needed the civil and criminal legal immunity the presidency conferred to avoid imprisonment for his corruption and that of his family. A number of my contacts reported that a soothsayer had said that Obasanjo would die either at the Villa or in jail. Certainly there was anxiety among Obasanjo's people as to what their own future would be if their *oga* was no long chief of state.

In March 2005, a visiting American academic expert on Nigeria told me there was a "permissive environment" for a military coup. And, in the 2005 Independence Day lecture six months later, Maduekwe asked, "Is Nigeria a failed state?" His response to his own question was no, but Nigeria danced on the brink.

By 2005, the possibility of an Obasanjo third presidential term had become part of the wider political debate. However, at no time did the president ever acknowledge publicly that he was seeking to remain in office. The heavy lifting of promoting Third Term[22] was done by his close associates at the Villa, certain big business personalities, and a few traditional rulers. I was pitched by a cabinet minister, a powerful traditional ruler, and two rich businessmen over an elegant lunch in Lagos. Their argument was that only Obasanjo could ensure that the economic reforms would continue, only he could keep the military from coming back, and he was pro-American. A Third Term candidacy also solved the lame-duck issue: everybody understood that, if he ran, the elections would be rigged to ensure that he won, as they had been in 1999 and 2003.

Obasanjo's silence was shrewd. His foreign friends, especially, told each other that the president had not said he would seek to remain in office. Some diplomats, myself included, thought that Obasanjo himself was of two minds, that agitation for Third Term came from Villa denizens who wanted to be able to continue to feather their own nests, not from the president, and that a word from Western heads of state might encourage him to leave office on time. But Obasanjo's silence about his future plans also provided little opening for a dialogue with foreign leaders on Third Term. A senior figure in the PDP told me that Obasanjo's conscience was torn between its good side (respect the constitution and leave—the "Mandela option") and its bad (change the constitution and stay—the "Mugabe option") and that he hoped the good side won. Given the course Obasanjo has followed ever since, there is little doubt in my mind now that he inspired and perhaps orchestrated the effort for Third Term and that, as numerous Nigerian politicians told me, he had made up his mind to retain the presidency indefinitely shortly after he narrowly won the PDP presidential renomination in 2003. Obasanjo is an authoritarian personality who regularly intimidated and humiliated his closest associates. It is inconceivable that Villa denizens would have launched the Third Term full-court press without their *oga*'s approval. Furthermore, Obasanjo never showed any interest in suggestions that he fill a prestigious international post after he left the presidency. Nevertheless, Obasanjo has consistently denied Third Term ambitions. More than a year after the issue had been put to rest by the Senate, shortly before I left the country, a Villa emissary assured me that he had never "actively" supported Third Term.

OBASANJO'S DEFEAT

After more than seven years in office, Obasanjo was nearly universally un-popular in Nigeria. His military style, his seemingly poor political skills, his inability or unwillingness to address domestic problems, his apparent goal of remaining president indefinitely, and the growing suspicion that he and his family were deeply corrupt made him a figure disliked or detested, even in Yorubaland. The political classes were in tune with the sentiments of the public. Under these circumstances, how could he contemplate a third term?

As the elections of 1999 and 2003 showed, and as that of 2007 would subsequently confirm, there was little relationship between votes cast and whom the Independent National Electoral Commission (INEC) declared elected to office. Elections were a kind of public ritual—not a way to deter-mine who would exercise political power. In addition, in a highly venial political atmosphere, Obasanjo's network had access to nearly unlimited funds for bribery, and he had successfully retained control over the security services and the army. Nigerian members of the National Assembly told their American embassy and other diplomatic contacts that the Villa would pay up to $1 million plus a building plot in the posh Asokoro section of Abuja to certain, influential senators in return for a favorable vote on the constitutional amendments necessary for Third Term. Obasanjo's unpopularity with most of the people of Nigeria was largely beside the point.

Much more serious was the consolidating opposition of Nigeria's political elites in the face of public anger, especially in the North, which, in the end, ensured that the constitutional amendments necessary for Third Term were defeated. Abdulsalami Abubakar, Babangida, Aliyu Mohammed, Danjuma, and Atiku Abubakar—Obasanjo's sponsors in 1999—all publicly or private-ly opposed Third Term. Danjuma was the quietest, but his wife, Senator Daisy Danjuma, was courageously outspoken against Third Term on the floor of the Senate. Atiku, Babangida, and Aliyu Mohammed openly sought the PDP presidential nomination for themselves. A vengeful Obasanjo ad-ministration successfully blocked Daisy Danjuma's party renomination as a senator and tried unsuccessfully to indict Babangida's son for corruption. Although he illegally tried to keep Atiku Abubakar's name from appearing on the presidential ballot, Obasanjo was unsuccessful because at the last minute the courts ruled in Atiku Abubakar's favor. In 2006, Obasanjo fired Gusau as his national security advisor, apparently because of the latter's presidential ambitions.

Given his then-glittering international reputation, why did Obasanjo go down the Third Term road? After all, he knew better than most the "no presidents for life" dictum in Nigerian politics. My view is that Obasanjo was increasingly cut off, and cut himself off, from the internal politics of Nigeria as he pursued the will-o'-the-wisp of African regional politics with the approbation of the international community. My contacts at the Villa and within the party told me that his circle of advisors was shrinking; he was listening to fewer people, and those were telling him what he wanted to hear: that he was indispensable to Nigeria and to Africa, a message echoed by his foreign friends. He progressively denied himself the advice and counsel of the most powerful *ogas* in the country. His sources of information also became fewer. He spent an ever-larger percentage of his time on international issues. For example, just before the National Assembly definitively defeated the proposed package of constitutional amendments in May 2006, he hosted an important Darfur peace conference in Abuja, where he brokered a deal between the Khartoum government and some of the rebel groups, to international accolades and indifference at home.

Obasanjo may have also been concerned about possible EFCC and other investigations of his family and himself once he had left office and lost his civil and criminal immunity to prosecution. The 2007 accusations of his daughter's corruption and the 2008 mutual accusations of the same by his son Gbenga and the latter's estranged wife add some credibility to this speculation—so, too, did March 2008 press reports that the EFCC was investigating allegations of his personal corruption, though he has never been formally indicted in a court of law. [23] Certainly, his days of living modestly were over. On the street, it was widely believed Obasanjo acquired a private jet early in 2008.

On Third Term, public opinion asserted itself in a way that the *ogas* did not ignore because they largely agreed with it. This was particularly clear in the North, where unrest and associated violence intensified so long as Obasanjo's Third Term ambitions remained alive. Local interests in some places told their senators that, if they voted for Third Term, they would be killed if they returned to their constituencies. (This story was repeated to me multiple times by members of the National Assembly.) Almost all of the media opposed Third Term, as did most of the leaders of civil society. [24]

By the end, May 16, 2006, when the requisite constitutional amendments were definitively defeated by the National Assembly, Obasanjo did not have with him a sufficient number of *ogas* to prevail. At the time, it looked closer than it does in retrospect. My Lagos lawyer contacts up to a few days before the National Assembly vote were predicting with chagrin that Obasanjo would succeed; a senator told me only twenty-four hours in advance that he and others opposed to the Third Term finally had sufficient votes to defeat the necessary constitutional amendments through the parliamentary procedure of tabling them. He said they would move the following day before ever-higher Villa bribes caused some of their colleagues to change their minds. And they so moved. Had Obasanjo in fact managed successfully to split the political class and achieve passage of the necessary constitutional amendments, I was told, the consequences would have been stark: business and legal contacts were predicting a military coup and, if that failed, a possible civil war. The winter and spring of 2006 were the most dangerous period in Nigeria's history between the Biafra war and the 2009–10 presidential succession crisis caused by Yar'Adua's failing health and subsequent death, to be followed by national elections in less than a year.

For Americans, Third Term posed a dilemma. Washington saw close collaboration with Abuja on regional issues such as Darfur and Somalia as an essential national interest, and there was the continued predisposition to take at face value Obasanjo's stated commitment to free and fair elections. Furthermore, any country has the right to amend its constitution, and ambassadors are rightly reluctant to intervene in the purely internal affairs of a friendly state where flagrant human rights violations are not the issue. Nevertheless, as I said publicly, U.S. policy in the developing world has been consistently to support term limits as a means of opening the political space for wider democratic participation. I also said repeatedly that, for Nigeria's friends, the methods by which the constitution was amended were crucial: was the process transparent and based on the rule of law, or was it done through bribery and intimidation?

WASHINGTON'S DILEMMA — AND THE EMBASSY'S

Alas, by early 2006, it was clear that the latter was the case, especially bribery. The challenge was how to signal to the elites and to the public that we knew what was going on and to support those Nigerians committed to a democratic process, without, of course, having evidence that could be used in a court of law. Washington continued to value the Obasanjo relationship, and I could not cut my ties irreparably with the Villa by directly accusing it publicly of corrupt and undemocratic behavior.

With those constraints, I decided to move the annual celebration of our National Day from July 4 to President's Day (Washington's Birthday) in February 2006.[25] My public excuse was that the weather is better for an outdoor reception in Abuja in February than in July, thereby saving us the expense of renting a hotel ballroom. The real reason was that I wanted a credible occasion to talk publicly about how presidential term limits promoted democracy. I took as my theme George Washington and his voluntary refusal to remain in office more than two terms and the way that decision had helped shape American democratic expectations of the presidency.[26] Ambassadors often give a history lesson about their own country in their National Day remarks, and I made no reference to Nigeria beyond the usual pleasantries about our close bilateral relationship. Nevertheless, our hundreds of Nigerian guests understood my meaning: when I finished, there was a collective gasp and then strong applause. There was no subsequent comment either from the Villa or Washington.

In hindsight, the United States did too little explicitly to oppose Third Term, and we thereby undermined our identification with democracy and the rule of law among many Nigerians. So far as I know, there were no high-level U.S. messages from the Bush administration (either oral or in writing) to Obasanjo advising him to stand down—nor, so far as I know, did the British, Dutch, and other friendly governments warn against his holding on to power. In our private communications with our Nigerian interlocutors, we emphasized the rule of law; free, fair, and credible elections; and the need to avoid violence rather than opposition to Third Term. The embassy did maintain its traditional contacts with Nigerian political figures demonized by the Villa; I continued to see regularly, if discreetly, Vice President Atiku Abu-bakar, General Buhari, and ex-governor Orji Kalu and the other actual or potential presidential candidates who had run afoul of the Villa over Third Term and in the run-up to the elections.

In late April 2006, the U.S. embassy issued a statement affirming the United States' view that "executive term limits should be respected in the interest of institutionalizing democracy and opening political space." Also, it noted that Obasanjo had made no public statement of his plans after his term ended.[27] The BBC noted that this statement was "the strongest yet from the U.S. government" on Third Term,[28] and it was immediately welcomed by the Conference of Nigerian Political Parties, one of the most important prode-mocracy nongovernmental organizations (NGOs).[29] Mild though the statement was, such was Washington's continuing concern about partnership with Obasanjo that, although I had cleared in advance the text with the Department of State, at least one high-level Bush administration political appointee objected to my having issued it.

Nevertheless, despite the obvious shortcomings of our low-key approach, Nigerians, who in general overestimate U.S. influence over everything, often gave us disproportionate credit for the defeat of Third Term rather than where it belongs: with themselves. Members of the National Assembly did tell me that, once they concluded that the Americans would not uncritically support everything Obasanjo did to retain power, they were emboldened to respond positively to what they and their constituents wanted—defeat of Third Term.

In the aftermath of Third Term, the United States was very popular in Nigeria, at least for the moment, even in the Islamic North: as a Northern interlocutor put it to me, "Too bad about Iraq, too bad about Abu Ghraib and Guantanamo; what matters is that you opposed Third Term." In the Delta, our opposition to Third Term seemed to trump the fact that two of the three biggest oil companies operating there are American. Delta opinion distinguished between anger at the oil companies on the one hand and praise for the U.S. position on Third Term on the other. [30]

After the May 16, 2006, tabling of the constitutional amendments in the National Assembly, Obasanjo publicly accepted that constitutional amendment was no longer possible, and so he moved on to Plan B. President for life was no longer possible; it remained to be seen whether he could be chairman of the governing party's Board of Trustees for life and thereby retain much of the substance—if not the ceremony and protocol that he loved—of presidential power. As he had with Plan A, Obasanjo remained silent on Plan B.

Chapter Seven

The "Election-Like Event" of 2007

On December 19, 2006, Olusegun Obasanjo's American friends saluted the Nigerian president at a gala in the Grand Ballroom of the Waldorf Astoria Hotel in New York. The dinner was hosted by the American civil rights organization the Leon H. Sullivan Foundation. It was supported by Goodworks, a lobbying firm under contract to the Nigerian government and led by Andrew Young, the civil rights leader, former mayor of Atlanta, and former U.S. ambassador to the UN. The guest list glittered and the security was tight. Speakers freely compared the honoree to Nelson Mandela. Hope Sullivan, president of the Sullivan Foundation and daughter of Leon Sullivan, an international civil rights leader, read a letter from President Bush. [1] There was a photographic exhibition of the highlights of the president's life, including a picture of the mud-walled Yorubaland compound where he was born in 1937, the Nigerian equivalent of the American log cabin.

PLAN B

By the time of this event, Obasanjo had abandoned his efforts to secure a third presidential term. He had already launched Plan B, whereby he would exercise influence from within the ruling People's Democratic Party (PDP) rather than the presidency. He had identified the party's chairmanship of the Board of Trustees as potentially a particularly powerful position, if in his hands. There is, so far as I know, no "smoking gun" that outlines the now former president's intentions. But the outlines of Plan B, like the efforts to implement Plan A, are clear from what Obasanjo and the people around him were trying to do. Moreover, as early as mid-2005, Nigerians interested in politics were talking to me about the possibility of Plan B as the way Obasanjo would hold on to power if he could not retain the presidency.

Just before leaving for the New York gala, running roughshod over party rules, Obasanjo imposed on the PDP as its presidential candidate Umaru Yar'Adua, an obscure Northern governor in ill health. For vice president, Obasanjo initially wanted Sir Peter Odili, the outgoing governor of Rivers state. Obasanjo and Odili had long been close personally. "Sir" Peter Odili, a papal knight, was the "sponsor" of the wedding of the only son of Obasanjo by First Lady Stella Obasanjo. But the Economic and Financial Crimes Commission (EFCC) head Nuhu Ribadu, in a sign of his growing political independence, dashed that possibility with his public charges that Odili was corrupt. So Obasanjo selected a Christian Ijaw, Goodluck Jonathan, the governor of Bayelsa state, for the vice presidential slot. Jonathan had been elected deputy governor in the rigged 2003 elections; when Obasanjo had the governor removed from office, ostensibly because of corruption, Goodluck became governor.

At the party convention in December 2006, the president's minions used intimidation to get other potential presidential and vice presidential candidates to withdraw. Nevertheless, Obasanjo still had to stifle opposition within the PDP to his "diktat." Obasanjo insiders have told me that the president was "genuinely surprised and angered" at the amount of opposition within the PDP to what he was doing, yet another sign of the president's isolation from domestic political realities. Expressing his own disappointment at the way events were unfolding, a senior PDP politician told me in January 2007 in Abuja that he consoled himself with the fact that at least Obasanjo would no longer be president by Inauguration Day, May 29, 2007, and "at this point, that is all that matters." It was also palatable that the Northern Muslim Yar'Adua and the Southern Christian Jonathan also respected the power-sharing principle of "zoning," whereby the presidency alternated between North and South, and if the presidential candidate were Christian, then the vice presidential candidate would be Muslim, and vice versa.

Free, fair, and credible elections in April 2007 were the goal for the many Nigerians devoted to democracy conducted according to the rule of law. They would argue that such elections would banish forever the specter of the return of military rule. They would establish a government with the popular legitimacy to address the impoverishment of most of the people, the insurrection in the oil-rich Delta, and the growing alienation in the North. For such Nigerians and their international friends, especially the United States, "free, fair, and credible" elections in the "Giant of Africa" were also to be a signpost of the way forward for the rest of the continent; they were supposed to inoculate the continent against the rigging characterizing the December 27, 2007, elections in Kenya, for example. For Washington, a stronger, ever more democratic Nigeria was to be a principal partner in Africa.

At the time of the Waldorf gala, among many Africa watchers in the Bush administration, if not at the U.S. embassy in Abuja, there was optimism that

Nigeria's April 2007 elections would, indeed, be free, be fair, and confirm Nigeria's democratic evolution. And there was a predisposition to give in advance much of the credit to President Obasanjo. As a Washington official put it to me, "He has always done everything he said he would." Right up to when the elections occurred, Obasanjo and Maurice Iwu, his chairman of the inappropriately named Independent National Electoral Commission (INEC), gave regular assurances that the elections would be free, fair, and credible. These were taken at face value by many in the Bush administration. On the other hand, much Nigerian opinion was already skeptical about the president's alleged commitment to, and the likelihood of, credible elections.

Washington and other international donors had provided significant, multiyear financial support for the electoral process. Washington and the European Union (EU) each contributed about $15 million, and the United Kingdom even more (if its bilateral contributions are added to its contributions through the EU). The U.S. mission provided political support for the process in speeches, informal conversations, and press events almost from the date of my arrival. So, too, did other representatives of the donor community. Western nongovernmental organizations (NGOs) had studied the 2003 elections and submitted proposal after proposal as to how electoral procedures could be improved. They conducted seminars and provided experts. At donor expense, foreign experts worked directly for INEC, although they were excluded from decision making. Nigerian NGOs and professional associations, such as the Nigeria Bar Association, offered to provide INEC with all possible support. And their activities also often received substantial international donor support, especially from European countries.

OTHER CANDIDATES

During the January–April 2007 campaign, there were dozens of presidential candidates, but only three were credible. Umaru Yar'Adua, handpicked by Obasanjo, was unknown in the country beyond having a famous name. During his eight years as governor of Katsina, he had had little contact with the political movers and shakers elsewhere in the country, and his personal patronage network did not extend beyond his own state. There was continuing speculation about the poor state of his health, given credibility by his collapse on the campaign trail in March 2007 that resulted in a secretive hospital stay in Germany. He was also unknown to the Abuja diplomatic corps. At a meeting of Western ambassadors I convened shortly after he had secured the PDP nomination, I asked for a show of hands of those who had met him. There was not one. Nevertheless, as the PDP presidential candidate, he had the grudging support of most of the elites that run Nigeria and wanted Obasanjo out.

General Muhammadu Buhari was probably the most popular political figure in the North. His supporters believed he was the presidential candidate in 2003 that won the most votes. He was a former military ruler known for his austere and upright lifestyle, and his clampdown on corruption was probably the most effective in Nigeria's history. A supporter of sharia law, the authenticity of his Islamic faith caused anxiety in the Christian South, where he was frequently called "Taliban Man."[2]

The third leading candidate was Vice President Atiku Abubakar, a rich businessman with oil interests in Angola as well as Nigeria. He was a consistent advocate for a democratic political culture in Nigeria. He had been a candidate in 2003 but had withdrawn in favor of Obasanjo in return for the latter's promise to support his presidential candidacy in 2007. But his advocacy for a multiparty, civilian democratic polity was overshadowed by the debate over Obasanjo's unsuccessful efforts to exclude him from the ballot altogether. A devout Muslim, Atiku Abubakar was sensitive to Christian concerns. For example, generally he did not use in public life the *alhaji* title to which he is entitled.[3] Especially after Obasanjo broke with him over Third Term, Aso Villa and its supporters maintained a steady drumbeat of accusation that he was personally corrupt to discredit him.

With respect to the three candidates' views of the United States, Yar'Adua's were largely unknown. Though he had made the hajj, he had never visited the United States, rare for a member of the Nigerian elite. A university lecturer with degrees in chemistry, there were rumors of a brief flirtation with Marxism when he was young. However, as a candidate and subsequently as president, he demonstrated that he wanted close ties with, and the approval of, the United States.

Buhari's viscerally pro-American views were characteristic of senior officers in the Nigerian military of his generation, though he had lingering resentment over what he saw as the American "tilt" toward Obasanjo and Washington's willingness (or, as his supporters saw it, eagerness) to accept the rigged 2003 elections.

Atiku Abubakar was unabashedly pro-American. He talked with pride and affection about his education by Peace Corps volunteers, and while he was vice president, he and I sought to invite the Peace Corps back to Nigeria. (The effort failed, apparently because of fear that the Peace Corps volunteers would take away jobs from Nigerian university graduates.) One of his four wives is American, and he has children with American citizenship. He has established an American-style, rigorously nonsectarian university in Yola, the capital of his native Adamawa state.[4]

I was privileged to enjoy cordial, indeed friendly, relations with all three candidates, with Atiku Abubakar and Buhari throughout my tenure as ambassador and with Yar'Adua from January 2007, after he had in hand the PDP presidential nomination. All three had the reserved, exquisite manners characteristic of the Northern elites.

FAILED ELECTIONS

INEC may have been so unprepared for the elections because its collective leadership, all put in place by President Obasanjo, had expected Plan A to work. That, of course, did not happen. Third Term was stopped by mid-May 2006, and the elections occurred only eleven months later. Up until the failure of Third Term, little or nothing concrete had been done to prepare for national elections or to address the administrative and technical failures of the 2003 elections to ensure they were not repeated.

There was a scenario that was supposed to shape the 2007 elections. First, there was to be a national census. Based on its results, electoral boundaries would be redrawn to account for population growth and shifts. Second, INEC would prepare new, accurate voter registration lists, which would be published and displayed for all to see. Finally, INEC would print the ballots and establish credible vote counting and tabulation procedures. Each portion of this scenario failed.

Nigeria has not had a credible census since a partial one in late colonial times. Previous efforts to conduct one ran afoul of ethnic and religious rivalries and ended in violence. The resulting counts did not command legitimacy. The census of 2006 sought to avoid those issues by posing no questions about ethnicity or religion. Only noses were to be counted by the Nigeria National Population Commission (NPC), which anticipated hiring a million enumerators (and thereby providing a huge opportunity for the NPC and the governing PDP to dispense patronage). The actual count was nondramatic, and there was little violence. But it is unclear how much counting actually occurred. The NPC announced the preliminary results in January 2007. It said that Nigeria's population numbered about 140 million, that men outnumbered women by a ratio of 105 to 100,[5] and that the population was growing at a rate of 3.2 percent per year. Obasanjo, who had routinely stated that the population of the country was 150 million, observed that his figure would be reached within a few years. More controversially, the census allegedly found that the North had a larger population than the South and that Kano state, rather than Lagos state, was the largest in the federation.

Numerous political leaders from the West, South, and East rejected the NPC findings. The governors of Abia and Lagos states did parallel counts that called into serious question the census results. Nevertheless, despite the alarums and excursions, the census had no direct effect on the April 2007 elections because the official results were not announced in time to do the constitutionally mandated revision of constituency boundaries.

INEC decided to create a new voter registration list, rather than updating or building on that used in 2003. It also looked to introduce voter identification cards that would be machine readable. INEC pursued various high-tech possibilities for registration, none of which proved to be practical in a country that lacks consistent electrical power. The registration process did not follow the legally mandated timeline, and it lacked uniformity from one part of the country to another. Domestic NGOs reported many abuses, including the mass registration of small children and babes-in-arms. Official lists of voters were not publicly posted in most parts of the country, as mandated by law. Nevertheless, in February 2007, INEC announced that 61 million Nigerians had registered to vote. As the National Democratic Institute (NDI) pointed out in its evaluation of the elections, INEC never posted publicly the complete roster nor explained the methodology by which the list of 61 million had been compiled.[6] On polling day itself, in many places diplomatic observers saw that the resulting voter registration lists were not used at all.

INEC was also responsible for the registration of candidates. At the presidential level, Obasanjo successfully pressured INEC to not register two of his enemies, Atiku Abubakar and Abia governor Orji Kalu, allegedly because they were under investigation for corruption by the EFCC and other agencies. This exclusion was patently illegal. In a sign of the increasing judicial independence of the executive, the courts ordered both to be placed on the ballot only a few days before the poll. Subsequently, INEC credibly claimed that the late rulings establishing the presidential candidacies of the vice president and the governor required the reprinting of tens of millions of ballots and contributed directly to the chaos of election day.

The entire election process—registration, production of ballots, polling, and counting—was a shambles. Up to the day of actual voting, there was popular concern that the elections would be postponed and speculation that Obasanjo was sabotaging the preparations so that he could justify remaining in office. And the pattern of incompetence and failure was so pervasive that these suspicions became credible.

The failure of every step was widely reported in the press, by NGOs, and by the U.S. mission back to Washington. The mission maintained close contact with the NGOs that the United States funded to support the electoral process. In the last few months before the elections, I chaired a weekly meeting of representatives of NGOs and embassy personnel following electoral developments. In addition, I chaired a monthly, later biweekly, and then weekly information-sharing meeting of the chiefs of mission of the principal donors to the electoral process. It was clear months in advance that the elections were in trouble. But the Villa and INEC insisted that all would be well.

INEC was anything but independent of the Obasanjo government. Under the electoral law, Obasanjo appointed its chairman and all of its regional commissioners; Chairman Iwu had no control over the regional commissioners. INEC's budget was part of that of the presidency, and the president controlled the disbursement of funds to it. In the aftermath of the bad 2003 elections, there were proposals for the reform of INEC to establish its independence. The National Assembly finally passed a watered-down version in June 2006 after the defeat of Third Term. That legislation was inadequate to establish INEC as a truly independent agency.

INEC chairman Iwu is a Christian Igbo from Anambra state. A pharmacist, he has advanced degrees from a British university. His specialty is pharmacognosy (medicinal plant research). In 1999, he announced prematurely that he had found a cure for Ebola at the International Botanical Congress in St. Louis. He is an American citizen.

Iwu had no obvious background in overseeing elections beyond his on-the-job training at INEC. His political sponsors appear to have been the Uba brothers, Chris and Andy, both Igbos deeply involved in Anambra politics. Andy Uba, who had done well in the United States as a physiotherapist, administrator, and medical entrepreneur, attached himself to President Obasanjo when the later was first released from jail. The two became close. During Obasanjo's second term, Andy Uba served as his special assistant for domestic policy and was a strong advocate for Third Term. Not least because of his sponsorship by the Uba brothers, Iwu was seen by many Nigerians as Obasanjo's man.[7]

As for the technical shortcomings of the 2003 poll that had been identified by numerous observers, INEC under Iwu's leadership was fascinated by the possibility of high-tech fixes rather than practical and concrete ways to improve the electoral process. INEC purchased high-tech equipment that was never used through impenetrable procurement procedures costing millions of U.S. dollars. Illustrative of its disorganized operating style, INEC accreditation of foreign elections observers was chaotic and last minute. Worse, the vital domestic observer organizations only received their accreditation cards the day before the April 14 poll and only after their participants had been screened by the State Security Service. Without accreditation cards, the security services could have excluded domestic observers altogether from polling places. By election day, ballot printing and distribution had generally broken down. Symptomatic of the chaos was that an aircraft ostensibly delivering ballots to the hinterland crashed the night before election day, with loss of life.

By early 2007, members of the National Assembly had lost confidence in Iwu. In the aftermath of the April elections, Iwu became a convenient scapegoat for all that went wrong, particularly for those who never intended for genuine elections to take place.

Nigeria's international friends had all turned a blind eye as the major parties ignored or violated their own rules with respect to candidate selection.[8] It was the Nigerian courts, especially at the upper levels, without any overt international support, that blocked the blatantly illegal attempt by the president to control who could run for the presidency. Though pre-election survey teams from the Commonwealth, EU, NDI, and International Republican Institute (IRI) sounded the alarm that the elections preparations were deeply flawed, too many in Washington took comfort in the president's and the chairman's assurances that all would be well and assiduously continued to court Obasanjo involvement in Darfur and Somalia.

On the morning of the April 14, 2007, elections, I wrote to Washington that Obasanjo and Iwu were saying that everything was in place for free, fair, and credible elections. However, I also reported that nobody outside the Villa or among Obasanjo's foreign acolytes had much hope that the elections would be anything but a shambles. There was a general expectation that Yar'Adua would be rigged-in as president. That previous day, Obasanjo sent the minister of the Federal Capital Territory, Malam Nasir el-Rufai, to see me with "polling data" that showed there would be a PDP sweep.

I met with the leaders and sometimes the rank and file of the numerous American election observation teams that came to Nigeria. These included many of the American academics who follow Nigeria closely. Some of them had observed all three elections since the ostensible restoration of civilian rule in 1999. Absent, however, was an observer team from the Carter Center in Atlanta. Following the bad 1999 elections, the Carter Center made recommendations for improvements in the election process that the Nigerian government has consistently ignored. Under those circumstances, the Carter Center has declined ever since to participate in election observation in Nigeria.

Typically, my meetings with election observers took place at the ambassador's residence, and I would have present members of the embassy staff. These conversations were candid. The election observers provided us with thorough oral briefings on what they were seeing. Often, they were angry at the "criminal duplicity" of those charged with conducting the polling.

The embassy in Abuja and the consulate in Lagos fielded more than fifty election observer teams, covering the country except for parts of the Delta where levels of violence and kidnapping were too high. The teams were thorough: each team visited its assigned site in advance of polling day, touching base with local civil society leaders, party workers, and INEC officials. They then returned on the day to observe the actual polling.

On election day, I sat in my office in Abuja as reports from the mission's election observers started to come in. In some places, our observers reported that there were no ballots at all. In others, observers on the scene saw that polls opened late and closed early, with potential voters still waiting in line. In yet other places, INEC distributed ballots to the state capital but not in the countryside. Here and there, notably in Lagos and Kano, both controlled by opposition parties, polling was more normal. In the early afternoon, I visited several polling places near the embassy in the "monumental core" of Abuja. Balloting there was also normal, though the lines of voters were short. As the Western media was concentrated in Lagos and Abuja, its early reports on the polling were optimistic. So, too, were those of some of the small embassies that did not have the resources to observe the polling beyond the capital and therefore based their reporting on what they saw in central Abuja. Early, optimistic reporting on the elections often reflected the wish by Nigeria's friends that the elections would be credible.

The rigging of the elections was massive: international and domestic observers estimated total turnout at no more than 14 million, and some observers argue that, in fact, it was as low as 5 million. Yet INEC announced that Yar'Adua won 24 million votes, Buhari about 6.6 million, and Atiku 2.5 million—a total of more than 33 million ballots cast. [9]

These figures destroyed any pretense that the elections were credible: Villa insiders with whom I met a day or two after INEC announced the victors expressed deep embarrassment and acknowledged that the results were not believable. They fell back on the argument that Yar'Adua would have won "anyway," citing the alleged polling data that el-Rufai had already shared with me. They pleaded for international "understanding" because Nigeria's democracy is "new." The tragedy from their perspective was that the rigging and fraud had been unnecessary and reflected, they argued, INEC's incompetence and Nigeria's "underdeveloped political culture."

The Transitional Monitoring Group (TMG), an umbrella of Nigerian civil society organizations that deployed fifty thousand trained observers, concluded that the elections did not meet the minimum standards required for democratic elections. [10] It called for their total cancellation at the national level and for a rerun of the lower-level polling in ten states. For the same reasons, the Joint Action Forum, another umbrella group covering fifty Nigerian civil society organizations, also called for a rerun of the elections.

The EU Elections Observation Mission said the presidential elections were "far short of basic international and regional standards for democratic elections," that the electoral process "cannot be considered to have been credible," and that "there can be no confidence in the results of these elections." [11]

The NDI observer team, led by former secretary of state Madeleine Albright, said, "The electoral process failed the Nigerian people," and "it is unclear whether the April 21 elections reflect the will of the Nigerian people." [12] The IRI's team, headed by former U.S. war crimes ambassador Pierre Prosper, characterized the polling as "below the standard set by previous Nigerian elections and international standards witnessed by IRI around the globe." [13]

The Commonwealth Election Observer Group, in its departure statement, characterized the elections as "a missed opportunity" and emphasized the low turnout of voters, as did the Economic Community of West African States (ECOWAS) Observer Mission. The preliminary declaration of the ECOWAS Observer Mission was less critical in tone than the others but called on INEC in the future "to ensure that the results to be declared truly and faithfully reflect the voter preferences"—thereby implying that had not been the case in 2007. [14]

The NDI and IRI are associated respectively with the Democratic and Republican parties and are entirely independent of each other. While they receive U.S. government funding, they jealously maintain their independence from any Washington administration in office. They cooperate closely with each other in observing elections, dividing responsibilities and turf. I met with Albright, the head of the NDI delegation, before and after the polling, and separately also with Prosper, the head of the IRI delegation. The purpose of the first meeting was for me to brief them on election preparations as the embassy saw them; at the second, they briefed me on what they had seen. Each issued a public statement after the elections. While as a courtesy I was shown the statements in advance, neither the embassy nor I had any input into them. This was as it should have been.

The U.S. mission teams had remained in close contact with other observer teams, especially those fielded by Nigerian civil society organizations. Other Western embassies in Abuja also fielded teams or hosted others from their home countries. The EU's team was especially large and experienced. Nigerian NGOs repeatedly told us that the visible presence of foreign observers meant less interference in their own work by the Nigerian security services. U.S. mission reporting on what our election observers saw was in classified channels. However, its assessment of the rigging of the elections did not differ materially from what the other international observation teams were saying in public. Among younger embassy officers, there was deep anger over what they saw, similar to that of their nonofficial American colleagues.

The bottom line is that domestic and international observers, official and unofficial, saw clearly how bad the elections were conducted in virtually all parts of the country, and they were in fundamental agreement that the 2007 polling was not free, fair, or credible. Despite embarrassing and patently false claims to the contrary from President Obasanjo, President-Elect Yar'Adua, and INEC chairman Iwu, there was a consensus that the elections of 2007 were the worst since the ostensible restoration of democracy in 1999. The EU statement on the elections was the most forthright. [15]

The dilemma we and other election observers faced was how to report to the world accurately what had happened yet keep the door open for dialogue with the Nigerian authorities on future improvements in the elections process. Albright was deeply impressed with what she saw of Nigerian civil society and their Nigerian election monitoring teams. For her, the contrast was breathtaking between the honesty, competency, and organization of the Nigerian civil organizations and the squalid rigging. NDI and IRI wanted to support Nigerian civil society in its efforts to overturn the most egregious election results through the judiciary. I shared their outlook. I also shared Washington's concern to keep the door open for dialogue with the Nigerian government on the regional issues with which we were still cooperating. For more than a week after INEC announced the election results, there was no U.S. official comment. Then the State Department spokesman referred publicly to Nigeria having "missed an opportunity to strengthen an element of its democratic process through a sound electoral process." He went on to characterize the elections as "seriously flawed."[16] Privately, I sympathized with the anger of my younger officers at the apparent weakness of the statement. But I understood Washington's need to play the trimmer.

My view is that the excessive rigging occurred because Obasanjo, the PDP, and INEC lost control: there was sequential rigging by officials and politicians at every stage of the balloting and the counting and tabulation process that culminated in the incredible final vote totals. Obasanjo had said the elections were "a life and death matter," and PDP and INEC operatives acted that way. They "over-egged the pudding" at every step. So, too, did all the other parties, when they could: the elections were characterized by "competitive rigging." None of the political parties were angels in the 2007 elections. But the advantage rested with the party of government, the PDP, because INEC and the security services were controlled by the Villa.

In the immediate aftermath, the Obasanjo government continued to show its characteristic political skills. Some of the PDP's party operatives wanted to rerun the elections in Lagos and Kano, the two largest cities in the country and where the PDP had lost. However, the Villa declined to overreach. Had the election results been set aside in those two, volatile cities, there might have been a popular eruption hard to control.

In his inaugural address, President Yar'Adua explicitly acknowledged the shortcomings of the elections and pledged reform. As in 2003, the U.S. Department of State urged Nigerians to seek redress in the courts, rather than taking to the streets, "to eschew violence or any other extraconstitutional actions."[17]

Public protests were remarkably few—nothing compared to the upsurge of popular anger and violence in Kenya after the stolen elections there later in the year. Strikes over economic issues in the aftermath of the polls—and some were disruptive, especially in Lagos—did not assume an overt political cast, perhaps because of a heavy security presence and the government's judicious use of its powers of detention. For example, the authorities arrested the general secretary of the Alliance for Credible Elections, an indigenous elections monitoring organization. He was soon released, but the message of intimidation was clear.

In fact, the street posed even less threat than in 2003. Certainly, there was violence during the election period—how many deaths, we do not know, with estimates ranging from 60 (official) to 200–300 (from international NGOs) to 1,500 (mostly from press observers and indigenous NGOs). Most of the deaths resulted from local rivalries, many without any national political meaning.[18] In many, maybe most, cases, the elections were the occasion rather than the cause of the violence.

When it was all over, a civilian, Yar'Adua, succeeded another, ostensible civilian, Obasanjo, as the president for the first time in Nigeria's history. Much was made of this in Washington and London. The Nigerian in the street took little notice.

The losing presidential candidates, Buhari and Atiku Abubakar, sued to have the presidential elections invalidated by the courts. Almost a year later, in February 2008, the Court of Appeals, sitting as an elections tribunal in presidential elections disputes, unanimously threw out their challenges on the basis that the election irregularities did not materially affect the outcome and also on various technical grounds. The plaintiffs then appealed to the Supreme Court. With respect to Buhari's plea, the body eventually upheld the elections by a vote of four to three on technical grounds. With respect to Atiku, the court ruled against him six to one. However, the court also issued a statement acknowledging that the 2007 presidential elections had been deeply flawed. Atiku Abubakar and Buhari accepted the ruling.

Public apathy continued to be remarkable. Following the presidential elections tribunal decision, there was no civil disturbance of any kind. Indeed, a decision favorable to the Villa had been nearly universally expected. The press was reporting general public relief that new elections would not be necessary.[19] The *New York Times* quoted as broadly representative of public opinion one Solomon Emifa, a thirty-five-year-old marketing manager in Abuja: "We have in the back of our minds what is taking place in Kenya, in Somalia, Chad. No one here wants to have that kind of experience. No one wants to die because of a political crisis. Because at the end of the day, these guys are very rich, we are the ones who are really going to suffer."[20]

My concern was that continuing public apathy likely reflected the growing disillusionment with democratic institutions that had already been documented by the polling organization Afrobarometer.[21] All three candidates were alike: Northern, Hausa-Fulani, and rich (even Buhari, in comparison with the mass of the population). The so-called campaign had not surfaced policy issues that captured the public imagination. Indeed, there were few speeches by the presidential candidates, and most of Yar'Adua's were delivered on his behalf by Obasanjo. Rallies were lackluster. The significance that Atiku Abubakar was civilian in outlook and an advocate for multiparty democracy was diluted by Yar'Adua's similar civilian status, despite the fact that his elder brother had been an army general and an active participant in a military government. And, with his modesty, Yar'Adua was already making a good personal impression both at home and abroad. So I concluded that for most Nigerians a stolen election was not worth a riot, a police beating, and jail. Their reaction was evidence of their divorce from their formal institutions of government. In the public's perception, the Nigerian government was now as "colonial," irrelevant, and exploitative as the British regime had ever been. Their defense was to have as little to do with the government or the state as possible, to migrate internally into the worlds of family, ethnic group, and religion. For the first time, I now understood what Nigerian radicals were talking about when they said the Nigerian people remained the victims of colonialism, only the masters were other Nigerians. It was this Nigerian popular passivity that illustrated the break in the contract between the government and the governed. For the first time, I became personally convinced of the possibility of state failure.

Shortly after the April elections, the Nigerian presidency floated a trial balloon by which President Obasanjo would bring the newly elected (but not yet inaugurated) Yar'Adua to London and Washington to "introduce" him. This went nowhere because of the lack of American and British enthusiasm in light of the elections. Indignant, if only for the moment, over the electoral travesty, Washington and London sent low-level representatives to the inauguration of Yar'Adua; by contrast, the U.S. delegation to the inauguration of Liberian president Ellen Johnson-Sirleaf a few months earlier had been led by First Lady Laura Bush. As a State Department spokesman subsequently put it, there was a "pause" in the U.S.-Nigerian bilateral relationship. [22]

However, with the regional importance of Nigeria and our need for Nigerian oil and peacekeepers, this pause did not last long. The new president met with the secretary of state on the margins of the UN General Assembly in October 2007, and President Bush invited him to the White House in December. The possibility was floated that Bush would include Nigeria on the itinerary of his 2008 Africa swing. That may have been seen as just too much, and it did not happen, ostensibly because of "scheduling constraints."

OBASANJO OUT

Instead of an election, the polling of April 14 and April 21 had been a pageant, an "election-like event," a "happening" with some of the trappings of an election but with little or none of the substance—and it generated little popular excitement. In 2007, the political will necessary for genuinely democratic elections was not there among the elites. By then, the *ogas* already had what they wanted: Obasanjo out of office and the presidency rotated to the North.

How can we account for the passivity of the Nigerian people? Despite Nigeria's dreary history of military dictatorship and growing disillusionment with the Obasanjo administration, Nigerians time and time again have demonstrated a thirst for democracy. During the various programs "to restore civilian democracy" sponsored by successive military dictatorships, Nigerians patiently waited for hours to cast their ballots, as I saw for the first time in 1988 in the Babangida-sponsored local elections in Lagos. And, though the elections of 1999 and 2003 were flawed or a sham, domestic and international observers alike recognized that the annulled election of 1993 had been credible, proof if any were needed that free and fair elections were possible in Nigeria. Their annulment by Ibrahim Babangida had provoked a serious domestic political crisis, a clear indication of how deeply the man and woman in the street cared about them.[23] It is against that background that the public apathy over the April 2007 elections and their aftermath is especially tragic.

A year after the Waldorf gala and following the rigged elections of April 2007 over which President Obasanjo presided, his international reputation had become tarnished. He was no longer uncritically placed in the international civil rights pantheon. Plan B was in effect but tattered. By August 2008, an important faction in the PDP was working for Obasanjo's removal from the Board of Trustees. This effort, however, was unsuccessful, a sign of his residual political strength. Nevertheless, Obasanjo was much diminished. What had happened?

In the past, Obasanjo had advocated a one-party state for Nigeria, and that achievement would be an element of Plan B.[24] After the failed elections of April 21, 2007, PDP operatives made overtures to Buhari and even former vice president Atiku Abubakar to rejoin the governing party, a step toward that goal. Those efforts came to naught, and Nigeria remained a multiparty state, though with the PDP far stronger than any of its rivals. Nevertheless, despite Obasanjo's frequent claim that it was the largest political bloc in Africa, the PDP remained institutionally weak, and it was far from being a totalitarian entity. Obasanjo dominated it, but the party did not dominate Nigerian political life. The patronage networks remained far more powerful, with the PDP being merely one venue among many for their competition and cooperation. The PDP, along with the other major Nigerian political parties, lacked the coherence, structure, and popular support of other African parties such as the African National Congress in South Africa or ZANU-PF in Zimbabwe. By 2007, the PDP stood for nothing except power for its leaders, and the public knew it. To me, there has always been an air of unreality about Obasanjo's apparent strategy to rule Nigeria through his party position.

PLAN B INCOMPLETE

Once he was out of office, there were many charges in the press that Obasanjo and his family were thoroughly corrupt. Following investigations of variable rigor, many journalists concluded that everybody in the Obasanjo family was guilty of corruption. For those commentators, the alleged behavior of the former president and his family made a mockery of the anticorruption campaign that Obasanjo had used to justify his presidency and continued political influence. Several commentators noted the fundamental hypocrisy of Obasanjo's having prosecuted the children of his predecessors as head of state, Sani Abacha and Babangida, for corruption while his own children were feeding at the public trough.[25]

Obasanjo's son, Gbenga, fed the press frenzy by accusing his father of adultery and incest. As part of nasty divorce proceedings, Gbenga accused his wife of having had sexual relations with her own father and with her father-in-law, then-president Obasanjo.[26]

Gbenga's charges against his wife, father, and father-in-law genuinely shocked Nigerians—especially Yorubas—and provided Obasanjo's enemies with a stick to use against him. Some Yoruba editorialists and columnists expressed deep shame over Obasanjo's alleged behavior as a reflection on fatherhood, their own gender, and their ethnic group. Though there were cautionary comments that the charges were unproven, many took them as credible because Gbenga had made them in a sworn affidavit. (Oaths retain sanctity in Nigeria.) In an effort to disassociate the former president from Yorubaland, they recalled that Obasanjo had never been a part of the Yoruba elite.[27]

Gbenga's charges also resonated because stories of the ex-president's sexual predation have circulated for years. In addition, in Nigeria, where the family is a supreme institution, the fact that a son made public charges against his wife, father, and father-in-law as part of a judicial process endowed them with a degree of credibility exceeding the usual gossip and hearsay characteristic of Nigerian public life.

Gbenga is, apparently, Obasanjo's first or second son.[28] A medical doctor with an advanced degree in public health from Johns Hopkins University, he gave up his U.S. medical practice and returned to Nigeria when his father became president in 1999. An unnamed *This Day* editorialist said he was close to his mother, whom Obasanjo discarded along with many other women, suggesting that this relationship provided some explanation for the virulence of his attack on his father.

Public discussion in Nigeria often has a strong moral—or moralistic—tone. The intermingling of charges of financial corruption with sexual perversion has precedent. In the case of the Obasanjo family, the bottom line of most of the commentary was that they are all rotten.[29] Commentators returned again and again to the theme of Obasanjo's hypocrisy: after all, he had built his international reputation in part on his alleged efforts against corruption, especially his early work on behalf of Transparency International abroad and, at home, the EFCC.

From the perspective of Nigeria's future, it hardly matters whether the sexual and financial charges against Obasanjo and the charges of financial corruption against his children are true. What does matter is that they were widely believed, and they led to the further discrediting of an already unpopular political figure, his family, and the political system that had allowed them to flourish.

In response to the scandal, a party elder statesman, former Kano state governor Abubakar Rimi, called on the governing party to cancel Obasanjo's election as its lifetime chairman of the Board of Trustees, as did the former chairman of the party, Solomon Lar, who said that Obasanjo not only had embarrassed the party but also was turning Yorubaland "into another Sodom and Gomorrah."[30] According to press reports, they were joined by former Senate president Ken Nnamani, former Speaker of the House Aminu Asari, and fourteen others in asking the party to repeal its reservation of the chairmanship of the Board of Trustees to former chiefs of state. Had this been successful, it would have been the prelude to Obasanjo's removal.

That effort failed, and Obasanjo has never been indicted for corruption in a court of law, though some of his children have been. In part, because of his continued control over the party machinery, his enormous wealth, and his ties with the military, he has continued to be an influential kingmaker. However, charges of corruption and sexual misbehavior by his own son contributed to his relative loss of power and helped limit Plan B. Further, Obasanjo, rich as he is, no longer enjoyed the direct and unlimited access to oil wealth available to a president. Now he was but one of a number of kingmakers.

With Obasanjo's increasing inability to pull the political strings and with President Yar'Adua's deteriorating health, the stage was set for the 2009–10 crisis of government authority that accompanied Yar'Adua's final illness and death. Obasanjo had dominated Nigeria after 1999. By 2008, that dominance was gone. In retrospect, only Plan A could have ensured that Obasanjo would retain power. But Plan A would have likely led to a coup or civil war. Paradoxically, with the failure of Plan A and Plan B, both catastrophes remained a possible outcome to the 2009–10 presidential succession crisis and subsequent national elections in 2011.

Chapter Eight

The Breakdown of the Nigerian Political System

President Yar'Adua's November 2009 hospitalization and his subsequent May 2010 death precipitated a period of profound political crisis that some Nigerians saw as portending the breakup of the federation. For foreign observers, the booming economy of Lagos and Ibadan—largely based on finance, real estate, and consumer spending along with high oil prices—overshadowed dysfunctional national politics. The North became the venue of a largely uncoordinated, radical Islamic insurrection that outsiders often lumped together under the moniker of Boko Haram. Not only could the federal government not contain the insurrection but its heavy-handed, often brutal tactics increased the latter's virulence and viciousness. Governor of the Central Bank Lamido Sanusi testified before the National Assembly that in the Niger Delta, oil theft (bunkering) deprived the state of up to 10 percent of its oil revenue. He also said publicly that the state agency and corporation that managed oil were so dysfunctional that nobody knew how much oil Nigeria actually produced, despite optimistic official statistics that claimed a production level of 2.7 million barrels a day. [1] Meanwhile, kidnapping in the Delta was again on the upswing.

There were signs of loss of confidence in the political system. Numerous reports and allegations of official corruption at spectacular levels undermined the already rapidly deteriorating credibility of the federal and many of the state governments. In the prosperous parts of the country, such as Yorubaland and Lagos, the Jonathan administration was widely viewed with indifference if not contempt. Elsewhere, especially in the North, it was actively hated, especially in the aftermath of the end of power alternation, commonly called "zoning," between North and South. The traditional Northern elites fractured, and some of the region's traditional rulers were co-opted by the

Jonathan administration. This only served to discredit them among much of the general population that increasingly turned to radical Islamic preachers. The Nigerian political system revealed itself to be more fragile than most observers had thought. Restoring confidence in it or building a replacement for it became a major challenge. By 2013, Nigeria was dancing closer to the brink than it had been in 2010 when the first edition of this book appeared; in parts of the North, it was over the brink.

Since independence, and especially since the end of the 1967–70 civil war, whether under military or civilian government, Nigeria had been ruled by networks of rival elites that cooperated just enough to ensure access to oil revenue. As discussed in chapter 3, there were rules: there were to be no presidents or military rulers for life; the lives and property of the heads of patronage networks were sacrosanct (though not those of their foot soldiers); and above all the informal system of power alternation among the elites, known as zoning, was to be respected. This was broadly characterized as rotation between Northern Muslims and Southern Christians, though with many nuances and exceptions. Aspects of this approach dated from the colonial period, and as Federal Character it was enshrined in the constitution. It ensured that state benefits were shared out by the elites. With respect to the presidency, zoning had no legal mandate, but it had been the standard practice of the People's Democratic Party, the ruling party since the restoration of ostensibly civilian government in 1998–99. It was an important tool for insulating contests for the presidency from the country's ethnic and religious rivalries that otherwise could be exploited by political figures to advance their own selfish interests while unleashing violence that nobody could control.

Federal Character and the practice of zoning provided some boundaries to the otherwise rampant winner-take-all political culture where the prize was the state and its oil revenue. The system allowed for the almost complete impunity from the law for the country's most important elites. Though this governance provided little or nothing for most Nigerians who were increasingly impoverished, and though ordinary crime and banditry increased, it kept the country together and avoided civil war. It also enabled Nigeria to play a significant role on the world stage. Most elites believed that Nigeria's size and peacekeeping contributions entitled it to a permanent seat on the UN Security Council. As a regional and continental power, Nigeria was the most important African strategic partner for successive Washington administrations.

The breakdown of Nigeria's governance via the crisis that began in 2009 proceeded by stages and acquired its own dynamic. The essential context was the collapse of the unity of the Northern establishment. It had always been more fragile than Nigerians from other regions feared. President Yar'Adua's illness and subsequent death exacerbated the personal rivalries in the North that fueled the collapse as they jostled for position. This Northern disunity facilitated Goodluck Jonathan's abandonment of the zoning agreement, which led him to run for the presidency in 2011 when it was the North's turn. The subsequent 2011 election split the country in two between the North and the South, Muslim and Christian. It also discredited much of the Northern traditional elite, whom many in the North saw as feathering their own nests by ignoring the interests of their own religion and region. Radical Islamic groups flourished. The security challenge they posed consumed the federal government, which became much less active on the international scene, and the diplomatic partnership with the United States withered.

THE LAST DAYS OF PRESIDENT YAR'ADUA

At the end of Obasanjo's second term, zoning called for a Northerner to be the next president. Yar'Adua was a Muslim Northerner who was handpicked by Obasanjo to be the PDP presidential candidate, and he was then rigged into office in the 2007 elections. Despite these inauspicious beginnings as a likely puppet of Obasanjo, Umaru Yar'Adua became surprisingly independent and started to change the direction of the presidency for the better. During his first year in office, he gradually extricated himself from Obasanjo's influence and remained relatively distant from the vice president, Goodluck Jonathan, whom Obasanjo had handpicked as his running mate. (Probably the most influential person around him was his wife, Turai Musa.) Much better educated than any of his presidential predecessors (he had an advanced degree in analytical chemistry), Yar'Adua's presidential style was genuinely civilian, almost for the first time since the end of the civil war. Fourteen years younger than Obasanjo, Yar'Adua seemed to mark the beginning of a generational change in the country's leadership. He was the first Nigerian president to declare publicly his assets; his net worth, less than $5 million, was not large for a senior member of a family long part of the Northern establishment.

President Yar'Adua's policies diverged from those of Obasanjo in important areas. His amnesty for Niger Delta militants did not include a political process to address Delta grievances, a major shortcoming. Nevertheless, it halted for a time the attacks on the oil infrastructure that was vital to the country's finances. Unlike his predecessor, he insisted that Supreme Court decisions be enforced, even when they were contrary to his own government's interests. Unlike Obasanjo, his focus was primarily domestic rather than the world stage; before his election he had never traveled to the United States.

All of these developments were positive for the growth of democracy and the rule of law in Nigeria, so Yar'Adua's death in 2010 was a significant setback. For at least a decade, his health had been poor. He suffered from a chronic kidney condition and visited hospitals in Germany and Saudi Arabia. Shortly before election day in 2007, he collapsed during his campaign and was evacuated briefly to Germany for treatment. In November 2009, he entered a hospital in Saudi Arabia for treatment of what his spokesman identified as pericarditis (inflammation of the lining around the heart).[2] He returned to Nigeria in February 2010, but died the following May.

The 2009–10 illness of President Yar'Adua resulted in a vacuum in executive authority. While hospitalized in Saudi Arabia, he had no contact with his government. He was unable or unwilling to hand over presidential authority to his vice president, Goodluck Jonathan. His wife Turai and a handful of personal retainers walled off the president from any outsiders. When a Nigerian, Umar Farouk Abdulmutallab, tried to destroy an aircraft over Detroit on Christmas Day 2009, there was literally nobody in charge in Abuja with whom the American president could talk. During this hiatus in authority, Jonathan was reluctant to assume presidential powers, perhaps because he doubted there was a political consensus in his favor. It was unclear whether the North would accept a Jonathan presidency so long as Yar'Adua was still living. After all, under zoning, it was still the North's turn to hold the presidency. At the same time, resentment was building in the South over perceived Northern efforts to exclude Jonathan from the presidency. Consistent with its vocation as the ultimate guarantor of the survival of the state, there is anecdotal evidence that elements of the army were preparing to step in to resolve this impasse.

The U.S. arrest of Abdulmutallab after his botched terrorist attack may have forced Jonathan's hand. Presumably responding to pressure from Washington, he ordered the Nigerian security services to cooperate fully with the United States, in effect a presidential decision. On February 9, 2010, the National Assembly voted to make Jonathan the acting president until President Yar'Adua resumed his duties or died. The National Assembly's action, led by David Mark, a retired general, the Senate president, and a Middle Belt Christian, was extra-legal, as there is no provision in the constitution for an acting presidency. And there was, in fact, a legal alternative: Yar'Adua could have been impeached on the grounds that he was no longer in contact with his government, though Northern sentiment strongly opposed that course of action. The vote to make Jonathan acting president did end the vacuum in executive authority and forestalled the possibility of a military coup. According to the BBC, many powerbrokers went along with Jonathan's acting presidency because he was not seen as a threat and he indicated he would not contest the 2011 presidential elections.[3]

On February 23, 2010, President Yar'Adua returned to Abuja. His plane arrived unannounced, after dark, parked at the far edge of the runway, and was immediately surrounded by troops from the Brigade of Guards, the president's personal guard force. He was loaded into a waiting ambulance and transferred to Aso Villa. The return had overtones of a countercoup to Jonathan's extra-legal acting presidency. It involved approximately 300 troops, and artillery was deployed throughout the city at the order of the commander of the Brigade of Guards and the chief of army staff. The chief of defense staff, the most senior officer in the military, was not informed in advance, nor was the acting president. After his return, nobody but his wife and a handful of personal attendants actually saw Yar'Adua. He continued to have no contact with the government nor to exercise any presidential duties. Stories of little credibility that he was playing with his grandchildren were apparently circulated by his wife, Turai.

Following Yar'Adua's return to Nigeria, there was seemingly a standoff between Jonathan and Turai, supported by her sons-in-law, both governors, and certain Northern politicians. The State Security Service ransacked Jonathan's office the day after the president's return and soldiers were stationed in front of the president's chair in the Presidential Chamber to prevent the acting president from sitting in it. Eventually Jonathan and Turai reached an understanding, and President Yar'Adua's spokesman then issued a statement on his behalf saying that Jonathan would continue to "oversee affairs of state."

Jonathan sought with success to build support. He met with the Nigeria Governors Forum and appointed a Presidential Advisory Committee. The latter demonstrated that Jonathan had won the support or acquiescence of some of the most powerful interests in the country, at least for the moment. Its chair was Theophilus Danjuma, a retired general and a Christian, but with links to the military and the traditional Muslim establishment. Other members included Basil Omiyi, former chairman of Shell Nigeria, and constitutional lawyer and political activist Ben Nwabueze. There were hints that Turai was trying to negotiate Yar'Adua's exit from the presidency in return for ruling party selection of one of her two sons-in-law as Jonathan's vice president.

The selection of one of the sons-in-law for vice president was an important issue. In the zoning system, the president and vice president were to be from different regions of the country. When a president's term of office was up, the vice president would be well placed to be the next PDP candidate for the presidency. Therefore, if one of the sons-in-law became Jonathan's vice president, when Jonathan stepped down in 2011, the son-in-law would be well placed for the PDP presidential nomination and certain election. During this period, Jonathan continued to let it be understood that, consistent with zoning, he intended only to finish-out Yar'Adua's term and he would not run for the presidency until 2015 when it was again the South's turn. In April 2010, Jonathan visited Washington, DC, for President Obama's nuclear summit where he made a good impression. He was received by the American president, vice president, and secretary of state, an indication, perhaps, of relief that Nigeria had avoided a coup. A succession crisis appeared to have been avoided.

PRESIDENT GOODLUCK JONATHAN

Yar'Adua's death in May 2010 made Jonathan the fully legal chief of state and seemed to promise some stability. Differences between Yar'Adua and Jonathan were obvious. The former was from Katsina, a sharia state in the far north, and was a devout Muslim. The latter was born in Bayelsa state in the Delta and is an Anglican Christian. But there were striking similarities as well. Jonathan, like Yar'Adua, was well educated, with a PhD in zoology. Yar'Adua was born in 1951, Jonathan in 1957, making both of them younger than the typical *ogas* that ran Nigeria. Both wives, Turai Yar'Adua and Patience Jonathan, were strong willed. Before being handpicked by Obasanjo, neither man had had a distinguished political career. Yar'Adua had been the low-key governor of a small state with little of the ethnic or religious challenges that make Nigerian governance so difficult. Jonathan had been a teacher and a school inspector.

That promised stability was shattered in 2011, when Jonathan announced that, contrary to his previous indications, he would run for the presidency in 2011, abrogating the zoning practice that had preserved consensus in Nigeria for so long. This change of heart surprised many. Jonathan did not seem to be consumed with presidential ambition. His political career was shaped by accidents. An undistinguished lieutenant governor of Bayelsa state rigged-in by a questionable election, he became the governor when his boss was removed from office for jumping bail rather than face money laundering charges in the United Kingdom. Then, Obasanjo handpicked him as PDP vice presidential candidate because he needed a Southern Christian to balance Yar'Adua, and his preferred candidate, "Sir" Peter Odili, was unavailable because he was facing corruption charges. Further, Jonathan was not personally associated with corruption, though his wife was suspected; she was under investigation for money laundering to the tune of $13.5 million in 2006—a case that has now gone away.[4] He was the first president from his Delta region and the first Ijaw. He had become president essentially by accident, and perhaps the people around him were not prepared to lose their own chance at the political trough so quickly. They likely pressured Jonathan to run in 2011, as they are likely again to do in 2015.

The Northern elite scrambled for a response to Jonathan's surprise candidacy for the 2011 presidential elections. First they tried to find a Northern unity candidate who could block his nomination by the PDP. They started their search at the Northern Political Leadership Forum, chaired by Adamu

Ciroma, an *oga* founder of the PDP and finance minister in Obasanjo's first government. The chief contenders to be the unity candidate were former military chief of state Ibrahim Babangida, former National Security Advisor Aliyu Mohammed Gusau, former governor of Kwara state and scion of a powerful political family Bukola Saraki, and former vice president Atiku Abubakar. Atiku Abubakar won the Forum vote, but reportedly by a margin of only one over Babangida.[5] (Babangida subsequently threatened to leave the PDP.) Abubakar became the Northern candidate for the PDP primaries, but the Northern elites did not appear to work very hard for his candidacy, while Jonathan did surprisingly well, especially in the Middle Belt.

The January 2011 PDP convention was the final showdown for the two candidates. The five thousand convention delegates gathered at Eagle Square, an outdoor stadium where military reviews take place. But the chips were stacked in Jonathan's favor. Many participants reported intimidation by Jonathan supporters, and the convention became essentially an auction for delegate votes. Jonathan, with access to unlimited oil revenues as chief of state, outbid Atiku Abubakar and secured the nomination. It was said that Jonathan offered delegates $7,000 for expenses while Atiku Abubakar offered $5,000. In purely pecuniary terms, the nomination was costly for Jonathan as he had to buy support to a greater extent than did most of his presidential predecessors. On the street, it is widely believed that the oil minister, Diezani Alison-Madueke, ensured Jonathan's access to the necessary oil revenue.

The PDP convention was about money, power, and patron/client relationships. There appears to have been no discussion of the difficult challenges that Nigeria faces, such as poverty or the sense of marginalization in the Delta or in the North. The convention appears to have been disconnected from the Nigerian people, and its leadership made no effort to appeal to the electorate. It was solely an episode of elite politics. What was new this time was not that it was awash with money, bribery, and intimidation, but rather that it ended zoning—and did not replace it with any other device for insulating presidential elections from Nigeria's ethnic and religious cleavages.

THE 2011 PRESIDENTIAL CAMPAIGN

Although Jonathan had won the PDP primary, there was a still a general election to win in April 2011. The PDP is the national party of the political establishment, and it has dominated electoral politics since a consortium of the military and big business established it after the death of Sani Abacha in 1998. Nevertheless, there were sixty-three officially recognized political parties in 2011, most of which were focused on "favorite sons" at the state and local levels. Of these, three parties had a broader, if still regional importance:

the Action Congress of Nigeria (ACN), with its base in the West; the All
Nigeria Peoples Party (ANPP), strong in the North; and the Congress for
Progressive Change (CPC), a much broader-based party, though strongest in
the North. Though these three parties have never elected a president, they
frequently elected governors, senators, and representatives in the National
Assembly, though never in the same numbers as the PDP, which remains the
only party with a genuinely national reach.

The North's response to Jonathan's capture of the PDP presidential nomination was to rally around the candidacy of Muhammadu Buhari, the former
military ruler who had run for the presidency in 2003 and 2007. Buhari is
probably the only Nigerian politician who is genuinely popular with non-
elites, and he might have had a chance had the elites supported him. But
Northern former PDP stalwarts such as Babangida, Gusau, and Saraki appear
to have sat on their hands; they had no love for Buhari, whose populism and
anticorruption platform threatened their interests. (It will be recalled that
Babangida staged a successful coup against Buhari when the latter was military chief of state.) In 2011, Buhari ran under the auspices of the CPC. The
ACN, dominated by former Lagos state governor Bola Tinubu, ran as its
candidate Nuhu Ribadu, a former chairman of the Economic and Financial
Crimes Commission and seen by many as the "clean government" candidate.
The ANPP's head, Ibrahim Shekarau, a former governor of Kano, was also a
presidential candidate for a time but eventually threw his support to Buhari.

To stand a chance of defeating a PDP presidential candidate, the ACN,
ANPP, and the CPC would need to rally behind a single candidate. Tinubu
refused to do so, apparently because Buhari would not give him what he
wanted during the pre-election political horse-trading. Nuhu Ribadu remained in the race but as a minor candidate, wining only one state in Yorubaland. The election was essentially a horse race between Jonathan and Buhari.
For the first time since the restoration of civilian government in 1999, the
presidency was a true contest between a Southern Christian and a Northern
Muslim rather than a simple alternation. The supporters of both sides appealed to ethnic and religious identities to bolster their candidates. The context was already escalating inter-religious and inter-ethnic conflict that had
been documented by the U.S. Commission on International Religious Freedom (USCIRF) and by the Nigerian Inter-Religious Council (NIREC).[6] As
American scholar John Paden observed, the Nigerian federal government
appeared to pay little attention to the warnings of the ethnic and religious
violence that would follow the April 2011 elections.[7]

The extent and quality of ethnic appeals during the campaign are difficult
to document; the evidence is almost entirely anecdotal. The use of religious
and ethnic identities by politicians to advance their own agendas was not new
in Nigerian politics, even if zoning had largely inoculated specifically the
presidential race against such appeals. As the U.S. Commission on Interna-

tional Religious Freedom concluded in its 2011 report, "religion and religious identity are intertwined in ethnic, political, economic and social controversies, and can be misused by politicians, religious leaders, or others to rouse their constituencies for political gain."[8] That is what was going on during the 2011 campaign season. In the Middle Belt, it seems clear that Jonathan's supporters used a common Christian identity to garner support from members of different ethnic groups. Additionally, it was commonly believed that Jonathan garnered the support of Muslim leaders like the sultan of Sokoto, the emirs of Kano and Zaria, and other traditional rulers with huge cash payments and the promise of constitutional recognition of the role of traditional rulers. They supported Jonathan, but much of the rest of the Islamic establishment and the broader Northern community went for Buhari.

In the North, imams and malams certainly urged their flocks to support Buhari. It was commonly thought in the North that Islam remained the majority religion in Nigeria and that all Muslims would fulfill their religious obligation to support Buhari. But electoral motives were always mixed. A Nigerian judge has commented, "in Nigeria, three things are intertwined; religion, politics, and ethnicity and the three are beclouded with corruption, poverty, and insecurity."[9]

THE 2011 GENERAL ELECTIONS

As the campaign wound down, the stage was set for the general elections in April 2011. After the blatantly rigged 2007 elections, the international community, led by the United States, the European Union, and Nigerian civil society, insisted that those of 2011 had to be better. There was a palpable sense that if the 2011 elections were as bad as those of 2007, the result would be significant violence, political instability, and the possibility of a military coup. From his first days as acting president, Jonathan made the delivery of credible elections one of his two primary goals (the other was improvement in the power supply). To that end, in July 2010, before he announced he had decided to run for the presidency himself, Jonathan appointed Attahiru Jega as chairman of the Independent National Electoral Commission (INEC). Jega—a former vice chancellor of Bayero University in Kano and a former head of the national Academic Staff Union, with a PhD from Northwestern University—was highly regarded for his integrity. However, neither Jonathan nor Jega could influence the commissioners who made up INEC, who were usually beholden to their state governors. The international community did its part by providing diplomatic and financial support, and Nigerian civil society also fully mobilized. For the first time in Nigeria's history, it used social media to counter blatant election abuse. The enthusiastic engagement of young people and women who hitherto had played lesser roles in Nigerian elections was a positive sign of change.

INEC claimed that it registered more than 73 million voters for the 2011 elections. In 2007, it had claimed that 61 million had registered. As for the polling, in 2007, it claimed that more than 33 million ballots were cast; as we have seen, independent observers thought the number was much lower. In 2011, INEC said that more than 38 million ballots were cast. The significant increase over 2007 combined with the voter turnout of less than half the alleged number of registrations raises questions about the credibility of both statistics. Nevertheless, the elections of 2011 were better organized than they had been in the past. Ballots and ballot boxes were delivered, and, more so than in the past, polls opened on time. When there were technical glitches early in the polling process, Jega was not afraid to postpone the elections by one week to resolve them. People cast ballots in areas where it previously had not been possible to do so. Nevertheless, as has been the case since 1999, the PDP candidate won. The official figures showed that the PDP candidate (Jonathan) garnered 22,925,275 votes, or 57 percent of the total; CPC (Buhari), 12,395,774 (31 percent); and for ACN and ANPP together (Ribadu), 2,984,035. Jonathan easily won an absolute majority of all of the ballots cast. [10]

Jonathan had had two constitutional hurdles to overcome if he was to avoid a runoff election. He had to win 50 percent of the total vote and 25 percent of the vote in two-thirds of the states. He met the first requirement by garnering up to 99 percent of the votes in those parts of the country that supported him. (Alleged voter turnout in those states was also substantially higher than in the rest of the country.) As for the second, he carried outright twenty-three states; he needed four more with 25 percent of the vote. In eight of the twelve sharia states, his vote exceeded 25 percent. In twelve southern states, Jonathan's totals ranged from 95 to 99 percent of the votes cast, recalling elections in the old Soviet Union and stretching credulity. So, too, did his high percentages in certain sharia states: 40 percent in Gombe and Jigawa and 44 percent in Kebbi. As in the past, PDP governors appear to have played a major role in ensuring that the balloting and counting came out right. (Gombe, Jigawa Kebbi, Kaduna, Katsina Soko, and Zamfara, all sharia states where Jonathan won 25 percent or more of the votes, had PDP governors.)

All was not well. Neither of the principal opposition parties accepted the results and instead went to court to challenge the results. Immediately following the polling, Nigerian civil organizations were claiming the likelihood of fraud, especially in the ballot collation centers. [11] And, of even greater long-term significance, for the first time Nigeria's presidential elections bifurcated the country along religious lines: the twelve sharia states of the North had majorities for Buhari; the other states, predominately but not exclusively Christian, voted for Jonathan. The exception was Osun state in Yorubaland, which voted for Ribadu.

Despite these facts, the voting results were hailed by the international community as credible, primarily because they were better than those of 2007. And within Nigeria, in most parts of the country, Jonathan's victory was also seen to be credible despite the numerous shortcomings of the polling and counting process. Not so in the North. The aftermath was the most violent of any election since 1999. When Jonathan's victory was announced, there were murderous attacks on PDP supporters, especially those parts of the Northern establishment that had supported him. The private houses of the sultan of Sokoto, the emir of Zaria, and the emir of Kano were torched. These essentially political demonstrations merged into tit-for-tat ethnic and religious murders, very conservatively estimated at around a thousand. And the violence and loss of faith opened the door for Boko Haram, which had predated by as much as a decade the elections of 2011, to gain widespread support.

The irony is that while the polling practices of the 2011 were much better than in 2007, the dire predictions about the results of bad polling came true anyway because of the abrogation of the zoning system. The country bifurcated along a regional and religious line with many, if not most, in the North denying the legitimacy of the elections. The violence was the worst since the civil war and was concentrated in the Middle Belt and the North. To cite only one example, in south Kaduna state, a predominately Christian area, Christians slaughtered at least eight hundred Muslims, including many women and children. [12] But there were deaths, often uncounted, in many other places as well. There were naive calls, especially by Western observers, for Buhari to "do something" to rein in his supporters but Buhari could not control Northern rage (and he certainly did not encourage it). During this time the army never formally took over the government, but the military presence throughout much of the country greatly increased, with martial law declared in some Northern jurisdictions.

The results of the 2011 election were devastating for Nigerian politics. The old political system that had held Nigeria together was in tatters. Presidential power alternation was gone. The Northern political establishment was largely discredited on the street. And, while the formal aspects of Federal Character were preserved, Jonathan surrounded himself with fellow Christians, mostly fellow Ijaws, rather than including a significant number of elites from all around the country. Ethnic and religious appeals had entered Nigerian politics in a big way.

THE JONATHAN PRESIDENCY

Following the elections, Jonathan faced several serious issues: increasing ethnic tensions, the rise of Boko Haram in the North, and, in the aftermath of the massive public spending associated with the elections, a true fiscal crisis. Rather than reaching out to the North to mend Nigeria's regional fractures, Jonathan concentrated on the economy. He embarked on a program of economic reform, reappointed Ngozi Okonjo-Iweala as finance minister, and retained Lamido Sanusi as the governor of the Central Bank. Most significantly, on New Year's Day 2012, he took the long-debated step of eliminating the federal petroleum subsidy, which had kept gasoline and other petroleum products available to Nigerians at substantially below market prices.

The end of the subsidy had been a hotly debated topic for many years. Despite the fact that Nigeria has an abundance of crude oil, it lacks refining capacity and spends billions importing fuel not only for transportation but also to power the diesel generators that provide much of the country's electricity. Economists and much of the international banking community argued the costs of the fuel subsidy impeded development and laid an unsustainable burden on Nigeria's finances. Dating back to the aftermath of the civil war, successive governments had tried and failed to eliminate it. Public pushback was significant: For most Nigerians the fuel subsidy was their only benefit from an industry that otherwise enriched a small number of *ogas*. Prominent religious leaders had long defended the subsidy as a moral and ethical right.

The end of the subsidy sent shock waves throughout the country. Within days, a liter of gas more than doubled in price. Popular anger at Jonathan surged. Organized labor, with the support of the Nigeria Bar Association and the National Medical Association, organized a week-long general strike that effectively shut the country down. There were popular protests in virtually all of Nigeria's major cities with a focus that broadened from the fuel subsidy to bad government. Protesters in Kano explicitly invoked the Arab Spring and the Occupy Wall Street movement. They called their encampment "Occupy Kano" and its venue as "Tahir Square." Protesters shut down economic activity in Lagos, Ibadan, and Kano.

This popular revolt had several positive results. First, it united the country in opposition to the Jonathan administration across ethnic, religious, and regional lines. In Kano, the protest was accompanied by an accord between Christians and Muslims. Christians provided protection while Muslim protesters prayed, and Muslims returned the favor in a city that had been a byword for religious hatred and Islamic radicalism. The same pattern could be seen in other cities. By the end of January the strikes and demonstrations were over. But they had demonstrated a new possibility for Nigerians to bridge ethnic and religious differences by focusing on governance issues. Second, Nigerian civilians had an important success using democratic, par-

ticipatory activism. In response to the protests, Jonathan announced the restoration of about half of the fuel subsidy, though he left open the possibility
that eventually it would all be eliminated. There were arrests and payoffs as
well, tactics that governments have long used in Nigeria to control labor
unrest. But protesters remained in touch through various forms of social
media and promised to take to the streets again if the government tried to end
the remaining fuel subsidy. Thus far, the Jonathan administration has made
no such move.

The government was left with serious financial challenges. Despite the
elimination of half of the subsidy at the beginning of 2012, by the following
October estimates of the backlog of subsidy payments owed to fuel traders
were as high as $18 billion or over half of the national budget for 2012. The
National Assembly ordered a probe of the operation of the fuel subsidy that
was expected to highlight widespread fraud, including at the highest level of
government. By late 2012, the report still had not been made public. The fuel
subsidy, and the quarter of the national budget devoted to the Northern
insurgency associated with Boko Haram, together were driving the Nigerian
government deeper into debt with consequences that were difficult to foresee.

Even with the national elections only a year behind them, by the end of
2012, Nigerians were focusing attention on the elections of 2015 and specu-
lating as to whether Goodluck Jonathan intended to run again. However, the
threat posed to the Nigerian state by the Boko Haram insurgency and the
prospect of renewed violence in the Delta lent an aura of unreality to that
discussion.

In many ways the elections of 2011 and their aftermath were a disaster for
Nigeria. Jonathan's decision to run in effect ended zoning. The elections
bifurcated the country along regional and religious lines for the first time in a
presidential election. The aftermath of the elections provided space for radical Islamic movements in the North to expand, a process that was encouraged
by the Jonathan administration's security approach to what was, in essence, a
political problem. Meanwhile, the Jonathan administration's well-intentioned
economic reforms were moving only slowly. A Petroleum Industries Bill
(PIB) that was to reform the industry and the relationship between the Nigerian government and the major oil companies was dead in the water because
of regional rivalries. By the end of 2012, expansion of the power supply had
only just started. The costs of the Northern insurgency and the fuel subsidy
combined with declining oil revenue because of theft were starving development initiatives of funding. The Jonathan administration was making little
progress trying to bridge the gap between the government and the Nigerian
people. There was little or no debate on education and health, where responsibility is divided between the federal government and the states but improvements in both were essential if Nigeria was to achieve the sustainable

economic development that might lift the overwhelming majority of its citizens out of poverty.

In February 2012 the National Bureau of Statistics (NBS) reported that the percentage of Nigerians living in absolute poverty rose to 60.9 percent in 2010 from 54.7 percent in 2004. Using the U.S. dollar-a-day poverty measure, the NBS estimated that poverty rose to 71.5 percent. It stated that the Northeast and the Northwest were the poorest regions in Nigeria.[13] Those regions are the heartland of Boko Haram.

Chapter Nine

Boko Haram

On Sunday, November 25, 2012, two coordinated suicide attacks on the Protestant church within the army cantonment at Jaji in Kaduna state killed up to 50 worshippers. The following day, unidentified gunmen attacked the Special Anti-Robbery Squad (SARS) head office in Abuja, killing up to 10 policemen and freeing some 150 suspected terrorists.[1] Jaji showed that no government facility or church in the North was safe from attack, and Abuja once again that no government facility was immune, even a police headquarters. While at the time no group claimed responsibility for these attacks, the Nigerian media assigned responsibility to Boko Haram and assumed that the two attacks were coordinated. However, a week later a hitherto unknown radical Islamic group, calling itself the "Jama'atu Ansarul Muslimina Fi Biladis-sudan" claimed responsibility for the SARS attack only.[2] In October 2012, the respected human rights organization Human Rights Watch estimated that since 2009, more than 2,800 people had been killed by Boko Haram or the security forces.[3] The Office of the Prosecutor of the International Criminal Court at The Hague in an October 2012 preliminary report accused Boko Haram of engaging in crimes against humanity, but it did not so cite the federal government.

What was Boko Haram? It remained shrouded in mystery for most Nigerians and outsiders alike. Its name appeared to cover political opportunists and criminals as well as radical Islamists, categories that often overlapped. Boko Haram numbered the followers of Malam Mohammed Yusuf but in common usage also included groups such as Jama'atu Ansarul Muslimina Fi Biladis-sudan. But, even with respect to Yusuf's core disciples, there was remarkably little hard information about their structure and leadership.[4] There is even less known about other groups, such the one claiming responsibility for the SARS attack.[5]

The Nigerian government and the press commonly labeled Boko Haram as an inchoate, grassroots rebellion and ethnic and religious conflicts of which Yusuf's followers were only a part. The revolt's foot soldiers likely came from the millions who made up the unemployed youth bulge throughout the North, whether or not they were followers of Yusuf. They easily identified with Boko Haram if they had attended Islamic schools where they learned little other than to memorize the Koran. Often they were children of peasants, rootless if not homeless in a big city. They could be bound together by a common Islamic sensibility, inchoate rage, and the prospect of earning a little money as terrorists. The vast majority could be only loosely tied, if at all, to Yusuf's disciples and could act with little or no outside coordination or direction. They could also be easily manipulated by political operatives.

The violence, of which Yusuf's followers were only a part, appeared to be shaped by the populist Islamic radicalism of the Sahel extending in various forms from Khartoum to Dakar. Radical Islam's specific appeal in Northern Nigeria owed much to the North's political marginalization, poverty, and bad governance. Their rhetoric did not refer directly to such secular factors, but that was the context for their own political and religious agenda that emphasized justice for the poor.

Within Islamic circles there was an ongoing theological dispute, sometimes violent, usually not. One side was populist and literalist in its religious thinking. It was commonly labeled "Salafism." The other was a more mystical and less literal religious approach, often called "Sufism." (The meaning and use of both terms had strayed far from their technical meaning within Islamic theology.) In common parlance, Salafism had long been associated with the poor for whom it demands justice. It tends to be parochial in outlook and leadership. Its mind-set reflects the austere environment of northeastern Nigeria with the Sahara creeping south. It is unsympathetic to ambiguity and especially values personal rectitude for which bribery and corruption were anathema. Sufism is more cosmopolitan and associated with the establishment. It has a higher level of tolerance for ambiguity and diversity of religious views within Islam. These rival approaches to belief are not rigidly segregated from each other and often overlap, though education solely based on memorization of the Koran probably inclined students more toward Salafist ways of thinking than Sufist.

Since the end of the civil war in 1970, Salafist Islam in Northern Nigeria and the broader Sahel region of West Africa had come to increasingly resemble Saudi Arabia's Wahhabism with its literal reading of the Koran and other sacred texts. Saudi missionaries and Saudi money had helped strengthen that approach by building mosques and Islamic schools. Salafists rejected the alleged "accretions" to Islam from African traditional religions that Sufism would tolerate, such as veneration of local saints. Hence Salafist radicals in Timbuktu in Mali destroyed ancient tombs of such saints in 2012. (The tombs were UNESCO World Heritage Sites.) Salafism in the Sahel was only a generation old, while Sufi roots went back through a thousand years of Islamic civilization in West Africa. Further fragmenting Islam in Northern Nigeria was the traditional rivalry for religious leadership and secular power between the sultan of Sokoto and the shehu of Borno, though both were part of the conventional Islamic establishment.

"BOKO HARAM"

The moniker "Boko Haram" was first applied in the Railway Quarter, a Maiduguri neighborhood, to the followers of a radical malam, Mohammed Yusuf. He was later murdered by the police in 2009 as they suppressed his bloody insurrection against the state. Boko is the Hausa word for "book" and commonly refers to Western education. Haram is the Arabic word for "forbidden." Some members of Yusuf's movement styled themselves as "People Committed to the Prophet's Teaching and Jihad." Others, however, have observed that the broader movement had no overarching name for itself. Instead, local people called it by many different names.[6] The moniker Boko Haram was adopted by the Nigerian government and by the media, and they applied it to virtually all antigovernment activity in the North, thereby imposing undue coherence on a diffuse, often localized revolt.

Mohammed Yusuf's specific group started as a small and marginal part of the larger movement of Islamic protest in the North that was, at that period, usually nonviolent. But, even before Yusuf's murder, he and his followers had evolved into a violent revolt against the Nigerian political economy, including both the Islamic establishment and the secular state. Boko Haram's transformation from a peaceful to a violent movement was encouraged if not caused by security service brutality. With its highly diffuse, religious, even millenarian dimensions, it might constitute a new type of revolution in Nigeria because it aimed at the creation of a polity through violence and rage but without a political program or even much of a structure. Intensely parochial, it defied conventional analysis based on the precedents of the French, Russian, or even Iranian revolutions. It did not fit with the Arab Spring, lacking any democratic aspirations. Nor did it fit into the internationalist al-Qaeda or jihadist framework, though it shared the same Islamic rhetoric. By October 2012, there were media reports that Boko Haram was taxing people where it could and that it had a flag.[7] It was still too soon, however, to say whether there were signs that the movement was seeking to establish itself as an alternative to the Nigerian state.

The relationship among the followers of Yusuf and other groups in revolt was shadowy. At a minimum, however, after his death the disciples of Yusuf appeared to acknowledge the spiritual primacy of Abubakar Shekau, who may have been his deputy. But other parts of the broader revolt were not necessarily responsive to the strategic or tactical leadership of Shekau.

The grassroots revolt of which Yusuf's followers were a part had no regionwide charismatic leader, no politburo, and no authoritative manifesto. It seemed to have few organizing principles beyond hatred for Nigeria's political economy and the Abuja government, and the aspiration to create a pure Islamic state based on sharia. It built popular support through field preachers outside the usual Islamic establishment. It likely attracted support from at least some politicians and patronage networks that believed they had been marginalized by the 2011 elections, as well as purely criminal gangs who claimed to act under its umbrella.

Its transformation from a grassroots revolt on the fringe to a movement powerful enough to credibly threaten the secular state owed much to changes in Nigeria's political arrangements. In a process beginning during his 1999–2003 first presidential term, Olusegun Obasanjo dismissed those military officers who had held civilian office during the years of military government. Most of them were from the North, and Northerners developed a deeply entrenched hatred for Obasanjo, believing that their dismissals were part of a systematic marginalization of the North. The end of zoning during the elections of 2011 seemed to be a continuation of this process of marginalization and raised the specter that it had become irreversible. That conclusion provided the foundation on which radical Islamic alternatives could build. In 2011, the Northern political establishment fragmented, with some supporting President Jonathan. Those who did lost local influence, with at least some Muslims turning toward radical Islamic preachers for leadership. Those among the Northern elites who did not support Jonathan were well disposed to acquiesce to or even support an insurgency against the federal government. Political and even purely criminal elements had also taken advantage of the general breakdown of order. Ethnic conflicts, often driven by land use disputes, also accelerated. Violence ostensibly in the service of true religion became self-reinforcing and self-justifying. Boko Haram fed off of it.

MOHAMMED YUSUF

Mohammed Yusuf was born in Yobe state in 1970. He had four wives and twelve children when he was murdered in 2009. He may have had Kanuri family ties; others say he was a member of one of the numerous minority tribes in the region. He was a malam (teacher), not an imam (worship leader). He was a charismatic preacher who appeared to draw on Salafist religious enthusiasm and its emphasis on justice for the poor through sharia. The BBC,[8] citing a Nigerian academic, reports that Mohammed Yusuf was well educated, spoke English, and lived lavishly; he may have even had a Mercedes-Benz. But these personal details, like his ethnicity, are not confirmed. His teaching may have been influenced by the course of Borno state politics. His disciples had a special enmity for then-governor Ali Modu Sheriff, whom many of them held as ultimately responsible for Yusuf's death.

During his career, Mohammed Yusuf was arrested numerous times but always released, presumably because of the intervention of his politically powerful friends. That pattern likely encouraged the police to kill him; they were frustrated by Yusuf's apparent immunity. With Nigeria's sclerotic judicial system, "jungle justice" (popular vigilante justice) followed by instant execution, or murder, occurs in public places. It is also widely believed that the police regularly murder suspects "trying to escape." The immediate aftermath of the murder of Mohammed Yusuf was captured by a cell phone camera and broadcast all over Northern Nigeria. It contributed to Yusuf's status as a martyr and the already widespread populist hatred of the security services. The police and the army, both national institutions, were the face of the Abuja government for many or most in the North.

A Nigerian commentator[9] credibly reports that Yusuf had initially believed that an Islamic state based on sharia could be achieved without violence through preaching and mobilization of the people. But his deputy, Abubakar Shekau, argued that success would require an armed struggle, and Yusuf's followers increasingly resorted to the murder of their critics and opponents. Repeated attacks by the army and the police on the group tilted the balance in favor of Shekau, resulting in the bloody insurrection of 2009. In the days following Yusuf's murder, the police also killed a number of other alleged leaders, include some of his family members, without reference to any judicial process. The police destroyed Boko Haram community property and arrested a large number of Yusuf's followers. The survivors went underground. Even so, the remnants of the community were still on the outer fringes of Northern Nigerian Islam, posing no threat to the Nigerian state. But a year later Yusuf's followers were back, in the new environment created by the end of zoning and the elections of April 2011. By 2012, Boko Haram operations had expanded to cover much of the North.

ABUBAKAR SHEKAU

Little is known about the immediate period after Yusuf's death when his followers went underground.[10] His successor was his deputy, Abubakar Shekau. The Nigerian security services had thought that Skekau had been killed at the same time as Yusuf, until he appeared in videos several months later. However, as late as the end of 2012, Shekau still had not been seen in person since the day Yusuf was murdered three years before. He normally communicated through videos. He spoke in Hausa and Arabic but not English. He did not appear to be educated beyond Koranic studies.

Shekau may have been slightly older than Yusuf. In 2012, estimates of his age ranged from 34 to 43. He was a Kanuri, and, according to the BBC, [11] he had been a theology student of pronounced radical views. After Yusuf was murdered, he may have married one of the former's wives and adopted his children.[12] In one of his few videos, he said, "I enjoy killing anyone God commands me to kill—the way I enjoy killing chickens and rams."[13] He appeared to operate through a cell structure, well suited to a diffuse, grass-roots movement that made use of unemployed youth. There were occasional references to a shadowy *sura*, or council. In the absence of hard information, it was suggested that his headquarters was in northern Cameroon. As a person and as a leader, he was swathed in myth, but not charisma. He was no Lenin, Mao, or Castro.

ORIGINS OF THE INSURRECTION

The long-term religious and political context for the expansion of violent Islam was the struggle in Northern Nigeria to restore sharia in the criminal domain after the end of military government in 1998 made it possible to do so. Like Salafism, the sharia impulse was driven by a popular search for justice in a region that was progressively impoverished and misgoverned. It was first promoted by a governor of Zamfara state in the service of his own political agenda, but it so caught the popular imagination that its spread could not be stopped until it was adopted by all twelve of the predominately Muslim states. The federal government never addressed contradictions between sharia and national law;[14] Olusegun Obasanjo, then the head of state, appears to have thought that the sharia enthusiasm would burn itself out if the federal government did not interfere. However, the Nigerian constitution recognizes absolute freedom of religion while sharia has dire penalties for those who renounce Islam, circumstances that would seem to make collision between the two inevitable. In fact, the governors kept the lid on the practice of sharia, especially its cruel and unusual punishments such amputation or stoning. The former was rare, and the latter has never occurred during the past decade. But adoption of sharia did not solve the fundamental problem of different standards of justice for the rich and poor. A consequence was a growing disillusionment with "political sharia" and stronger advocacy for sharia that truly would not distinguish between rich and poor. True sharia would provide real justice for the poor and thereby would advance the establishment of God's kingdom on Earth. Frequently advocates of sharia urged that the system be extended throughout the country, including areas with a Christian majority.

The so-called Nigerian Taliban appeared within two years of the sharia wave when it was becoming clear how little had changed. There are similarities between it and Yusuf's movement, which may have evolved out of it. Salafist and violent, the Nigerian Taliban was suppressed by the military and melted back into the countryside. But it proved to be the opening of a new round of the grassroots rebellion against Abuja that culminated in accelerated Boko Haram attacks starting in 2009.

Until 2012, a large majority of Boko Haram's victims were Muslims with links to the government. Boko Haram viewed the traditional Islamic establishment as the greatest enemy of all. From its perspective, the sultan and his emirs had exploited the poor, failed to implement sharia, and sold out to Jonathan in 2011. Boko Haram murdered the brother of the shehu of Borno and tried to kill the shehu himself and numerous other traditional rulers. By 2012, it appeared to be trying to take away the religious functions of the sultan of Sokoto and transfer them to a religious council that would sit in Yobe and that Boko Haram would dominate.[15]

POLITICIANS

After 2011, there is some evidence that at least a few Northern politicians and heads of patronage networks attempted to make use of Boko Haram to advance their own agendas. President Jonathan complained at various times that his administration and the ruling PDP were "infiltrated" by Boko Haram. In August 2012, the Adamawa state governor in a major newspaper accused "corrupt politicians and political opportunists" of "hijacking and criminalizing" Islam to perpetuate violence and instability to settle political scores.[16] Shuaibu Mohammed Bama, characterized by the Nigerian security services when he was arrested in October 2012 as a "high-ranking" Boko Haram operative, was apparently in hiding at the home of his uncle, Senator Ahmed Zannah Khalifa.[17] Mohammed Ali Ndume, a senator representing south Borno, was arrested and charged with links to Boko Haram in March 2012. An alleged Boko Haram informant had told the security services that the senator was a major sponsor of the sect, a charge which Ndume has denied. Moreover, during the pre-trial legal maneuvering, he claimed that the vice president, Namadi Sambo, was aware of his contacts with Boko Haram, ostensibly to arrange a cease-fire.[18]

It was widely believed in Nigeria that relations between some Northern politicians and Boko Haram were close.[19] Jonathan acquired the support of Northern elites in the elections of 2011, but other Northerners, including many politicians of lower rank, remained hostile to his government. There is a reasonable probability that disaffected Northern politicians were sympathetic to some of the Boko Haram attacks. Their goal would have been to destabilize the Jonathan administration and enhance their own local standing. The chicks hatched by the end of zoning thus may have come home to roost. However, it is unlikely that politicians or patrons would take direction from Shekau, though they may well have shared his religious outlook.

Boko Haram is usually seen as a deadly enemy of the Abuja government and the PDP that controls it. However, in a twist, a spokesman for the Borno state government in mid-November 2012 claimed that the ruling PDP was murdering its political rivals claiming they were part of Boko Haram. The Borno state government was one of those in the North controlled by the opposition All Nigeria Peoples Party (ANPP). The Borno state commissioner for information, Inuwa Bwala, told press reporters that "politicians find in Boko Haram the perfect alibi to commit all sorts of crimes. Armed robbers found Boko Haram a perfect alibi to loot and attack banks. Businessmen who had disagreements with their business partners found Boko Haram a perfect alibi to unleash terror on them. To the effect that you cannot clearly define in this configuration which one is a Boko Haram and which one is not." In fact, a large number of the prominent victims of assassination in Borno were ANPP.[20]

CHRISTIANS

The Boko Haram revolt received its greatest notoriety in the West from its attacks on Christians. Among the Salafists in general there was considerable ambiguity about Christians, who probably constitute the majority of the population of Nigeria. The more moderate recognized that Christians were a "people of the book" and as such were entitled to toleration, but certainly not the full rights and privileges enjoyed by Muslims. Such moderates seemed to envisage the system under the Ottoman empire, where Christians were tolerated but subject to heavier rates of taxation and other burdens. However, a more radical strain wanted to exterminate Christianity, at least in the North. They were prepared to murder converts to Christianity from Islam and to destroy churches.

Stories, many credible, circulated among Christians of Boko Haram operatives forcing conversions to Islam. Death was the alternative, and some Christians chose it. Among Muslims, however, other stories circulated that church bombings were carried out by Christian agents provocateurs for motives that were entirely local and therefore variable. For those for whom the goal was the destabilization of the Jonathan administration, escalating conflict between Muslims and Christians advanced that agenda.

Ethnic hatred, easily stirred by the unscrupulous, also likely played a role. While Christians could be found nearly everywhere in the North, often their numbers were small, and their place of origin was outside the region. From the last names published in the press, many of the victims appeared to have been Igbo or Yoruba. Christians were, of course, also identified with Good-luck Jonathan's government.

By 2012, attacks were causing large numbers of Christians to leave the North, even if temporarily. Insofar as attacks on churches were designed to produce a Christian backlash, that strategy, at least through 2012, failed. While some Christian leaders threatened wholesale mayhem against Muslim communities outside the North, actual violence was limited. An exception was Plateau state, long a theater of murderous conflict where religious, ethnic, and occupational boundaries coincided.[21] Largely ignored by the Western media, villages around Jos were the venue of murderous ethnic cleansing perpetrated by both sides.

CRIMINALS

There was almost certainly an important criminal element in Boko Haram that probably increased with the progressive breakdown of order in parts of the North. Northern Nigeria has long been the venue of important smuggling routes. Kidnapping purely for ransom has occurred for centuries. Recently with respect to the kidnapping of expatriates, the federal government has been quick to blame Boko Haram. A disastrous 2011 attempt to free British and Italian hostages by a joint UK and Nigeria military operation was justified on the basis that the kidnappers were part of an al-Qaeda-linked operation. In fact, the evidence points to the kidnapping as being purely mercenary and without a political dimension. However, in December 2012 a group that kidnapped a French national claimed to have links with al-Qaeda in the Islamic Maghreb. Organized criminal gangs may also have had links to disaffected politicians. Without an improvement in conditions in the North, it is plausible that criminal activity will broaden, perhaps extending to narcotics trafficking, as it has in Mali.

SCIENCE AND TECHNOLOGY

Among participants in Boko Haram, there was also ambiguity about modern technology. Shaykh Ibrahim Datti Ahmad, of whom ostensible Boko Haram leaders speak with approval, had attacked the World Health Organization's campaign to wipe out polio through vaccination in 2003. Datti Ahmad claimed that polio vaccination was part of a campaign by the West in cahoots with the Abuja government to limit Muslim births, and he had spoken favorably of the Nigerian Taliban. Yet he was a medical doctor with a degree from the University of London. If he did not resort to violence, some of his rhetoric suggested he was prepared to do so. But if this strain of radical Islam represented by Datti Ahmad rejected polio vaccination, it embraced the AK-47 and used social media to tactical advantage. As for Datti Ahmad, an important political leader, it was never established that he was part of Boko Haram, though he appears to have been close to it. He may also have been a personal friend of Mohammed Yusuf. [22]

MONEY AND WEAPONS

Up until 2012, Boko Haram attacks appeared to be largely funded by bank robberies. One commentator credibly estimated that there had been several dozen since 2011. [23] Remittances from abroad have played little if any role in Boko Haram's financing, nor is there evidence of significant subventions from the international jihad movement. The Nigerian diaspora in the developed world is overwhelmingly Christian, and there is no evidence of significant overseas remittances from them to Boko Haram.

Boko Haram has successfully looted weapons from arsenals. Explosive materials and expertise were readily available in Northern Nigeria, where there has long been a mining industry. The more systematic effort to raise funding by levies and bounties reported in October 2012 may indicate that the expansion of Boko Haram operations was outstripping their more traditional approaches of bank robberies and breaking into armories.

New has been Boko Haram use of suicide bombers. Suicide is anathema to West African culture and was almost unknown as a weapon of terror in Nigeria before the 2011 attacks on the police headquarters and the UN headquarters, both in Abuja. The use of suicide bombers has continued since then. At the time of the first attacks there was speculation that this new tactic reflected new or closer ties between Boko Haram splinters or spin-offs with other jihadist movements such as al-Qaeda in the Islamic Maghreb (AQIM), the al-Qaeda affiliate operating closest to Nigeria.

Boko Haram in fact had little need for outside help. Its operations, though lethal, were relatively cheap. Vehicles used as car bombs were often stolen. Explosives were cheap. Foot soldiers for operations could be hired cheaply from the legions of unemployed youth, especially those who were products of the Islamic schools. And patrons who supported Boko Haram could call upon their clients.

OPERATIONS

Though bank robberies and jailbreaks had been ongoing, the tempo of violent attacks ascribed to Boko Haram or claimed by it escalated dramatically beginning in December 2011. Before then, attacks had mostly been on symbols of government authority, such as police stations. Individuals targeted for assassination were usually Muslims. After December 2011, however, churches were increasingly the targets of Boko Haram, and the death toll dramatically increased.

The location of the attacks also spread steadily toward the West from those areas dominated by the Kanuri in the East. By 2012, they were taking place in Sokoto, the home of the sultan.[24] However, evidence that this move was part of a coordinated, centrally directed strategy is lacking. With Boko Haram so highly decentralized, and with the possible emergence of splinter groups, it may be that the insurgency was spreading on its own accord at local initiative and direction.

Boko Haram operations were also increasing in sophistication. In mid-2012, for example, Boko Haram attacked the towers that play an essential role in Nigeria's wireless telecommunications networks. Thereafter it became increasingly difficult to communicate with the North or within the North by cell phone.

By the end of 2012, there had been no Boko Haram operations in Lagos, the heart of Nigeria's modern economy. Boko Haram was clearly capable of such an attack because of its now frequent use of suicide bombers, and such an attack would likely have had devastating consequences for the country's economy and the continued attraction of foreign direct investment. But Lagos is far from the North and is not a party to the "civil war" within Northern Islam. From that perspective, Boko Haram may have regarded Lagos as irrelevant. However, that could change as Boko Haram continues to evolve. A stronger nihilist dimension in a Boko Haram splinter could lead to an attack on Lagos even if to no purpose.

INTERNATIONAL JIHADIST LINKS?

With its huge, impoverished Muslim population, Nigeria was bound to be of interest to the international al-Qaeda movement. Osama bin Laden had called for the overthrow of the secular government in Abuja. The shared Islamic rhetoric of Boko Haram and Shekau's aping of Bin Laden's style in his videos suggested links. And al-Qaeda affiliates operated near Nigeria in southern Algeria. Northern Mali, now ruled by al-Qaeda allies and affiliates, is only a few hundred miles away from Northern Nigeria.

Starting in 2011, Boko Haram's tactics became more sophisticated, and it started using suicide bombers. These innovations suggested that Boko Haram was receiving assistance from some part of the jihadist movement.

Nevertheless, up to the end of 2012, there continued to be little evidence of meaningful links between Boko Haram and the international jihadist movement. There had been no operations carried out in Nigeria by AQIM. This may be changing. In December 2012, a group claiming to be affiliated with AQIM kidnapped a French national. By 2012, Shekau used anti-American rhetoric, but it was much less prominent than his denunciation of the Abuja government. The government of Niger did arrest Nigerians it accused of traveling to Mali for terrorist training in September 2012.[25] But the numbers—five persons—were very small.

With West African borders being so porous, travel between Nigeria and areas where AQIM operates is easy. Yet there was little sign of increased al-Qaeda influence up to the end of 2012. This could change in the future, depending on developments in Mali or if the Nigerian security services are able to drive Boko Haram underground, as happened in 2009.

Instead of the international jihad, and reflecting its parochialism, Boko Haram continued to be focused primarily on internal Nigerian issues. It showed little interest in Southern Nigeria, let alone Europe or the United States. Boko Haram attacked no Western facilities in Nigeria. Fundamentally, the world outside of Northern Nigeria was irrelevant to Boko Haram's goals. However in the future that could change if the North comes to see the United States as supporting the policies of the government of Goodluck Jonathan that Muslims regard as repressive. In an ominous development, in November 2012 Shekau in a video bitterly attacked the United States and linked together presidents Obama and Jonathan.[26]

FISSURES

By 2012, there was speculation that Boko Haram was starting to splinter, with some elements within it objecting to the high casualty rates its attacks were inflicting on innocent Muslims.[27] Some argued that Boko Haram had up to three different elements, with Shekau's the most bloodthirsty. Others, however, have argued that Boko Haram's loose cell structure precludes splintering, just as it does central direction and coordination.

There have been calls for negotiations between the government and Boko Haram. Former president Obasanjo led one such effort; his Boko Haram interlocutor was murdered the day after their initial meeting. In July 2012 the newly appointed national security advisor, Sambo Dasuki, sought the help of Islamic scholars and prominent Salafists to broker a cease-fire. In August, Vice President Sambo went to Saudi Arabia for negotiations. Both initiatives were to no avail. Not only did Shekau not participate in these negotiations but Boko Haram bombed Sambo's house. Shekau's spokesman characterized Sambo's interlocutors in Saudi Arabia as false. In November 2012 there was another attempt by a third party to arrange negotiations, this time with Muhammadu Buhari as intermediary. However, neither Buhari nor the government had been consulted in advance, and nothing came of that initiative. In any event, by late 2012, Boko Haram was continuing its war against the

Nigerian state, though it was unclear what victory would look like or what its consequences would be.[28]

THE FEDERAL GOVERNMENT'S RESPONSE

The federal government over the past decade has addressed Boko Haram and its predecessors as a security problem, not as a symptom of Northern political marginalization and impoverishment. Since the colonial period, the main mission of the army has been to maintain domestic order. There is a national police force, but it is undertrained, underequipped, and underpaid. Hence it has been the army and the State Security Service (the secret police during years of military rule) that the federal government has used against Boko Haram. The Jonathan government in December 2011 suspended constitutional guarantees in parts of four states for six months. The suspension, which had little impact on reducing violence and was unpopular, has been lifted. In April 2012 the federal government granted emergency powers to the security forces to counter Boko Haram.

The heavy security presence in these areas has become dysfunctional. There was a downward spiral, with soldiers resorting to brutality amongst an increasingly hostile population. Too often, after a Boko Haram operation, soldiers rounded up young men who simply "disappeared." On the other hand, soldiers and police were primary targets of Boko Haram, and their casualty levels were high. Northern governors increasingly called for the departure of the army from Northern cities because they believed that the security presence aided Boko Haram recruitment. But, had the military left, Boko Haram would have been left in control—if control was what it wanted. It certainly would have murdered as many of its perceived enemies as it could.[29]

By the end of 2012, an endgame was hard to foresee. In the past, millenarian Islamic movements had burned themselves out, often under military pressure. But there was no sign that this process was under way. Instead, there were signs that Boko Haram might move toward the establishment of an alternative government. On the other hand, Boko Haram did not seem to be consolidating. Instead, it appeared to be a grassroots revolution but without a political infrastructure and mostly fed by popular rage with a dose of Islamic fervor. And the military appeared incapable of controlling it.

However, the fact that Boko Haram operations continued largely to be in the North meant that much of Nigeria could simply ignore it.

In effect, Boko Haram and the government's response to it have been slowly bifurcating the country between North and South, Muslim and Christian. Should that continue to happen, the 70 million Nigerians in the North, already impoverished, faced an increasingly bleak future without access to oil revenue.

Chapter Ten

Washington and Abuja

Nigerians widely believe that free and fair elections are the way to restore public confidence in their government and avoid sliding into failed-state status. Yet none of the four elections—those in 1999, 2003, 2007, and 2011—that have taken place since the country's ostensible return to civilian rule has met international standards for credibility, though those of 2011 were better than their predecessors. At best, they were "election-like events." Each time, however, the international community led by the United States looked the other way. Nigeria's next elections, scheduled for 2015, are also likely to be problematic.

BILATERAL RELATIONS

Since independence, U.S.-Nigerian official bilateral relations have usually been good, though cooler under military rulers and uniquely bad during the later years of Sani Abacha's dictatorship with his flagrant violation of human rights. This usually positive relationship has largely been based on our parallel interests since the end of the civil war: African regional stability through conflict prevention or resolution; exploitation of the region's petroleum resources; and, under President George W. Bush, the addressing of public health challenges, especially HIV/AIDS and malaria. Though conventional wisdom was that Democratic administrations accorded Africa more attention than Republican ones do—former presidents Jimmy Carter and Bill Clinton are Nigerian national heroes—in fact, U.S. assistance to Africa reached its highest level than ever before under President George W. Bush, and that is being sustained by President Obama.

The U.S. embassy in Abuja and the Nigerian embassy in Washington each occupy new buildings, a sign of the closer, post-Abacha diplomatic partnership. The Nigerian embassy is widely admired as one of the more architecturally distinguished buildings in Washington. The American embassy in Abuja, reflecting the post-9/11 security requirements, resembles a bunker devoid of grace and has a line of visa applicants snaking around its perimeter walls. Nigeria also maintains consulates in New York and Atlanta, while the United States has one in Lagos. The American consulate occupies the 1960s chancery of the former embassy before the capital moved to Abuja and badly needs renovation. In President Obama's first term, Secretary of State Hillary Clinton approved the establishment of a consulate in the North, probably Kano. But budgetary and security constraints have stalled its construction.

The Department of State has the lead in the conduct of U.S. foreign relations. However, given Nigeria's size and importance, multiple federal agencies play a role in policy formulation. The National Security Council at the White House is charged with interagency coordination and usually shapes diplomatic activities directly involving the president, such as communications with another head of state, receiving high-level foreign visitors, and presidential trips overseas. The National Security Council played an important role in securing debt relief for Nigeria during President Obasanjo's second term. State recommended it, and the Treasury opposed it. State saw debt relief as an aspect of international support for Nigeria's new, nominally democratic government that was embarking on important economic reforms. Treasury objected because Nigeria did not qualify for debt relief under the criteria set by the international financial institutions. The impasse between the two cabinet departments was broken only when the National Security Council adopted State's position.

At other times during President Bush's two terms, however, there was institutional and personal friction between parts of the National Security Council and the leadership of State's Africa bureau that discouraged information flow and hindered policy coherence. Often, personality differences combined with poor communication and mutual suspicion between career professionals and political appointees were more important than disagreements over policy.

The Department of Defense's role increased in West Africa after 9/11. Defense has much greater fiscal and bureaucratic resources than the other federal agencies, and that provided challenges and opportunities for the U.S. mission as a whole. On my watch, other agencies represented at the embassy and the consulate included the Federal Bureau of Investigation; the departments of Agriculture, Commerce, Health and Human Services, Justice, and Treasury; the Drug Enforcement Administration; and U.S. Agency for International Development (USAID). Personnel from all agencies in Nigeria were under the direct authority of the ambassador. Relations among the personnel of the various agencies in Nigeria were good. Notably, there was not the friction between the civilians and the military that exists elsewhere.

As ambassador to Nigeria, I reported to the secretary of state through the assistant secretary for African affairs. Because of long-standing management issues within the embassy and the consulate, I also worked closely with, but did not report to, the undersecretary for management and his staff. The undersecretary outranked the assistant secretary, but they had separate reporting chains to the secretary. As his or her title indicates, the former was concerned with operations of the mission as an institution, including such issues as consular operations, personnel, housing, and transportation, all of which required much of my time and energy. The latter was concerned with policy, especially the bilateral relationship. Over the past decade, the undersecretary and the assistant secretary have usually been political appointees.

Of the three who occupied the office of assistant secretary for African affairs while I was in Nigeria, one was a career civil servant,[1] one was a highly distinguished development professional, and one came from the National Security Council. The assistant secretary is the "boss" of all the ambassadors serving in countries covered by the bureau and writes (or, more often, just signs)[2] the mandatory annual professional evaluation report on each that is the basis for performance pay and promotion. The assistant secretary is supported by a principal deputy assistant secretary and two or three deputy assistant secretaries. One of the latter usually has a focus on West Africa in general and Nigeria specifically. Of the deputy assistant secretaries, one is usually a political appointee with African interests while the others are career foreign service officers.

With some forty-two countries covered by the Africa bureau, an assistant secretary's personal involvement in a particular bilateral relationship can vary depending on events and his or her interests, background, and agenda. One of the three assistant secretaries I worked under met with me every time I visited Washington. The meetings would last at least an hour as she asked probing questions. These face-to-face meetings were supplemented by telephone calls and informal, written communications when I was in Abuja. She understood the implication of Nigeria's internal developments to the viability of our diplomatic partnership and to stability in West Africa. With another, however, I had only minimal contact. In that case, the Nigeria water was carried by the principal deputy assistant secretary.[3]

Within the Bureau of African Affairs, there is an Office of West African Affairs that includes the Nigeria desk along with desks covering the other countries in the region.[4] When I was ambassador to Nigeria, the office had a director who reported to the principal deputy assistant secretary or to a deputy assistant secretary. The Nigeria desk itself had one or two desk officers who reported to the office director or the latter's deputy.[5] The Nigeria desk is usually the first point of coordination with the many other State offices interested in Nigeria, and it takes the lead in ensuring Washington support for the U.S. mission in Nigeria. During my tenure, despite turnover of personnel and chronic underresourcing, the Nigeria desk and the Office of West African Affairs provided the mission with strong support. The desk was the vital hinge between Embassy Abuja and Consulate General Lagos and the Washington bureaucracy. It was, however, overstretched in comparison with other country desks. For example, the Bosnia desk at that time had eight officers; the Ukraine desk, six. In the Obama administration, Secretary Clinton has mitigated somewhat these staffing shortages, ensuring that the second desk position is filled and augmenting it with an additional, part-time officer.

Other agencies headquartered in Washington devoted varying numbers of personnel to the bilateral relationship, with USAID and the departments of Defense, Commerce, Energy, Treasury, and Health and Human Services usually having the largest. Even so, the executive branch personnel who spent much of their time working on Nigeria fit easily into a large conference room.

The Department of State, other federal agencies, and the embassy have access to the U.S. federal government's repository of experts and factual information about virtually all aspects of Nigeria, and its richness is probably unequaled anywhere else in the world. However, too often, the scattered information and insights are not brought together quickly enough or in a form that can be used by decision makers. In addition, the federal treasure trove is frequently underused because of personnel shortages among those working on Nigeria in Washington, Abuja, or Lagos combined with short deadlines that are often in turn driven by the media news cycle. The short-term focus also militates against using or trusting expertise developed over years that can illuminate the bewildering complexity of an issue at best only half understood by a decision maker. And email favors quick, if facile, answers to difficult questions over research and reflection.

In my experience, interagency coordination varied. It worked well at the embassy or consulate level, less so in Washington. Most officers from agencies working on Nigeria in Washington tended to be midlevel or even junior. While there were honorable exceptions, too often their bureaucratic masters would not empower them to make decisions. Too often administration political appointees were skeptical about the advice of the career professionals closest to an issue. The resulting need to refer routine issues up the chain of command could be time consuming and frustrating. With more difficult issues requiring a high-level decision, too often the substance was sacrificed for the sake of form as principals' staffs packaged them into a memorandum of one or two pages. Anything longer risked remaining unread and decisions unmade.

At State during Bush's second term, there were frequent changes of personnel dealing with Nigeria. During the thirty-eight months I was ambassador, there were two secretaries of state, two assistant secretaries of African affairs, and one acting assistant secretary.[6] There were also three different principal deputy assistant secretaries and three different deputy assistant secretaries with primary responsibility for Nigeria. There were two different West Africa office directors and two different senior Nigeria desk officers. In the department, as at the embassy, there were numerous staffing gaps resulting in large part from the personnel demands of operations in Iraq and Afghanistan. With chronic understaffing, personnel burnout was an ever-present concern.

Turnover was also characteristic of the position of ambassador to Nigeria. My thirty-eight-month tenure was longer than that of any of my predecessors over the previous twenty years, save for Walter Carrington, who served forty-eight months.[7] The frequent turnover of U.S. executive branch personnel at all levels dealing with Nigeria, the short period of time they served, the frequent and often unpredictable staffing gaps, the challenges of interagency coordination, and the informal and sometimes undisciplined nature of ubiquitous email communication encouraged a largely unexamined emphasis in the U.S. government on short-term rather than long-term interests. The undermining of the democratic process in Nigeria from 2005 to 2007 was gradual, and the issues were complicated. For those new to Nigeria, it was tempting to "see no evil" with respect to the seemingly ambiguous and confusing internal affairs of a country where our common interests in Darfur or Somalia seemed more important.

While I was ambassador, a few members of Congress expressed a particular interest in Nigeria, and some congressional staffers with an African focus had been in place longer than their executive branch compatriots. Senator Russ Feingold (Democrat of Wisconsin) served as the chairman of the Africa Subcommittee of the Senate Foreign Relations Committee. He and his staff followed Nigerian and African developments closely, and the senator regularly spoke out on humanitarian issues and in support of democracy and the rule of law in Nigeria. Congressman Donald Payne (Democrat of New Jersey) chaired the U.S. House Foreign Affairs Subcommittee on Africa and Global Health. He and his staff, too, were particularly knowledgeable and outspoken about Nigeria. Congressman Ed Royce (Republican of California), Payne's predecessor as chair of the Subcommittee on Africa, had traveled to Nigeria in 1999 to observe that year's elections. He also headed a congressional delegation to Darfur in 2005 and led the effort in the House of Representatives to bring former Liberian tyrant Charles Taylor before the Special Court for Sierra Leone for war crimes. Other members of Congress also had links to Nigeria. Senator James Inhofe (Republican of Oklahoma) briefly visited Nigeria in 2004 in part to maintain contact with certain Christian clergy. Senator Bill Nelson (Democrat of Florida) visited as part of his agency oversight responsibilities and met with the newly inaugurated

Yar'Adua in 2007. The Congressional Black Caucus, a group of African American members of the House (with one senator), all Democrats, were also concerned about Africa, though less specifically about Nigeria.

Until his electoral defeat in 2010, Senator Feingold kept Nigerian issues before Congress by scheduling hearings and issuing statements. Confirmation hearings for American ambassadors, all but three of whom in sub-Saharan Africa were usually career diplomats,[8] were the occasion for thoughtful, bipartisan discussion of African issues. Both Senate and House Africa subcommittees would regularly invite administration figures to testify. Nevertheless, in my view, consecutive administrations did not sufficiently reach out to members of Congress with an interest in Africa. Some in the Bush administration, like their predecessors, feared that members of Congress would use an African issue for partisan political purposes. Others tended to be focused on high-profile issues with humanitarian, human rights, or security dimensions. Hence, Darfur, Somalia, or Southern Sudan generally commanded more widespread interest than Nigeria.

Because the U.S.-Nigeria bilateral relationship has become so multifaceted, the conventionally diplomatic dimension is becoming relatively less important than it was a generation ago. In that sense, there is the beginning of similarities to our bilateral relationships with Ireland or Italy, where the official is only one thread in a rich tapestry of mostly private interchange. Reflecting this new reality, the U.S. mission in Nigeria includes U.S. federal agencies whose primary focus is domestic, not international. The Centers for Disease Control, with a negligible presence when I arrived, had become one of the larger agency presences by the time I left because of our expanded health relationship with Abuja. Most of the other "civilian" agencies came, or greatly expanded their presence, after the restoration of ostensibly civilian government in 1999.

Foreign affairs agencies also grew rapidly. In 1998, USAID had less than five employees in Nigeria, only one of whom was American. Ten years later, it had some 120 American and Nigerian staff. In our embassy in Abuja and consulate in Lagos, on my watch the foreign affairs and security agencies remained the largest in terms of numbers of personnel. State was by far the biggest component of the mission because it had responsibility under U.S. law for the visa and other consular functions and it filled many or most of the administrative functions in-country for the other agencies.

The ambassador is personally responsible for interagency coordination at an overseas post. I chaired twice weekly a meeting of the heads of all of the agencies and other relevant personnel, the so-called Country Team. In addition, I often chaired smaller groups drawn from different agencies working on the same problem, such as embassy monitoring of preparations for Nigeria's 2007 elections.

Official U.S. assistance was valued at almost half a billion U.S. dollars by 2007–8. I administered it primarily through USAID, the Department of Defense,[9] and the Centers for Disease Control using Nigerian and American partners, both private (such as Catholic Relief Services or the Anglican Diocese of Kaduna) and public (such as the Nigerian Federal Ministry of Health). There were also a few partners from other developed nations, especially the UK. Humanitarian assistance was a major focus of the American embassy's leadership. I chaired a weekly steering committee of all the mission elements involved with the President's Emergency Plan for AIDS Relief (PEPFAR), which used the lion's share of U.S. relief dollars in Nigeria. The federal minister of health and I formed a "court of last resort" when our staffs were unable to resolve a particular issue. Our emphasis was that PEPFAR and other smaller assistance relationships was a partnership with both sides having obligations and responsibilities. Over the long term, I am convinced, these humanitarian activities do much to build our relationship with the people of Nigeria who are not part of the charmed *oga* circle.

The growing number of American citizens of Nigerian origin has directly contributed to the growth of the mission's consular burden. As Nigeria became a source of immigrants for the United States, family unification, welfare, and other issues increased. For example, some American women marry Nigerians who are studying in the United States and return with them to Nigeria.[10] Children of that marriage are regarded by the Nigerian authorities as Nigerian, by Americans as American. In the event of divorce, it might be difficult for the American spouse to return to the United States with her Nigeria-born children, and she might seek U.S. consular intervention. Such cases are often bitter and difficult to resolve because the family laws of the United States and Nigeria do not fit well together and emotions, naturally, are high.

The impoverishment of Nigeria has also spurred emigration to the developed world, especially the United States, the UK, and the European Union. (Many more Nigerians immigrate informally to elsewhere in Africa.) A Nigerian remarked to me, "Any Nigerian with a modicum of education wants to get out, and America is the first choice because it is less racist than any other country in the developed world." Around the world, visa applications for travel to the United States declined in the aftermath of the terrorist attacks of 9/11—except in Nigeria, where they increased.

U.S. consular law defines who may come to the United States as a temporary visitor. For Nigerians, usually their greatest difficulty is to convince the visa officer that, following a temporary visit, the applicant would return to his home country. Any nonimmigrant visa applicant has to overcome the law's presumption that all visa applicants are, in fact, intending to immigrate. Considering Nigeria's widespread poverty, this is a high bar, and the nonimmigrant visa refusal rate accordingly is high.

Other Nigerians, especially close family members of American citizens, are eligible for immigrant visas. But there is usually a waiting period of some years. There is also the official visa lottery, which distributes immigrant visas to a lucky few by chance.

Too many Nigerian immigrant and nonimmigrant visa applicants procure fraudulent documents to strengthen their case. Benin City is a center of the engraving industry, and practically any falsified document can be procured there, from birth certificates to diplomas. A very high percentage of Nigerian visa applicants submit fraudulent documents, even when there is no need to do so because the applicant is fully qualified. Yet the submission of fraudulent documents renders a visa applicant ineligible. Furthermore, because visas are such a valuable commodity, there is often connivance by Nigerian officials in visa fraud. For example, a low or midlevel official at a ministry might add ineligible names to a list of official travelers he submits to the embassy's consular section for diplomatic or other special U.S. visas.

Ogas derive prestige from their ability to secure visas for their clients and dependents. (They themselves are almost always eligible, not least because they will always return to Nigeria, the locus of their power and wealth.) Even government ministers routinely tried to pressure me to intervene on behalf of an ineligible "nanny" or "executive assistant" who, in at least one case, turned out to be a girlfriend.

On the U.S. side, visa adjudication is usually done by first-tour junior officers, who could interview seventy applicants a day and often more. At the U.S. mission in Nigeria, which suffers from a chronic inability to fill all of its positions, supervision of those junior officers is thin. There are simply too few officers for the visa burden, and the physical facilities are inadequate, especially in Lagos.

Despite these shortcomings, the consular operation has improved, in large part because the Department of State has diverted resources to Nigeria, recognizing how dire the consular situation had become, and because of the initiative and oversight provided by my deputy chief of mission, who made improving the consular operation his personal crusade. Nevertheless, immature officers could show cultural insensitivity, and mistakes were made—all the time.

My most embarrassing moment occurred when President Olusegun Obasanjo's personal staff showed me that a consular officer had issued a visa to a serving cabinet minister restricted to a single entry to the United States. The consular officer apparently had taken that step out of frustration with the volume of fraudulent documents submitted by her particular ministry in support of ineligible visa applications.

Successful visa fraud carries little shame in Nigeria. Nigerians firmly believe that immigration is a fundamental human right and that American visa requirements are a game to be won like any other, by guile, humor, stealth, and even divine intervention, if necessary. More than once at church on a Sunday morning, I heard a variation of the following prayer: "O Lord, soften the heart of the American ambassador here among us so that our brother Joshua may obtain a visa to go to New York so he can support his family here."

Security issues, real or suspected, may also bar an applicant from a U.S. visa. Since 9/11, U.S. security agencies have consolidated their formerly separate databases covering those, inter alia, ineligible for admission to the United States. Many Nigerian applicants with names common throughout the Islamic world have found themselves subject to U.S. interagency scrutiny that delayed the visa process by months. Too often the U.S. agencies involved had insufficient personnel and technical infrastructure in place to resolve such cases quickly. Increasingly, distinguished Nigerian Muslims have decided not to travel to the United States because of the rigor of the visa process. At the same time, Umar Farouk Abdulmutallab and his al-Qaeda-sponsored effort to bring down an American aircraft on Christmas Day 2009 showed that visa screening is not always effective. The rigor of the U.S. visa process combined with inadequate resources devoted to it threatens to make what has been a minor irritant in the bilateral relationship a major one, especially in the predominately Muslim North. I know a number of distinguished Nigerian Muslims formerly well disposed toward the United States who now decline to put themselves through the visa process with its bureaucratic rigors and accompanying delays. Rather than Disneyland, they now go to Dubai.

At my first press conference and at my last, more than three years later, reporters asked me the same questions: given the importance of Nigeria's oil, was the U.S. intent on establishing a military presence in the Gulf of Guinea or elsewhere in Southern Nigeria? Follow-up questions ranged from the faintly plausible—was there a U.S. naval presence in the Gulf of Guinea?—to the fanciful or even paranoid: what was the purpose of the secret U.S. Marine base in the Delta? Or, tell us about the secret tunnel the United States is digging in the Delta. (The location of that tunnel moved around, in the questioners' minds, at least, and it sometimes popped up in other African countries such as Congo.)

Elite Nigerians are conscious of their country's military and political weakness, and they are uneasy about our military power and deeply suspicious of our ultimate intentions wherever oil is involved, especially in the Niger Delta and the Gulf of Guinea. This ubiquitous suspicion, found even in the generally pro-American South, is stronger still in the Islamic North.

Nigerian elites also commonly regard their country as the West African hegemon and dislike rivals for influence in the region. For years, that suspicion and dislike focused on France, which Nigerians believed was too deeply involved in the affairs of the Francophone states that surround Nigeria. Paris had also openly supported Biafra's bid for independence during the 1967–70 Nigerian civil war. However, as the last remaining superpower, the instigator of the war in Iraq, and a seemingly uncritical advocate for Israel from the Nigerian perspective, the United States has now displaced France.

In March 2005, the National Intelligence Council (NIC), an advisory body constituted by the U.S. government whose views were not definitive, published a conference report, "Mapping Sub-Saharan Africa's Future."[11] The report raised the possibility that Nigeria could become a failed state through a junior-officer military coup. It included speculation about the possible consequences for West Africa if such an event occurred. In May 2005, President Obasanjo sent copies of the report to members of the Senate, he said, to caution them about such a possible future scenario.

The result was a media firestorm. Senators, the media, and many ordinary Nigerian citizens were hurt and offended that the United States could even contemplate the possibility of a junior-officer coup. A delegation of senators paid a formal call on me to ask, in effect, for assurance that "it isn't so." The embassy and I went into overdrive to make the point that an NIC conference report did not define the policy of the U.S. government. However, I added that the contributors to the conference were academics, journalists, and other Africa experts. It would be well to pay attention to their views under the rubric of "seeing yourselves as others see you."

Obasanjo's decision to send the NIC report to the Nigerian Senate raised a number of questions. Had he not done so, nobody in Nigeria likely would have paid any attention to it—none had in the two months that it had already been posted on the Web. Some speculated that it was somehow part of his campaign to win Senate support for constitutional amendments that would enable him to retain the presidency. A frequent argument from his circle was that only Obasanjo could provide the stability Nigeria needed to keep the "army boys" from coming back, the possibility the NIC report had raised. Regardless of Obasanjo's motivation, the episode illustrated how much the Nigerian elite care about U.S. opinion—and also how frightened they remained about the possibility of a junior-officer military coup.

In June 2005, we closed briefly the American Consulate General in Lagos because of a credible security threat, news of which we received from Washington. Nigerians reacted with embarrassment. From their perspective, the closure implied that security in the country was poor. Our response was to emphasize the close and ongoing cooperation between Nigerian and U.S. security agencies with respect to our diplomatic establishments in Nigeria. Nevertheless, one influential journalist[12] linked the NIC report, failure of the Bush administration to support the then current Nigerian candidate for the head of the African Development Bank, the consulate closure, and our "lukewarm" approach to debt relief to evidence that the United States did not take

Nigeria seriously enough. The gist was that the United States did not love Nigeria as much as Nigeria loved the United States. [13]

Nevertheless, bilateral U.S.-Nigerian diplomatic relations were good during my years in Abuja. Nigeria's processing of visa applications from U.S. citizens was timely and efficient and largely devoid of political interference. On my watch, the American embassy could always get appointments with government ministers, and even the president, often on short notice. Under Ibrahim Babangida and Abacha, the stonewalling of such requests had been routine.

Both military and civilian governments have been positively involved in West Africa and on the continent. Babangida, Abacha, and Obasanjo all played a role in peace efforts in Liberia, for example. Nigeria had been a staunch opponent of the South African apartheid regime, and Obasanjo had sought to facilitate its transition to nonracial democracy. More recently, Obasanjo was one of the few African heads of state willing to speak out against the excesses of Zimbabwe's dictator, Robert Mugabe.

For Obasanjo, diplomacy mostly involved face-to-face contact with other African leaders, leavened by visits to the UN General Assembly and attendance at African Union meetings in Addis Ababa, Organization of Petroleum Exporting Countries (OPEC) meetings in Vienna, the World Economic Forum at Davos, and largely ceremonial trips to capitals around the world. He provided strong leadership for the Economic Community of West African States (ECOWAS), especially on security matters. [14] His official travel seemed to become more incessant the longer he remained in office. His absence from Abuja combined with his centralized, military style of governance and a lack of trust in his associates and subordinates contributed to the sclerosis of the federal government. He did not see much role for institutions such as the foreign ministry, and he reserved for himself all important foreign policy decisions.

Under these circumstances, perhaps Obasanjo's most successful foreign minister was Joy Ogwu, a highly respected academic from the Nigeria Institute of International Affairs. She focused primarily on improving the foreign ministry as an institution, in which she had considerable success. President Umaru Yar'Adua subsequently made her ambassador to the United Nations.

Obasanjo made serious use of his national security advisor, Aliyu Mohammed Gusau, at least for the first six years of his administration. Gusau was deeply involved with security issues, terrorism, and "difficult" states, such as Libya. He had a close, productive relationship with the American embassy. Gusau, a retired army general and a Northern Muslim, had a power base of his own. He was also close to former military head of state Babangida and had played a role in Obasanjo receiving the People's Democratic Party (PDP) presidential nomination in 1999. He broke with Obasanjo over the latter's Third Term ambitions, and his departure probably weakened the last months of the Obasanjo presidency. (Gusau became an informal presidential candidate in 2007 and tried again in 2011.) Obasanjo replaced Gusau with another retired general, Sarki Muktar, who, though clearly able, lacked the personal power base of his predecessor.

President Yar'Adua did not employ the same hands-on approach to foreign affairs as had Obasanjo. He chose as his foreign minister Ojo Maduekwe, the secretary-general of the ruling party who was also pro-American, and ceded greater scope to the foreign ministry. Yar'Adua retained Muktar as his national security advisor. [15]

Among the political classes, Obasanjo's activism on African regional issues produced an ambivalent reaction. On the one hand, they took pride in their country's role in the African Union, ECOWAS, and the UN and its position as a regional hegemon. The ending of Nigeria's international pariah status with the coming of civilian government in 1999 was a positive consequence of the end of military rule. They could hold their heads high again in Mayfair and on Rodeo Drive. On the other hand, especially outside the military, there was resentment at the enormous resources consumed by Nigeria's high-profile, international political and security posture. I frequently heard complaints that Obasanjo's diplomatic activism, like that of Abacha and Babangida, had as its goal the enhancement of his own personal, international prestige rather than the interests of Nigeria. Other, perhaps kinder critics ascribed Obasanjo's emphasis on his international role as a compensation for his inability to deal with Nigeria's intractable domestic problems.

Obasanjo did enjoy widespread support from the elites where his goal was clearly to enhance Nigeria's international power and prestige. Obasanjo's campaign for a permanent African seat on the UN Security Council, implicitly understood to be held by Nigeria as the "Giant of Africa," was popular right across the ethnic, religious, and political spectrum. Unusual in nonracist Nigeria, advocacy for it was often expressed in racial terms: black people deserved a permanent seat at the Security Council table, and Nigeria was the logical candidate because it was by far the largest black nation in the world. Nigerians would bolster that argument with references to their country's contributions to UN peacekeeping.

Nigerians did not understand American reluctance to expand the Security Council and its unwillingness to endorse the Nigerian candidacy for a permanent seat. The Nigerian campaign for a permanent seat on the Security Council faded in the aftermath of the bad 2007 elections. But as a popular aspiration it remains. In September 2007, assistant secretary of state for Africa Jendayi Frazer, at a press conference at the UN in New York, acknowledged the possibility of Nigeria becoming a permanent member of the Security Council someday if it followed through with electoral reforms, strengthened the institutions of democracy, ensured stability, and contributed to international peace and security. This highly qualified response made the headlines in the important Lagos daily *This Day* as "US: Nigeria Fit for Permanent Member of the UN Security Council."[16]

PRESIDENTS BUSH AND OBASANJO

The Bush administration found President Obasanjo to be a congenial partner. Obasanjo was strongly supportive of the Bush administration's war on terror. He was the first African head of state, and one of the first from anywhere in the world, to call on the president at the White House in the aftermath of the 9/11 terror attacks on New York and Washington. Obasanjo's antiterrorism rhetoric remained impeccable throughout his administration, though operational cooperation had its difficulties, reflecting among other things the limits of the Nigerian president's control over those who remained profoundly suspicious of U.S. intentions in the Niger Delta and the Gulf of Guinea.

Perhaps one of Obasanjo's most important attributes for the Bush administration was his commitment to regional peacekeeping, especially where a U.S. role had to be limited. For Obasanjo, peacekeeping had advantages. It increased Nigeria's international prestige. The salary and perquisites that the UN provided Nigerian peacekeepers were important benefits that Obasanjo doled out to particular officers and units to better manage his relationship with the military. For the two presidents, Nigerian peacekeeping was win-win. The Bush administration's bottom line, expressed succinctly by a high-level political appointee at the Department of State, was "Obasanjo may be disliked at home, but he is good for Africa."

Obasanjo's opponents—civil society democracy advocates, marginalized Northern Muslims, those convinced he intended to illegally remain in office for life—associated the United States with his increasingly discredited administration. I had to regularly field complaints that the United States had sold out its commitment to democracy and rule of law in Nigeria because of our need for Obasanjo's oil or his peacekeepers. There were also complaints that the Bush administration's acquiescence to Obasanjo encouraged him to overreach.

The close relations between Obasanjo and Bush tended to mitigate Nigerian suspicion of the United States' military intentions in the upper reaches of the former's government. Nevertheless, there could also be considerable operational friction between the two governments, even when the goals were the same. Because of Obasanjo's centralized decision-making authority, Washington frequently assumed he would or could carry out any commitments he made. But, like his predecessors, Obasanjo's hold on many of the levers of power was tentative at best. He, too, was beholden to the interlocking networks of *ogas* who call the shots in Nigeria. More than once the military supported by parts of the political class simply did not carry out presidential directives—and there was little that Obasanjo could do about it.

Obasanjo's inner circle and the broader political classes had a tendency to overestimate U.S. support for Nigeria. They lacked understanding of the complexity of American governance and were disposed to viewing the friendship of the two presidents as ensuring the United States would toe the Nigerian line. If the United States was not forthcoming, there was disappointment and bewilderment on the Nigerian side. This was the case for issues such as a permanent Nigerian seat on the UN Security Council and support for a Nigerian candidate to head the African Development Bank (who did not even have the support of all the other African stakeholders).

Obasanjo was remarkably successful in applying "African solutions to African problems," albeit according to an African timeline, rather than Washington's. For example, he and Cameroonian president Paul Biya worked out the orderly transfer from Nigeria to Cameroon of the disputed Bakassi Peninsula ordered by the International Court of Justice. But they took longer to do it than interested Western observers expected, which gave rise to doubts about the good faith of one or the other heads of state. (Cameroonians also tried unsuccessfully to manipulate Washington into putting pressure on the Nigerians.) Obasanjo played a highly positive personal role when political thuggery endangered elections in Liberia and Benin and in seeking a resolution to the ongoing crisis in Darfur. He strongly supported the creation of a West African Standby Brigade—though Nigerian contributions were slow. (Then chief of defense staff General Andrew Azazi announced early in 2008 that sixteen West African countries had joined together to establish such a force, and the Gulf of Guinea countries were moving toward the establishment of an international Gulf of Guinea Guard, as Obasanjo had long advocated.)[17]

CHARLES TAYLOR

Obasanjo's emphasis on "African solutions to African problems" strained relations with parts of the American government over the disposition of the Liberian war criminal Charles Taylor. In 2003, at the request of West African regional leaders and some in the Bush administration, Obasanjo, with reluctance, agreed to give Taylor asylum in Nigeria. Taylor's removal from Liberia was essential to end the long civil war there. However, Taylor was widely hated in Nigeria because he was responsible for the deaths of many civilian Nigerians living in Liberia and Sierra Leone as well as deaths of Nigerian peacekeepers. To mitigate somewhat the domestic political liability of taking in Taylor, Obasanjo asked for and believed that he received assurances, particularly from Washington, that there would be no official, public criticism of Taylor's asylum.

However, with the establishment of the UN Special Court for Sierra Leone, Taylor's crimes in Sierra Leone received increased attention from the Bush administration. As urged by the special prosecutor, an American, David Crane (2002–5), and subsequently by another American, Stephen Rapp, after 2006 there was also growing sentiment in the U.S. Congress that Nigeria should turn Taylor over to the Special Court for trial. Many in the administration and the Congress concluded that Taylor was also trying to destabilize Liberia's transition to democracy. This put pressure on the Department of State to convince Obasanjo to hand over Taylor to the Special Court.

Obasanjo was skeptical about claims that Taylor was meddling in Liberia. He repeatedly asked to see our evidence that Taylor was doing so. An interlocutor in the president's office observed to me that the information we shared was credible "only if you had already made up your mind that Taylor was meddling in Liberia." Obasanjo also believed that Taylor's potential to destabilize West Africa was best minimized by keeping him in Nigeria. The Villa argued that to turn Taylor over to the Special Court without the support of the other African states involved in Liberia would undermine Obasanjo's credibility as an African regional leader.

People around Obasanjo, if not the president himself, were also concerned that trying a former African chief of state in an international court would create a precedent that would make arranging the "voluntary" departure of other tyrants more difficult in the future. Obasanjo's critics or enemies even suggested that the president was concerned that the precedent of holding Taylor internationally accountable could be applied to himself once he was out of office.

As pressure for Taylor's extradition became more intense, many Nigerians feared the United States would take the situation into its own hands and kidnap the former Liberian chief of state. That possibility became a theme of the press's interaction with me. Along with denying there was a secret U.S. Marine base in the Delta, I now had to deny we were plotting to kidnap Taylor from the territory of a friendly state.

The weekend before a scheduled Obasanjo visit to Washington in March 2006 to meet with President Bush, the Nigerians removed Taylor's guards— by whose authorization remains unclear. Two days later, the night of his departure for Washington, I called on Obasanjo in his private quarters. He was reading the Book of Job. Among other issues, we went over old ground on Taylor. That evening, Taylor fled. The Bush administration and members of Congress were furious, and upon his arrival in Washington, Obasanjo learned that a scheduled meeting between the two presidents was in jeopardy.

A few hours after he fled, Taylor was apprehended in Northern Nigeria, near the Cameroonian border, by a joint Nigerian customs and border patrol.

He was accompanied, according to security operatives, by a female companion and $50,000. Both the companion and the money immediately disappeared, seemingly without a trace. The Nigerians later in the day of Taylor's capture turned him over to the Special Court. The meeting of the two presidents went forward. However, Obasanjo remained deeply angry at the American officials in Washington who had pressured him to recapture Taylor seemingly as a condition for a presidential meeting.

The circumstances of Taylor's quick recapture are murky. My view is that Obasanjo was happy to have Taylor flee, probably to Libya, thereby relieving him of an irritant. I also think it was serendipitous that Nigerian security people recognized and apprehended Taylor and that Obasanjo did not orchestrate a scenario of escape and recapture.

U.S. MILITARY

The activities of al-Qaeda and its franchisees in the western Sahel made the region a concern for United States European Command (EUCOM). In addition, the increasingly popular view that the Gulf of Guinea's oil and gas reserves could provide an alternative to Middle East oil intensified U.S. military interest in the region. Once EUCOM "discovered" these reserves and their strategic importance, a visit to Nigeria apparently became an imperative for its senior officers if for no other reason than to be able to say they had been there. In 2004, especially, despite the cautions conveyed by the embassy, there were so many high-level U.S. military visits from EUCOM that Nigerian suspicions were raised. The U.S. visits, from a Nigerian perspective, seemed to have little purpose, encouraging speculation that the motives were sinister. The stated U.S. intention, to establish a personal relationship between top U.S. and Nigerian military personalities, rang hollow on Nigerian ears. As ambassador, in theory I had the ability to stop such visits. In practice, however, an ambassadorial veto of a military visit is almost impossible to sustain when the prospective travelers are high ranking.[18]

While military assistance is generally welcome, Nigerians themselves want to determine what and how it is spent. The United States should merely write the check. The U.S. military—and the U.S. Congress—has a different view. U.S. assistance money requires formal procedures, audits, and reports, which the Nigerian side resents. There are also clashes of style. The imperial retinues sported by high-level U.S. military visitors did not help. They traveled with huge staffs, dedicated aircraft, special communications, and schedules so tight they often dictated time and place of meetings with Nigerian interlocutors. Nigerians saw such visits as manifestations of pervasive American arrogance.

Early in my tenure, I worked to remove congressionally mandated restrictions on U.S. training for the Nigerian military. In 2001, a Nigerian army unit had massacred civilians at Zaki Biam,[19] and, to the justified anger of members of the U.S. Congress, the Obasanjo government refused to hold the perpetrators accountable. The professional military regarded the atrocities as the result of orders given by the upper reaches of an ostensibly civilian Nigerian government, if not by Obasanjo himself. They deeply resented being made the scapegoat, as they saw it, for decisions taken elsewhere. Though there was an official investigation of the massacre, mostly the result of pressure from the international community, its results were never released, and nobody has ever been punished for the cold-blooded murders.

Eventually, the Department of State and the embassy brokered an agreement between interested members of Congress and Obasanjo by which the restrictions would be lifted in return for an explicit, presidential public statement affirming civilian control over the Nigerian military. By 2004, the time was right. The military had not engaged in any repeat bad behavior, and Nigeria was continuing to play a central role in international peacekeeping. After Obasanjo made such a statement in October 2004, Congress lifted the restrictions. However, Nigerian resentment lingered that they had been imposed in the first place and that congressional opinion held the military, rather than the presidency, responsible for the atrocity.

Not least because of its own internal rivalries, parts of the Nigerian military were prepared to obstruct Nigerian operations that the United States wanted, and the government of President Obasanjo was too weak to prevent it. In October 2004, the United States offered to provide airlift for Nigerian troops to Darfur. Obasanjo and the African Union set the date for deploying Nigerians to Darfur, apparently without consulting broadly enough with the Nigerian military. In response, the Nigerian military authorities stonewalled a U.S. Air Force team's request to survey the airports from which it would carry Nigerian troops to Darfur and refused, until the last moment, to provide diplomatic clearance for U.S. planes to land and pick up the troops. The Nigerian Air Force wanted to do the deployment itself and wanted the United States and the British to provide it with the necessary capacity to do so. That, from an American perspective, would have taken too long, given the magnitude of the calamity in Darfur and perhaps also in light of the upcoming American presidential elections.

Parts of the Nigerian military also remained deeply concerned about American "spying" in preparation for some future, sinister operation motivated by alleged U.S. oil requirements. U.S. proposals to establish a separate military command for Africa—U.S. Africa Command (AFRICOM)—further fed Nigerian paranoia about U.S. intentions. For example, a Nigerian army general commented to me that AFRICOM was "unacceptable to Africa and that Africa itself should continue to defend its own sovereignty." Another called AFRICOM "an invading army." Despite U.S. assurances that AFRI-COM's purpose was largely humanitarian and to facilitate U.S. training of African militaries as requested by their own governments, official Nigerian reaction to the idea was similarly negative. In late 2007, Foreign Minister Maduekwe stated flatly that such a command was unnecessary and that Nigeria would not host it under any circumstances. Sentiment in the National Assembly and among the "chattering" classes in the media was largely the same.

Nigerians did not find credible the U.S. arguments for AFRICOM. The new command's bureaucratic sponsors did not sufficiently take into account the need to build a favorable consensus for it in West Africa, a process likely to take years. President Yar'Adua appeared to open the door to AFRICOM following his meeting with President Bush in Washington in December 2007. This, however, made the situation worse. Nigerians viewed it as an example of a weak president folding under American pressure. Since then, official Nigerian statements on AFRICOM have backpedaled furiously from the alleged sympathy shown by Yar'Adua.

In his second term, Obasanjo and his inner circle became intrigued with the possibility of a partnership with China, which has been seeking to establish a presence in the Nigerian oil industry, without notable success. The Chinese are not popular in Nigeria. They are commonly regarded as racists, and Nigerians have accused them of providing few jobs in the enterprises they have established. They are popularly blamed for the destruction of the textile industry in the North because they flooded the local market with cheap, allegedly smuggled imports. Obasanjo's interest in building a Chinese relationship became notably stronger toward the end of his administration when the United States had insisted on his turning Taylor over to the Special Court, opposed his Third Term aspirations, and publicly called for free and fair elections. He made a high-profile visit to China and shortly thereafter a number of high-senior Chinese officials visited Abuja. A variety of agreements were signed but with little long-term significance. The Chinese dimension may become an important element in Nigeria's foreign relations and its economic development in time, but so far it has not been.[20]

FOCUS OF THE BUSH ADMINISTRATION

Despite Bush's expanded outreach effort to the Islamic population of Northern Nigeria, considerable assistance for the elections of 2007, and consistently urging military restraint in Delta, the Bush administration focused mostly on Nigeria's role in West Africa. Little of the official dialogue was about democracy or governance. Even with respect to the 2007 elections, the administration was reluctant to acknowledge even the most obvious indicators that they were destined to fail. It preferred to take at face value the assurances of Obasanjo and Maurice Iwu that all would be well.

The administration's focus on regional security rather than on democracy and governance in its official relations with Nigeria in part reflected the primacy of short-term over long-term planning. West Africa was riddled with conflicts and accompanying demands that the administration "do something." But, with its commitments in the Middle East and South Asia, the administration could do little directly. Nigeria under Obasanjo, however, was willing and able. He sent peacekeepers where we would not. He traveled incessantly in the region to resolve conflicts and roll back coups. The Bush administration's proclivity was to accept, even celebrate, Obasanjo's diplomatic activism and largely ignore Nigeria's internal dissolution. The shortage of U.S. government resources devoted to Nigeria and the rapid turnover of the senior personnel who were responsible for Nigeria also encouraged this view.

Nigeria's crisis of 2010–12 is the consequence of President Obasanjo's efforts to retain power by securing the rigged election of his handpicked and weak candidates for president and vice president. That process undermined democracy and retarded the development of good government, with only a late and muted response from the Bush administration. The administration's inattention to Nigerian internal developments was unwise. Nigeria was dancing on the brink. If it went over the cliff, it could no longer "partner" with the United States on West African issues. And that is what happened under President Yar'Adua. With a weak or nonexistent presidency, religious and ethnic violence in the North, and the continued alienation of the Delta, Nigeria largely abandoned its leadership role in the region. It did little when Guinea was racked by a military coup in 2008 and did not play a leading role in countering the military coup in its neighbor, Niger. Despite U.S. requests, it played little role in the search for peace in the Horn of Africa. Subsequent to Obasanjo, it also played a diminished role in the search for a solution to the crisis in Sudan. With the presidential succession crisis in 2009–11 and the subsequent unrest in the Delta and North, Nigeria is currently unable or unwilling to be the strategic partner the United States seeks in Africa.

Chapter Eleven

Dancing on the Brink

On July 17, 2007, two days before I relinquished my duties and left the country, I paid the customary ambassadorial farewell call on President Umaru Yar'Adua. He received me in his conference room at Aso Villa, from which he had removed the memorabilia of former president Olusegun Obasanjo. The logistical arrangements were smooth. The president arrived exactly on time and accompanied by only a small entourage. As always, he was gracious. A few days earlier, the incoming foreign minister, Ojo Maduekwe, whom I had first met fifteen years previously when he was a young human rights lawyer, hosted a farewell dinner for the departing Canadian and Israeli ambassadors and me. In those last few days, I also held farewell press conferences in Lagos and Abuja as well as farewell receptions for Nigerian contacts, the diplomatic corps, and the American community. Nigeria did not feel like a failing state.

Yet, for many Nigerians, the constitutional crisis provoked by President Yar'Adua's ill health, Jonathan's acting presidency, the end of zoning, the divisive 2011 presidential elections, intensified insurrection in the North, and the prospect of renewed militant activity in the Delta were cumulative signs of impending state implosion. In the media there was debate over the viability of the Nigeria Project that had evolved out of the British amalgamation of the country in 1914.

A FAILING STATE?

Even before Yar'Adua's illness, that Nigeria was a failing state had long been almost a given among the "chattering" classes. For example, Ujudud Shariff wrote in the *Daily Trust* (Abuja) in 2004, "by now, it appears beyond all reasonable doubt that Nigeria is not only becoming a 'failed' state but also is fast slipping into anarchy."[1]

State failure is like obscenity: hard to define but you know it when you see it. In 2012, the confluence of Boko Haram depredations in the North, intensified ethnic and religious violence in the Middle Belt, the prospect of renewed insurrection in the Delta, and the paralysis of the presidency posed a greater threat to Nigeria's survival as a state than at any time since the civil war. The violence in the North and the Middle Belt was chronic rather than episodic, and it was acquiring a distinctive religious dimension. In the Delta, various parties were rearming themselves or had never disarmed, despite the federal government's amnesty. Weak executive authority in Abuja was foreseen to last at least until the elections of 2015. The Nigerian state has responded in the past to individual challenges of a similar magnitude. What is dangerous about the present is the confluence of four at the same time.

The Fund for Peace in collaboration with *Foreign Policy* magazine publishes annually the Failed State Index, based on objective political, economic, and social criteria. In a 2006 interview, Pauline H. Baker, president of the Fund, provided a helpful approach to state failure. She said,

> There is no universal definition of a failing or failed state, but there are a lot of attributes that scholars agree upon, such as losing control over the territory that you have jurisdiction over, not having full physical control over it, or not having a monopoly on the use of force because there are rival militias or rebel groups that have operated in the country, or lacking legitimacy for a large proportion of the population.[2]

She cautioned that the Failed State Index was a tool for analysis, not for prediction of the future.

Using this approach, the Fund for Peace has charted Nigeria's steady decline, despite the apparent air of normalcy in government offices in Abuja and Lagos and Nigeria's continued participation in the international diplomatic ballet, which, however, largely ceased with President Yar'Adua's Saudi hospitalization. By national ranking, with the first being the worst, Nigeria has been steadily closing in on the top, jumping from twenty-two in 2006, to seventeen in 2007, and to fifteen in 2009 to fourteen in 2012. The top of this list has been held by Sudan (2006, 2007) and Somalia (2008, 2009, 2012), which were venues of civil war at the time.[3]

Stephen Ellis observed that the international community tends to view failed states as broken machines "that can be repaired by good mechanics" within a short time frame.[4] He suggested that, instead, failed states are more like sick people, with diseases of varying causes, intensities, and consequences. Recovery is often slow and progress is uneven. Like ill people, failed states continue to function in various ways even while they are failing in others. This analogy fits Nigeria well. Up until Yar'Adua's final hospitalization, Nigeria continued to play an international role, if shrinking, even while government authority slowly ebbed away at home. The increasing emasculation of the state has not been just the consequence of militant activity in the Delta or uprisings by radical Islamic groups in the North. It has owed much to ubiquitous corruption and the government's inability or unwillingness to control it. Indeed, the criminality of Nigerian politics and the rampant corruption of officials at all levels have been both the cause and the effect of the alienation of the Nigerian people from their government.

Family, ethnic, and religious identities are trumping a sense of national allegiance in large part because the state no longer addresses the basic concerns and needs of the people. The renewed, probably sentimental interest in Biafra, with the Movement for the Actualization of the Sovereign State of Biafra (MASSOB) flying that flag, is but one sign of malaise about the future of the state.[5]

Genuinely national institutions are few and weak. The national university system has never recovered from the days of military dictatorship. Private universities try to fill the gap but benefit mostly the privileged and a few lucky scholarship students. The integrity of a universal National Youth Service, supposedly the capstone of tertiary education, has been undermined by exemptions or exceptions for those with the right connections. The health system is only slowly recovering from almost complete disarray. Its flagships, its response to HIV/AIDS and malaria, have been supported massively by the United States and other international donors. Two major health accomplishments, the virtual elimination of river blindness and guinea worm infestation, have been led by Nigerian and American nongovernmental organizations (NGOs), especially the Carter Center and the River Blindness Foundation, rather than the Ministry of Health. The national postal service still exists, but Nigerians have increasingly turned to private services, such as FedEx or UPS. The civil service, the police, and the military, intended to be truly national entities, have been underfunded for a long time, and promotion based on merit has been repeatedly compromised. Nigerians have comforted themselves by seeing the military as the guarantor of state survival—maybe so, but only if the military, especially the army, remains cohesive. But after 2011 the religious and ethnic fissures that affect Nigerian society were manifesting themselves in that institution, too, in the North and the Middle Belt. And the idea of the army as the ultimate savior of the Nigerian state is hardly congruent with democratic values.

The only national hero, Murtala Mohammed, the general who overthrew the Gowon military government and pledged to restore democracy, was assassinated in a failed coup. But he did not play the role of a Gandhi, Ataturk, or Mandela in promoting a common national identity (nor was his role in national life comparable to theirs; he was chief of state for only a few months before he was murdered). The founding fathers, such as Obafemi Awolowo,

Nnamdi Azikiwe, and Ahmadu Bello were heroes, but mostly to their fellow ethnic groups, rather than the nation as a whole.[6]

The Nigeria Project, an attempt to promote a national identity through government institutions, failed largely because poor governance wounded its spirit and made it largely irrelevant to most people. Three poor-quality elections since 1999 following a generation of military rule drove home the message to the Nigerian people that they had little role in choosing who would govern them. Most Nigerians stayed home for the April 2007 polls. The resulting Yar'Adua government lacked the credibility elections bestow, even if it enjoyed a degree of acquiescence. The elections of 2011, technically better than those of 2007, divided the country and were followed by the worst violence since the civil war.

The Nigerian people are not even tied to their government by taxes, which few pay. Instead, the federal government dispenses revenue, mostly from oil and gas, almost as though it were largesse. And state and local officials are rarely held accountable for how revenues are spent.

If a primary characteristic of a failed state is that its government has little or no control over a significant part of its territory, Nigeria's condition is not good. Until its high-profile 2009 amnesty offer, the federal government had not credibly addressed Delta violence and disruption of, at times, up to a half of Nigeria's oil production. It remains to be seen whether the 2009 amnesty will be a sustainable solution. However, as of 2012, little of the government's promised training for ex-militants had resulted in their finding alternative employment and reintegrating themselves into society. In parts of the North, the federal government retains control of the big cities only through a huge military presence in the face of the radical Islamic insurgency of Boko Haram. In the Middle Belt, the government is powerless to bring the ethnic and religious violence under control. Ethnic and religious strife scattered across the federation has resulted in the estimated 1.2 million internally displaced persons. And crime has remained ubiquitous in urban areas as has banditry on the highways. The federal government has failed to provide basic security for its citizens and has lost its monopoly on violence, two basic attributes of a sovereign state.

State failure can take many different forms. Despite the agitation of MASSOB or of marginal Ijaw groups, the federal government's failings do not appear to be leading to a replay of the Biafra war—the coherent secession of territory dominated by a single ethnic group to create a new nation-state. States of the federation, because of their access to oil revenues through a national formula for its distribution, have become a focus of elite and ethnic competition, rather than the building blocks for secession. Instead, the federal government's power and influence is increasingly being replaced by substitutes at the state and local level. This process appears most advanced in those parts of the North most effected by Boko Haram. Many thoughtful

Nigerians are afraid that their country is going the way not of Biafra but of the Congo, where Kinshasa's writ runs in only certain parts of the country and only for limited purposes.

Unlike in Congo or the Great Lakes region of Africa, none of Nigeria's neighbors meddle in its internal affairs, at least directly, which has helped Abuja to maintain a semblance of national coherence. Thus far, non-Nigerian terrorist groups like al-Qaeda have not established themselves, though in the North that remains a danger. Up to now, the very size and ethnic diversity of Nigeria has resulted in little coordination among the multiple challenges to the power and authority of the state. Militias in the Delta have not been linked to any external groups, nor have there been signs of meaningful cooperation with radical Islamic groups in the North. This may be changing. The Nigerian and international press are reporting that Middle Belt militants are trying to procure weapons from the Delta.[7] Should a relationship develop, antistate cooperation among militant groups in the Delta, the Middle Belt, and the North would pose another potentially lethal challenge to Abuja. More generally, as more Nigerians "withdraw" from citizenry into religion and their ethnic group and family, the state simply becomes less important to them. Rather than revolutionary sentiment, there is popular inertia about a nation that was a British construct and never did command deep loyalty.

In April 2008, a conference was held at the prestigious Nigerian Institute for International Affairs (NIIA) that addressed the possibility of a social revolution. The event was chaired by former vice president Atiku Abubakar and participants included General Danjuma, the current and former governors of Lagos state, other former governors, and prominent lawyers. Nearly all had participated in the establishment of the Fourth Republic, and all were now in some way in opposition. The gist of their deliberations was that "revolution" is the only way out of Nigeria's current predicament, though they differed as to what that might mean. Some argued for violence, others for civil disobedience, and others for a revolution of "ideas and moral conduct."

The Lagos press reported Ben Nwabueze, a prominent lawyer and author, as saying,

> Obasanjo emerged as a dictator because the people and institutions such as the Supreme Court and National Assembly failed to check dictatorship. We all contributed to the emergence of dictatorship in this country. We are too passive and too concerned about our individual interests. We need to evolve an ethic of resistance, an ethic of civil disobedience, to be on the street to protest if the President tyrannizes us. We need a peoples' revolution. The rot in this country can only be cleansed by blood. Mark it, one day it will happen.[8]

This willingness to discuss the possibility of violent revolution came from the cream of the Nigerian establishment, each an *oga*, but now disaffected.

More hopefully, the participants did seem to take for granted that "Nigeria," the nation rather than the government, would endure in some form.

Preservation of national unity up to now has been in the interests of the *ogas* that dominate Nigerian political life. The Nigerian state guarantees access to oil and gas money by those elites outside of the Delta through the principle of Federal Character. By being the largest country in Africa in population and with the continent's second-largest economy, Nigeria provides the necessary platform for those elites who aspire to play a role on the African or world stage that would be unavailable to the citizens of the small states more typical of postcolonial Africa. So Nigeria has stayed together for more than fifty years, despite a bloody civil war, because that is what the *ogas* have wanted. Now, in the aftermath of Third Term, failed elections in 2007, a presidential succession crisis, polarizing elections in 2011, ethnic and religious conflict, and Boko Haram, some *ogas* want the current system overthrown because it is inadequate and resistant to change for the better. But they are not ready to storm the barricades.

However, the NIIA conference is one sign that the *oga* consensus that has held Nigeria together may be unraveling. The Northern elite have already split over the elections of 2011, with those who supported Jonathan losing their credibility with many of their followers, who have since turned to radical alternatives. A precipitous, sustained decline in international oil prices, resulting in the drying up of the glue that holds the elites to the Nigerian state, could be the backdrop to radical political change. The last time oil prices dropped dramatically for a long period, the military's commitment to the restoration of civilian democracy evaporated, and the way was open for the brutal Abacha dictatorship, which, in turn, brought the country close to a violent upheaval. The oil price drop of 2008–9 was the backdrop to President Yar'Adua's offer of amnesty to Delta militants. Since then, oil prices have recovered somewhat, though the state is still short of money.

Until the advent of Yar'Adua and Jonathan, Nigeria's top political personalities largely remained the same since the end of the civil war—they merely aged in place. And no charismatic opposition leader has emerged that galvanizes Nigerians, though Muhammadu Buhari partially filled that role in the North. Should such a leader appear, he might be like Mandela or Lech Walesa. Or he could recall Fidel Castro or Hugo Chavez. Given the misery of ordinary Nigerians, the latter two are at least as likely as the former.

OTHER ALTERNATIVES

Is there a way out? Yes. Although reshaping political culture and breaking the stranglehold of patronage networks is hard, Nigerian state failure is not predestined. The politicians are replacing the men on horseback. The National Assembly blocked Obasanjo's Third Term ambitions in response to public anger, and, even though it was of questionable constitutionality, the National Assembly in February 2010 made Jonathan the acting president, ending the impasse in presidential authority. Jonathan's presidential oath taking after Yar'Adua's death was uneventful.

The strengthening of democratic institutions, of which these are hopeful signs, could go far toward bridging the current gap between the Nigerian people and those who rule them and thereby open the door to redressing the consequences of generations of bad government and lack of development. Indeed, just one genuinely free and fair national election that results in a credible new federal government could go a long way toward building popular confidence in democracy and its identification with the Nigerian state. The growing independence of the National Assembly and of the judiciary is helping to create a democratic culture—so, too, did President Yar'Adua's emphasis on the primacy of the rule of law. These are all hopeful signs of an alternative to a doomsday scenario.

Nigeria has never been a totalitarian state; its weak institutions and bureaucratic structure preclude it. Radio and the press are mostly free, and freedom of speech is largely recognized, though it is undermined by the persistence of thuggery and violence often instigated by political figures. Nevertheless, space persists for organizations of civil society, and they were crucial to the improvement in the polling in 2011. We have already seen the positive role played by the Nigerian Bar Association and the numerous civic organizations that monitored—and denounced as fraudulent—Nigeria's 2007 and 2011 elections. Furthermore, a few of these civil organizations are national in scope, rather than tied to a particular ethnic group or religion. The Nigeria Bar Association is a good example. It has branches in every state of the federation and the Federal Capital Territory. With 55,000 members, it is probably the largest professional association in Africa. And, by definition, its membership advocates for the rule of law and the continued existence of the Nigerian state.

In the business community, many are modernizers. They see the relationship between the rule of law, sanctity of contracts, transparent trade, and investment policy and accountability by all levels of government for its expenditure as basic to Nigeria's development. They support democracy conducted according to the rule of law, not least because such a culture is good for business—and, therefore, themselves. Nevertheless, many of them show little interest in the North, regarding it as a nest of obscurantism and the venue of Boko Haram terror, while they cheerfully pursue business opportunities from Ghana to Angola.

If oil prices recover and then stay high, if the military does not intervene directly in governance, there may be space for some of the political elites and the modernizers to foster a more democratic culture. They might form and support an opposition party that could challenge the ruling PDP. Already opposition parties hold many governorships, including most in the Southwest of the country and Lagos. A vibrant opposition party could promote more credible elections that, in turn, would be a positive step toward establishing popular confidence in the Abuja government. The governing party might respond to a credible opposition party with even more egregious rigging. But an opposition would be unlikely to remain silent, undermining the current popular indifference to fraudulent elections. If the National Assembly and the court system continue to grow in independence and demonstrate more integrity, they will encourage the growth of popular support for democracy. And credible elections would enhance the authority of the president and his government.

Nigeria is hobbled by itself and by its history, not by present-day external actors, including alleged al-Qaeda affiliates. Though the international community would pay a steep price for Nigerian state failure and the likely humanitarian calamity, it can do little except at the margins to prevent it. Nigeria is too big, the issues are too complex, and the international community is too distracted by seemingly more urgent matters.

Nevertheless, the argument in this book has been that Nigeria is important to the United States and the international community and that the Obama administration should pay more attention to it. Nigeria is the Giant of Africa; its success or failure is a compelling example to other multiethnic, multireligious African states. Nigeria has been central to U.S. energy security. And Nigeria has the heft to be Washington's partner on African security issues ranging from Darfur to Congo to Somalia. On the other hand, a failed Nigeria would likely unleash religious and ethnic conflicts generating refugee flows with the potential to destabilize its fragile neighbors.

What can the United States do to help Nigerians forestall state failure? The watchword must be, first, do no harm. This means Nigeria's friends must shun initiatives, no matter how well intentioned, that could exacerbate Nigerian instability. Because of abiding, widespread suspicion of U.S. intentions in the Gulf of Guinea over oil, the United States should avoid the appearance of a permanent military presence in the region. The U.S. Africa Command (AFRICOM) should remain headquartered in Germany until the West African states, including Nigeria, see the operational utility of having it in their region. Persuasion will require AFRICOM to conduct a sophisticated and sustained outreach campaign directed toward a broad spectrum of Nigerians. The modest U.S. military overtures in 2009–10 to provide training for the Nigerian military were steps in the right direction.

Similarly, the U.S. military should calibrate carefully the frequency of high-level visits to the country, which almost inevitably generate suspicions about U.S. intentions. Better for building personal relationship and rapport with senior Nigerian military personalities—the ostensible reason for many of the U.S. visits—is to host them in Europe or the United States.

More generally, the Obama administration should focus on Nigeria as itself, rather than on it primarily as its proxy in various regional crises or as the potential venue for al-Qaeda terrorism. On occasion, the Bush administration appeared beholden to President Obasanjo because, at U.S. urging, he agreed to the deployment of Nigerian peacekeepers. At the same time, the Bush administration was largely silent about his undermining of a culture of the rule of law at home, thereby damaging the United States' credibility as an advocate for democracy. The Obama administration should take into greater account what the Nigerian government is doing domestically before embracing Abuja too warmly.

President Bush's 2003 visit to Nigeria in the aftermath of Obasanjo's fraudulent reelection fostered the Nigerian perception that their president had the United States in his pocket. It may have also encouraged Obasanjo to think he could get away with manipulating the constitution to remain in office indefinitely. On the other hand, President Obama's June 2009 visit to Ghana rather than to Nigeria sent a salutary message to Nigerian elites that Washington's patience with failed elections and bad government is not infinite. Among some Nigerians, however, the Obama administration's 2010 close embrace of the extra-legal acting presidency of Jonathan reawakened skepticism about American commitment to democracy in Nigeria. And close American identification with the Nigerian security services risks alienating Africa's largest Muslim population.

The Obama administration should acknowledge and praise Nigeria's progress toward better governance. Specifically, it should continue to emphasize that the succession of one civilian chief of state by another in May 2007 and February 2011 was a step forward, even if the means by which that happened were not democratic.[9] The Obama administration should not repeat the mistake its predecessor made with President Obasanjo and take what the chief of state says at face value.

A possible model for the Obama administration to follow in Nigeria is the Clinton administration's approach in South Africa in the last years before the transition to nonracial democracy in 1994: correct relations and cooperation on issues of mutual concern with the official government of the National Party and support for those government officials working for the democratic transition, including the then state president, F. W. de Klerk. At the same time, the Clinton administration enhanced its support for South African civil organizations working to build a democratic culture and maintained an extensive dialogue with the then opposition African National Congress of Nelson Mandela and the Inkatha Freedom Party of Chief Mangosuthu Buthelezi.

As part of such an approach, the Obama administration, foundations, and other NGOs should broaden and strengthen their support for the National

Assembly, the court system, and carefully vetted state governments that are practicing good governance. Targeted assistance programs have their role: for example, by providing word processors to courtrooms, donors facilitate speeding up trials, thereby enhancing their credibility as instruments of justice. But Nigeria's friends should also be prepared to ask hard questions when any of the three branches of government appear to deviate from the way of democracy and the rule of law, especially for apparent, short-term political advantage. Here, official press statements are important, not least because Nigerians pay attention to what any U.S. administration says. But the administration must strike a balance between friendly concern and stridency, which is likely to be counterproductive. Timing of administration statements should be carefully considered. If U.S. spokespersons repeat the message too often, it will lose its savor.

The Obama administration should strengthen its ties to Nigerian civil society. This can be done through "soft diplomacy," such as facilitating more exchanges and providing more grants to those actively working to create a democratic culture. In a poor country starved of books, the United States should expand the number of its reading rooms, called "American Corners," at institutions around the country.

More specifically, the Obama administration should rationalize and properly resource the U.S. visa application process in Nigeria and, indeed, in the rest of the Islamic world. The delays and indignities faced by Nigerian Muslims who want to travel to the United States risk our outreach to the North and are contrary to the spirit of the long-term American policy of encouraging legitimate travel. More consular officers are needed to adjudicate visa applications within Nigeria. More U.S.-based personnel are required to manage the various security watch lists.

Complicating a strategy of cooler relations with official Abuja and warmer ones with civil society will be the U.S. program of bilateral humanitarian assistance, now more than half a billion U.S. dollars annually. It is heavily weighted toward health. Much of it is implemented through Nigerian and American NGOs, but Abuja plays an important coordinating role. Nigerians believe that the focus of U.S. humanitarian assistance reflects American preoccupations and priorities; the overwhelming majority of the funding is part of the President's Emergency Plan for AIDS Relief (PEPFAR).

In Nigeria, PEPFAR has become a treatment delivery system rather than the means by which public health is transformed. Absent better prevention strategies, the PEPFAR caseload will expand into the indefinite future as older victims kept alive by new therapies are joined by new victims of the disease. As a practical matter, the United States now has few options with respect to containing the size of the program and derives little leverage thereby over the Nigerian government. PEPFAR cannot be suspended or ¹uced significantly because, were that to happen, large numbers of people would die. At some point, a U.S. administration must ask the Nigerian government to shoulder a larger part of the PEPFAR financial burden. Such a conversation will likely be unwelcome to Abuja, which will argue for the primacy of its own development priorities.

Friendship for the United States is much stronger in the Christian South than in the Muslim North, and the escalating poverty of the latter makes it vulnerable to penetration by international terrorism in the future. Hence, especially in the North, the administration needs to continue its outreach in the traditional areas of support such as the education of Muslim girls or agricultural development. It should greatly expand U.S. efforts on behalf of Islamic high culture, such as facilitating more exchanges between Northern imams and malams and their American equivalents. It should support indigenous Muslim institutions—especially museums, with a focus on the preservation and cataloging of Islamic manuscripts. These efforts convey a deep respect for the rich Islamic culture of the Sahel and bring Islamic cultural leaders into direct contact with Americans. Admittedly, these initiatives are hard to undertake when the security environment in the North is very bad, as it was in 2012.

Finally, in the Delta, virtually all of the parties except the Abuja government want greater American involvement because they think it will strengthen their hand and advance their own agendas. The Delta is a swamp, literally and metaphorically. Accordingly, the Obama administration's role should be limited to facilitating communication among all parties when asked, reiterating the unacceptablity of violence and the need for a political solution, and providing technical assistance to promote greater official transparency in the expenditure of revenue by the states. But the United States must proceed with caution. The Obama administration can help only at the invitation of the Abuja government, which must be persuaded that outside assistance can help a failing state "recover." And direct U.S. intervention on the ground would suck the Obama administration into yet another quagmire. Developing the "architecture" of a Delta solution must be a Nigerian responsibility.

It is by remaining true to the ideals of democracy and the rule of law that foreign friends can assist those in Nigeria working to establish a democratic culture. Nations are sometimes lucky. It was common at the time to predict that England would suffer a violent social revolution after the defeat of Napoleon in 1815 and during the massive social dislocations resulting from the agricultural and industrial revolutions. The nightmare of a British equivalent to the Bastille haunted establishment imaginations—including Wordsworth's. The crown and parliament were discredited, the economy was depressed, government was reactionary, and crime was so high that the gallows and the Australia prison ships worked overtime. Yet, for reasons variously ascribed to the rise of Methodism or to an unpredictable flexibility within the political system to growth and transformation of the economy, Armageddon was avoided. It is to be hoped that the same confluence of positive, if now poorly identified, factors will be true of Nigeria.

A democratic Nigeria characterized by the rule of law would promote economic development, encourage alleviation of poverty, and address the people's alienation from their government. The Giant would have freed itself from its hobble, and the dance would be moved back from the brink. Nigeria indeed would become for the international community that African example of progress and peace that was the hope of the visionaries of the Nigeria Project. The shadow of state failure would fade like the smile of the Cheshire cat. Nigeria would become a nation rather than merely Awolowo's "geographic expression" and would shine as the beacon for African democracy.

Notes

INTRODUCTION

1. The custom is for U.S. ambassadors to go to their post of assignment as soon as possible after they are sworn in. In many countries, including Nigeria, newly arrived ambassadors can cool their heels a long time before presenting their credentials.

2. While awaiting presentation of credentials, newly arrived ambassadors take charge of the internal operations of their mission. However, the chargé d'affaires (usually the departing ambassador's deputy) continues to be responsible for official exchanges with the host government.

3. For Americans, therefore, ambassadors in their country of accreditation outrank visiting cabinet officers, including the secretary of state. Here, the protocol parts company with reality; in the Washington context, a secretary of state far outranks any ambassador and it ill serves a chief of mission to forget it.

4. There are two letters from an American president addressed to the host country's chief of state: one that recalls the new ambassador's predecessor and one that designates the new ambassador as the president's personal representative to the chief of state with full diplomatic powers, "extraordinary and plenipotentiary." In Nigeria, as elsewhere, a new ambassador provides the chief of protocol with copies of these letters upon arrival in the country. In some countries, this presentation allows a newly arrived ambassador to begin performing most of his official functions—but not in Nigeria.

5. The Yoruba is one of the three largest ethnic groups in Nigeria. It is centered in southwest Nigeria. Lagos is a predominately Yoruba city. President Obasanjo is Yoruba.

6. Both are distinguished career diplomats. Lyman was subsequently director of the Bureau of Refugee Programs, ambassador to South Africa, and assistant secretary for international organizations. Walker had been ambassador to Senegal before Nigeria and to Côte d'Ivoire subsequently. Lyman and Walker had each also served as deputy assistant secretary in the Bureau of African Affairs.

7. These were Nigerian civil servants, Nigerian and other diplomats, professionals (especially lawyers and journalists), "professional politicians" out of office and waiting for the departure of the military, a few military (the governing Armed Forces Ruling Council tried to avoid us), businesspeople, some traditional rulers, and academics.

8. Most of the embassy's contacts were shielded from the worst aspects of the eroding purchasing power of official salaries. However, for those who were not shielded, the decade of the 1980s was hard in comparison with the years of the oil boom. An academic at the University of Ibadan told me that he was on the "1-0-1 plan," that is, he ate breakfast and dinner but no

lunch so that he could adequately feed his children. Funding for higher education collapsed during the decade and has not entirely recovered.

9. These concerns were far from baseless, as the failed coup of 1990 showed.

10. The victorious presidential candidate was Moshood K. O. Abiola, a civilian, Muslim, Yoruba businessman with close ties to parts of the military. He was imprisoned and subsequently died in 1998 under suspicious circumstances.

11. Abacha's hanging of Delta Ogoni activist Ken Saro-Wiwa led to the Commonwealth expelling Nigeria.

12. This was especially true of politicians, including those within the ruling People's Democratic Party. The Northern establishment was close to political rebellion. The Delta would have an insurrection by the end of 2005. Many human rights advocates were critical of what they saw as a consistent pattern of the Obasanjo administration's violation of the rule of law. The exceptions to this pessimism were the economic "dream team," U.S.-based, Nigerian technical experts brought in from the international financial institutions to reform the economy, notably finance minister Ngozi Okonjo-Iweala, governor of the Central Bank Charles Soludo, and Obi Ezekwesili, who held a variety of high-level posts. All three were outsiders tied to President Obasanjo and lacked a political base of their own.

13. Evidence is anecdotal. Nigeria's crime statistics are notoriously unreliable.

14. It is widely believed that Abacha was murdered.

15. The previous civilian governments were the First Republic, which lasted from independence in 1960 to 1966; the Second Republic, from 1979 to 1983, under the civilian president Shehu Shagari; the Third Republic, a brief interlude in 1993 between the military dictators Babangida and Abacha; and the Fourth, dating from 1999.

16. The civil war was caused by the Eastern Region, subsequently called Biafra, attempting to secede from the federation. Probably the best estimate is that 500,000 to 1 million Nigerians on both sides died during the conflict. See John de St. Jorre, *The Brothers' War* (1972). I am grateful to Jean Herskovits for the reference.

17. Mugabe, the dictator of Zimbabwe, has manipulated the political system to remain in power indefinitely. In Nigeria, the "Mugabe option" is contrasted with the "Mandela option," the scrupulous adherence to the law, including presidential term limits.

18. This definition of democracy is from Robert A. Dahl, *Polyarchy: Participation and Opposition* (New Haven, CT: Yale University Press, 1971).

19. Depending on how "ethnic group" is defined, the estimated number ranges from 250 to 380. See William Graf, *The Nigerian State: Political Economy, State, Class, and Political System in the Post-colonial Era* (London: James Currey Press, 1988), 5.

20. The line dividing Christians from Muslims that starts in the Sudan continues straight across West Africa.

21. The Hausa-Fulani is a Northern, Muslim, Hausa-speaking ethnic group, one of the "big three," along with the Yoruba and the Igbo.

22. Odunayo Ogunmola, "34,000 Nigerians Killed Unlawfully since 1999, Says Group," *Nation* (Lagos), March 24, 2010.

23. "Nigeria: Criminal Politics: Violence, 'Godfathers' and Corruption," Human Rights Watch Report 19, no. 16(A) (October 2007): 18, http://www.hrw.org/reports/2007/10/11/criminal-politics.

24. Mike Okiro, BBC News broadcast, November 15, 2007.

25. The U.S. imports far more oil from Canada than any other place. Saudi Arabia is usually second; Mexico, third; Venezuela, fourth; and Nigeria, fifth. For the period January–September 2007, the United States imported an average of 1.084 million barrels of petroleum per day from Nigeria, in comparison with 2.460 million barrels per day from Canada. See U.S. Energy Information Administration's "Petroleum Navigator," at http://www.eia.gov/petroleum/index.cfm (accessed July 23, 2010).

26. In fact, in early 2010, Nigeria was the second-largest supplier of imported petroleum to the United States. Canada was first.

27. Given the importance to the United States of Nigeria's peacekeepers, at first glance it is surprising that the U.S.-Nigerian military relationship is relatively underdeveloped. In part, this is the result of the Nigerian military's poor human rights record and resulting U.S. congression-

al sanctions. It is also a result of deep Nigerian military suspicion about U.S. intentions in the oil-rich Gulf of Guinea.

28. Few Nigerian Muslims have immigrated to the United States, legally or illegally. Islamic Nigerians are oriented toward Saudi Arabia, the Persian Gulf, and, among the elite, the United Kingdom rather than the United States. In addition, from 1994 until 2006, there was no U.S. consulate facility in the North, requiring all regular visa applications to be made in Lagos.

29. Commonly known as AGOA, it is based on congressional legislation that encourages and facilitates African exports to the United States.

30. It was a matter of pure chance that no American polio cases were of Nigerian origin.

31. The story told on the street is that one of Obasanjo's military colleagues held a pistol to his head when he tried to overturn the process and stay in office. Whether true or not, this story was believed by at least some members of the National Assembly during the Third Term crisis.

32. On the international community's high expectations for Obasanjo in 1999, see Jean Herskovits, "Nigeria's Rigged Democracy," *Foreign Affairs* 86, no. 4 (July/August 2007): 116–17.

33. As of 2009, the U.S. Department of State is considering the reestablishment of a consulate in the North. With the escalating violence in the Delta, as of 2009 there is still no official, diplomatic travel in that region.

34. The embassy did make such points with regularity.

35. The speech runs to more than seventy closely printed pages. It is summarized in *This Day* (Lagos), February 13 and 20, 2005.

1. "UN PEU D'HISTOIRE"

1. For the period in which the British amalgamated Nigeria, see John M. Carland, *The Colonial Office and Nigeria, 1898–1914* (Stanford, CA: Hoover Institution Press, 1985). See also Eghosa E. Osaghae, *Crippled Giant: Nigeria since Independence* (Bloomington: Indiana University Press, 1998), 1–28.

2. To the east of Yorubaland, the Oil Rivers Protectorate includes the Niger Delta. While the largest tribe is the Igbo, it is also the home of numerous other ethnic groups.

3. Lugard's ideas about indirect rule are found in his *Dual Mandate in British Tropical Africa*, 5th ed. (Abingdon, Oxon, UK: F. Cass, 2005).

4. For a succinct discussion of the role of the Sokoto caliphate, see John N. Paden, *Faith and Politics in Nigeria: Nigeria as a Pivotal State in the Muslim World* (Washington, DC: U.S. Institute of Peace Press, 2008), passim, but especially 27–28.

5. John Reader, *Africa: A Biography of the Continent* (New York: Knopf, 1998), 581.

6. John D. Hargreaves, *Decolonization in Africa*, 2nd ed. (London: Longman, 1996), 11.

7. Reader notes that the area of modern Nigeria includes the linguistic cradle of the Bantu family of languages (see Reader, *Africa*, 667).

8. On the origins of Nigerian federalism, see "Nigeria's Faltering Federal Experiment," International Crisis Group, Africa Report 119, no. 25, October 2006, http://www.crisisgroup.org/en/regions/africa/west-africa/nigeria/119-nigerias-faltering-federal-experiment.aspx.

9. J. F. Ade. Ajayi and A. E. Ekoko argue that this regional approach was supported by Nigerian nationalists. See their "Transfer of Power in Nigeria: Its Origins and Consequences," in *Decolonization and African Independence: The Transfers of Power, 1960–1980*, ed. G. Prosser and W. R. Louis, 256–62 (New Haven, CT: Yale University Press, 1988).

10. Ajayi and Ekoko, "Transfer of Power in Nigeria," 256–62.

11. David A. Low argues that agitation for independence in Ghana led by Kwame Nkrumah convinced the British to accept rapid decolonization there and in its other West African colonies. See David A. Low, *The End of the British Empire in Africa* (Cambridge: Cambridge University Press, 1993), 33–40, 201–29.

12. Ajayi and Ekoko argue that pressure from Nigerian nationalists played a major role in the British decision to leave Nigeria. See Ajayi and Ekoko, "Transfer of Power in Nigeria," 245–49.

13. Maitama Sule, a participant in the independence talks, movingly recalled the aspirations behind the Nigeria Project in remarks at a dinner I hosted in Kano in 2004. On the failure of Nigeria to develop national politics at the time of independence, and the growth of ethnically based or regionally based political movements instead, see Hargreaves, *Decolonization in Africa*, 75–77, 132–37, 175–77.

14. In the countercoup, 39 officers and 171 enlisted men were murdered, as was Ironsi. Of them, 27 of the officers and most of the enlisted men were Igbo. M. Crawford Young, *The Politics of Cultural Pluralism* (Madison: University of Wisconsin Press, 1979), 470.

15. William Graf, *The Nigerian State: Political Economy, State, Class, and Political System in the Post-colonial Era* (London: James Currey Press, 1988), 43.

16. However, other elements of the U.S. embassy were not reduced. I am indebted to Walter Carrington, who was then ambassador, for the distinction between the USAID mission and the rest of the embassy.

17. In a country with so many ethnic groups, it is hard to see where this process of state creation will end. For example, there is agitation for the establishment of the new state of South Kaduna. Like the rest of the Kaduna state, South Kaduna is dominated by minority ethnic groups. But South Kaduna would be predominately Christian, while the rest of Kaduna is mostly Muslim.

18. Numerous human rights contacts told me upon my return to Nigeria that the country had been close to violent insurrection in the last months of Abacha's regime.

19. There continues to be advocates for a return to a parliamentary system as an antidote to excessive executive power. Maitama Sule, for example, characterizes the presidential system as "eurocentric and alien to the culture of Nigerians because it tends to abhor opposition views." See "Mark, Sule, Others Assess State of the Nation," *Guardian* (Lagos), May 30, 2008.

20. Falae, a graduate of Yale, is a banker and farmer. In the 1999 elections, he swept his native Yorubaland but gained little traction or was rigged out in other parts of the country.

21. For a discussion of this perspective, and a fascinating on-the-ground report from an observer, see Joel E. Starr, "'What Do You Have for Me Today?': Observing the 1999 Nigerian Presidential Election," *Stanford Journal of International Law* 35, no. 2 (1999): 389–97. I am grateful to Starr for supplying me with a copy of his article.

2. IF NIGERIA IS SO RICH, WHY ARE NIGERIANS SO POOR?

1. "Indicators: Dollar per Day," Nigeria Statistical Data Portal, National Bureau of Statistics.

2. National Population Commission (Nigeria) and ICF Macro, *Nigeria Demographic and Health Survey 2008* (Abuja, Nigeria, 2009).

3. The age cohort was women ages 25–49.

4. National Bureau of Statistics, *Nigeria Poverty Assessment: Quantitative Aspect* (Abuja, Nigeria, 2004).

5. "UNESCO on Poverty in Nigeria," *Daily Champion* (Lagos), January 27, 2010. UNESCO stated that 92 percent of the population was living on less than $2 a day and 71 percent was living on less than $1 a day.

6. I am grateful to M. Crawford Young for this label.

7. Nina Budina, Gaobo Pang, and Sweder Van Wijnbergen, "Nigeria's Growth Record: Dutch Disease or Debt Overhang?" World Bank Policy Research Working Paper 4256 (June 2007), http://elibrary.worldbank.org/content/workingpaper/10.1596/1813-9450-4256.

8. Azoma Chikwe, "Nigeria Health System a Wretched 187 out of 191 Nations—United Nations," *Sun News* (Lagos), March 22, 2010.

9. For complicated medical procedures that could be carried out only in London or Johannesburg, the mission community, Nigerian and American, would participate in fundraisers or otherwise contribute to the costs.

10. I was told by Lebanese community leaders that those who had left went to Abuja or Lagos, and, during the calm period, the older and richer returned to Lebanon.

11. At that time, the exchange rate was about N130 to US$1.00.

12. "Nigeria Riots Toll Passes 200," *BBC News*, November 24, 2002, http://news.bbc.co.uk/2/hi/africa/2508131.stm.

13. My interlocutor was a resident in Kano. Our conversation took place in 2004.

14. Chineme Okafor, "Nigeria: Power Generation Rises to 4,349.7 Megawatts," *This Day* (Lagos), December 19, 2012; "South Africa," Country Analysis Brief, U.S. Energy Information Administration, October 5, 2011; "Nigeria," Country Analysis Brief, U.S. Energy Information Administration, October 16, 2012.

15. Alarms are sounded about alleged Chinese attempts to muscle into oil and gas. Thus far, that has not happened. Despite dramatic announcements of Chinese credits (which Nigeria declines to accept) or of purchase of oil blocks at auction with sweeteners usually involving infrastructure construction or repair, the Chinese have yet to bring on line significant oil or gas production. And "Chinese" ownership of soil blocks often disappears.

16. For the World Bank's view, see especially Budina, Pang, and Van Wijnbergen, "Nigeria's Growth Record."

17. Paradoxically, Nigerians not part of the financial sector believe the naira is undervalued, recalling the days immediately after independence in which the naira was at par with sterling. And Nigerians blame "the government" for the decline in the naira's value.

18. The survey looks at the ease of conducting business in a variety of areas, such as starting a business, construction permits, enforcing contracts, registering property, and paying taxes.

19. "Doing Business 2013: Smarter Regulations for Small and Medium Size-Enterprises," World Bank Doing Business Project (October 23, 2013), http://www.doingbusiness.org/reports/global-reports/doing-business-2013.

20. We sent a cable advocating support for Nigerian debt relief in July 2004 before the issue was likely discussed in an interagency context in Washington. Our arguments were more political than economic.

21. The accusations of corruption had no credibility. Especially after Obasanjo started using allegations of corruption against his political enemies, such accusations became a ubiquitous part of the political dialogue.

22. Budina, Pang, and Van Wijnbergen, "Nigeria's Growth Record," 8.

23. Abdul Fattah Olajade, "Jonathan Attacks Obasanjo's Reforms," *Daily Trust* (Abuja), May 13, 2008.

24. *Africa Confidential* 53, no. 20 (October 5, 2012).

25. *Africa Confidential* 53, no. 20.

26. John L. Allen, "Africa's Bishops Tell West to Offer Help, Halt Exploitation," *National Catholic Reporter*, October 20, 2000.

3. WHO RUNS NIGERIA?

1. John Stuart Mill, *Principles of Political Economy, with Some of the Applications to Social Philosophy* (London: Longmans, Green, 1909), 754.

2. These personalities are perennial. In 2010, while acting president Goodluck Jonathan turned to Danjuma to chair a presidential advisory council and reappointed Gusau as national security advisor. The customs service and the police are national institutions. The employees of both services are subject to military-style discipline and organization.

3. On patron-client networks in Nigeria, see Richard Joseph, *Democracy and Prebendal Politics in Nigeria: The Rise and Fall of the Second Republic* (Cambridge: Cambridge University Press, 1987).

4. I am grateful to John Paden for his insight on the use of *oga* in the North and to Tade Aina of the Carnegie Corporation for its use in the rest of the country. Because *oga* is commonly used in Lagos and Abuja, I use it in this book to describe the ruling oligarchs.

5. Biafra dictator Chukwuemeka Ojukwu pursued a military career, though he was the son of an Oxford-educated Igbo businessman who was one of Nigeria's richest men in the late colonial period.

6. Looming over the American embassy's recreational facility, a palace was under construction during most of my Lagos tour. It was built by a colonel.

7. For example, Senator Steven R. Owie believes the corruption started during Murtala Mohammed's administration and then was "perfected" by President Obasanjo. See Simon Ebegbulem, "Murtala Instituted Corruption, Obasanjo Perfected It, Declares Rowland Owie," *Vanguard* (Lagos), March 31, 2008.

8. In principle, Nigerian law follows the same approach as most countries (except the United States) on ownership and access to natural resources. I am grateful to Olav Ljosne for this insight.

9. The federal government takes 58 percent of 87 percent of the Nigerian state's total petroleum revenue. These percentages are from the Central Bank of Nigeria.

10. George Packer, "The Megacity: Decoding the Chaos of Lagos," *New Yorker*, November 2006: 62–75.

11. Obasanjo apparently played no role in the Murtala Mohammed coup or in the coup that brought Abacha to power.

12. *Forbes* identified Saudi national Mohammed al Amoudi as the world's richest black person. He is of Ethiopian/Yemeni descent. *Forbes* ranked him 97. "The World's Billionaires," *Forbes*, April 10, 2010.

13. Simon Kolawole, "Forbes Names Dangote Richest African," *This Day* (Lagos), March 7, 2008. See also "The World's Billionaires," *Forbes*, March 5, 2008.

14. Jonathan Elendu, "Yar'Adua Relocates to Dangote's Mansion," *Elendu Reports*, January 27, 2007.

15. "Nigeria: Criminal Politics: Violence, 'Godfathers' and Corruption in Nigeria," Human Rights Watch Report 19, no. 16(A) (October 2007): 27, http://www.hrw.org/reports/2007/10/11/criminal-politics.

16. Since the 1970 end of the Biafra war, Murtala Mohammed is the only head of state to be assassinated, though Abacha was almost certainly murdered.

17. Shehu Yar'Adua, the older brother of President Umaru Yar'Adua, had been the head of a powerful Northern network that opposed Abacha's consolidation of power. Abacha destroyed him. Fragments of the old Yar'Adua network gravitated to Atiku Abubakar, rather than to Umaru Yar'Adua. I was told repeatedly that personal relations between the two Yar'Adua brothers had not been close.

18. Apples do not grow in Nigeria. A luxury food, they are much prized.

19. "Nigeria: Criminal Politics."

20. Marwa established, in 2003, and supports, the Marwa Africana Lecture Series at the University of Kansas. I am grateful to Richard Joseph for drawing this to my attention.

21. Ribadu, a lawyer, was Nigeria's assistant commissioner of police and the head of the legal and prosecution department of the Nigeria Police Force. He was promoted to assistant inspector general of police in 2007.

22. Eziuche Ubani, "Nuhu Ribadu on the Cross," *This Day* (Lagos), July 9, 2004. Citing the Lagos newspaper *Punch*, Ubani states that presidential special advisor Julius Ihonvbere called Ribadu on his discussion in a public lecture of distortions in Nigeria's award system "where thieves of yesterday become government officials of today and how that reinforces corruption."

23. I am grateful to M. Crawford Young for this observation.

24. The judiciary's handling of election challenges was seen as successful by the Bush administration and, apparently, played a role in the warming of ties to the Yar'Adua government at the end of 2007. See Assistant Secretary of State Jendayi Frazer's favorable comments "Nigeria at a Crossroads: Elections, Legitimacy and a Way Forward" (testimony before the House Foreign Affairs Subcommittee on Africa and Global Health, Washington, DC, June 7, 2007).

25. The cabinet must include a minister and a minister of state (junior minister) from each state in the federation—hence its huge size.

26. The Department of State cost of living allowance is determined by a complex formula that excludes certain costs at post, such as housing, which is provided by the U.S. government.

27. Villa denizens were thinking of the Latin American model for coups. However, coups may no longer require troops in the streets. Ernest Shonekan's interim presidency ended when

Babangida and Abacha held a conversation with him and politely told him he had to go. I am grateful to James Sanders for this insight.

28. Akinola was outspoken about the Abacha regime, much less about his fellow Yoruba and Christian Obasanjo. His closeness to Obasanjo, I was told, contributed to his defeat for the presidency of the Christian Association of Nigeria by the Roman Catholic archbishop of Abuja, John Onaiyekan, in 2007.

4. FAITH

1. Adam Nossiter has investigated Abdulmutallab's background in detail. See his "Lonely Trek to Radicalism for Nigerian Terror Suspect," *New York Times*, January 17, 2010, New York Edition, (A)1.

2. When I was ambassador there were ten American Corners in Nigeria; six were located in the North, namely, in Abuja, Bauchi, Jos, Kano, Maiduguri, and Sokoto. The other four were situated in the South in Lagos, Calabar, Ibadan, and Port Harcourt.

3. "America's Image Slips, but Allies Share U.S. Concerns over Iran, Hamas," Global Attitudes Project Report, Pew Research Center, June 13, 2006, http://www.pewglobal.org/2006/06/13/americas-image-slips-but-allies-share-us-concerns-over-iran-hamas.

4. Nigeria's Anglican archbishop, Peter Akinola, famously led a revolt against the ordination of gay bishops in the United States by the Episcopal Church. In the North, conviction of homosexual practice will lead to a death sentence by the sharia courts. For more on these issues, see Lydia Polgreen, "Nigerian Anglicans Seeing Gay Challenge to Orthodoxy," *New York Times*, December 18, 2005.

5. Starting with Zamfara state in 2000, eleven other Northern states ostensibly declared sharia as a parallel law to the federal constitution in the criminal domain.

6. "Nigeria: Criminal Politics: Violence, 'Godfathers' and Corruption in Nigeria," Human Rights Watch Report 19, no. 16(A) (October 2007), http://www.hrw.org/reports/2007/10/11/criminal-politics. See also Odunayo Ogunmola, "34,000 Nigerians Killed Unlawfully since 1999, Says Group," *Nation* (Lagos), March 24, 2010.

7. In fact, the cartoons were never published in Nigeria, raising doubts as to whether they were the real causes of the violence. However, the cartoons could be viewed in Nigeria on the Internet.

8. John N. Paden, *Faith and Politics in Nigeria: Nigeria as a Pivotal State in the Muslim World* (Washington, DC: U.S. Institute of Peace Press, 2008), 26.

9. On the caliphate, see John N. Paden, "Contemporary Relevance of the Sokoto Caliphate: Rule of Law, Federalism, and Conflict Resolution," opening speech at the International Conference of Scholars on the Sokoto Caliphate and Its Legacies 1804–2004, Abuja, Nigeria, June 14–16, 2004.

10. For background on Borno, see John N. Paden, "Nigerian Unity and the Tensions of Democracy: Geo-Cultural Zones and North-South Legacies," in *Dilemmas of Democracy in Nigeria*, ed. Paul A. Beckett and Crawford Young, 244–57 (Rochester, NY: University of Rochester Press, 1997).

11. See John N. Paden, *Muslim Civic Cultures and Conflict Resolution: The Challenge of Democratic Federalism in Nigeria* (Washington, DC: Brookings Institution Press, 2005), 65.

12. On the special intermixture of Islam, Christianity, and traditional religion in Yorubaland, see J. D. Y. Peel, *Religious Encounter and the Making of the Yoruba* (Bloomington: Indiana University Press, 2000).

13. See Paden, "Nigerian Unity."

14. Other scholars lump the Middle Belt with the North, as the British did in the colonial period.

15. The caliphate supplied the chiefs of state who, in aggregate, ruled the second longest: General Murtala Mohammed, who ruled from 1975 to 1976, when he was assassinated; President Shehu Shagari, who governed from 1979 to 1983, when he was deposed; General Abdul-

salami Abubakar, who headed the interim government from 1998 to 1999; and President Umaru Yar'Adua, "elected" in 2007. All, of course, were Muslims.

16. That is, reform movements separate from Izala and the Tijaniyya Brotherhoods. However, there is substantial overlap between the reforms advocated by the two traditional groups and the new ones.

17. Tashikalmah Hallah, "Sultan—No Al Qaeda, Taliban in Country," *Daily Trust* (Abuja), November 15, 2007.

18. Philip Jenkins, *The Next Christendom: The Coming of Global Christianity* (Oxford: Oxford University Press, 2002), 67–195.

19. The power of the African church was manifested during the row over homosexuality with their Western counterparts. With a flock of 18 to 20 million, Archbishop Peter Akinola proved to be very influential.

20. While both buildings were constructed with "private" donations, there were complaints that Obasanjo was heavy handed in his role as chief fundraiser. When the Muslim Umaru Yar'Adua became president, he took pains to assure Christians that the Villa Chapel and the Christian National Ecumenical Center would remain Christian worship venues and that the official role that Obasanjo had played would be assumed by Vice President Goodluck Jonathan, a Christian. The National Mosque in Abuja, much older that the Christian National Ecumenical Center, was constructed in part with Saudi money. The two buildings anchor an Abuja neighborhood that someday will include other cultural institutions such as the National Library.

21. Jenkins, *The Next Christendom*, 67–195. The apparent surge of Christianity was partly a result of the recognized value of education provided by the missions, especially in the previously non-Christian Middle Belt. For more on religion in Nigeria, see Helen Chapin Metz, ed., *Nigeria: A Country Study* (Washington, DC: Federal Research Division, Library of Congress, 1992).

22. See Pew Research Center's Forum on Religion and Public Life, *Tolerance and Tension: Islam and Christianity in Sub-Saharan Africa* (Washington, DC: Pew Research Center, 2010). It finds that 46 percent of the population was raised Christian and is currently Christian. Fifty-two percent were raised Muslim and are currently Muslim. See p. 19 of the "Executive Summary."

23. Jenkins, *The Next Christendom*, 195. Jenkins cites David B. Barrett, George T. Kurian, and Todd M. Johnson, eds., *World Christian Encyclopedia: A Comparative Survey of Churches and Religions*, 2nd ed. (New York: Oxford University Press, 2001).

24. Nigeria has three cardinals. Anthony Okogie, the archbishop of Lagos, and John Onaiyekan, the archbishop of Abuja, are the others.

25. After the civil war, military governments secularized missionary schools and hospitals. President Obasanjo during his first term allowed the establishment of private universities, all but one of which is connected to a Christian denomination.

26. For a review of scholarly views on the Maitatsine, see Mervyn Hiskett, "The Maitatsine Riots in Kano, 1980: An Assessment," *Journal of Religion in Africa* 17, no. 3 (1987): 209–23.

27. "Nigeria's Kano State Celebrates Sharia," BBC News, June 21, 2000, http://news.bbc.co.uk/2/hi/africa/798630.stm.

28. Phillip Ostien, *Sharia Implementation in Northern Nigeria, 1999–2006: A Sourcebook*, 5 vols. (Ibadan, Nigeria: Spectrum Books, 2007), viii.

29. The powerful emir of Kano, and indeed most of his followers, opposed Bin Laden's call to arms from as early as 2001, even though the war in Afghanistan was seen in many quarters as unfairly targeting Muslims. See Mark Doyle, "Nigeria's Emir Opposes Bin Laden," BBC News, November 23, 2001, http://news.bbc.co.uk/2/hi/africa/1672191.stm.

30. Bin Laden's comments were made on Al-Jazeera on February 11, 2003. They were also carried by the Nigerian press. For example, see "Danger in the Horizon," *News* (Lagos), March 4, 2003.

31. Maiduguri has been a flash point for violence before. The Maitatsine rioters of the 1980s also used Maiduguri as a base because of its proximity to Nigeria's borders with Chad and Cameroon. The city provides a gateway for militants to melt into the populations of its neighbors, then reappear to continue their indoctrinations when tensions subside.

32. Abdullahi Bego, "'Taliban' of Nigeria: Who Are They?" *Weekly Trust* (Kaduna), January 3, 2004; "Troops Kill 5, Arrest 47 Islamic Radicals in Yobe," *Vanguard* (Lagos), January 7, 2004; "Nigeria Security Forces Kill 27 'Taliban' Militants, Says Police," Integrated Regional Information Networks (IRIN), September 24, 2004, http://www.irinnews.org/Report/51490/NIGERIA-Security-forces-kill-27-Taliban-militants-says-police. The details—numbers killed, weapons captured by the radicals, and so forth—are inconsistent among the three reports, though the magnitude is roughly the same.

33. Andrew Ahiante, "Police Arrest Taliban Leader," *This Day* (Lagos), September 30, 2004; "Taliban Attack Police Patrol, Take Hostages," *Vanguard* (Lagos), October 11, 2004.

34. Paden, *Faith and Politics*, 35.

35. For press coverage, see, inter alia, Aminu Mohammed, "Cleric's Murder—Accused Denies Bail," *This Day* (Lagos), July 21, 2007; "Nigeria: Sokoto Demolishes Shiite HQ," *This Day* (Lagos), August 4, 2007; "Nigeria: Demolished Shiite Hqrts Now Clinic, Police," *Daily Trust* (Abuja), October 24, 2007; "Sokoto Shiite Leader, 112 Others Get 8-Yr Jail Term," *Daily Trust* (Abuja), May 28, 2008.

36. Quoted in Karl Maier, *This House Has Fallen: Nigeria in Crisis* (Boulder, CO: Westview Press, 2002), 170–71.

37. For a thorough discussion of the polio immunization crisis, see Judith R. Kaufmann and Harley Feldbaum, "Diplomacy and the Polio Immunization Boycott in Northern Nigeria," *Health Affairs* 28, no. 4. (2009): 1091–1101.

38. The federal government procures the vaccine through the World Health Organization.

39. See the emir's interview in *Vanguard* (Lagos), October 23, 2003.

40. Yusha'u Adamu Ibrahim, "Emir Backs Calls for Polio Vaccine Suspension," *Daily Trust* (Abuja), September 10, 2003.

41. "Atiku Tasks Polio-Infected States," *This Day* (Lagos), July 24, 2003.

42. "WHO Seeks 'Traditional Rulers' Support on Polio Eradication," *Daily Trust* (Abuja), August 26, 2003.

43. Sani Babadoko, "Polio—Nigeria Medical Association to Sanction Supreme Council for Sharia Leader Dr. Datti," *Daily Trust* (Abuja), September 15, 2003.

44. "What Has Polio Vaccine Got to Do with Infertility, AIDS?" *Weekly Trust* (Kaduna), August 9, 2003.

45. Vaccination was not an issue among the Muslims in Yorubaland.

46. UN Integrated Regional Information Networks on October 27, 2003, reported a Kano technician as saying, "We have not forgotten that an American company came here a few years ago to experiment with some drugs on our children, some of whom died while others were disabled." The American pharmaceutical company Pfizer subsequently made an out-of-court settlement for $75 million while admitting no culpability. I am grateful to John Paden for this update.

47. "Danger in the Horizon," *The News* (Lagos), March 4, 2003.

48. Ibrahim Shuaibu, "SSS Arrests Suspected Al-Qaida Members in Kano," *This Day* (Lagos), October 31, 2007.

49. Mohammed Lawal Shuaibu, "Nigeria: Terror Suspects Get Bail," *Daily Trust* (Abuja), March 13, 2008; "Nigeria: Suspected Terrorist Seeks Bail after 3 Years in Custody," *Daily Trust* (Abuja), February 19, 2008; "Nigeria: Al-Qaeda Suspect Tortured by SSS Gives Evidence Today," *Daily Trust* (Abuja), February 18, 2008; Funso Muraina and Kazeem Sulaiman, "Nigeria: Accused Alleges Torture by SSS," *This Day* (Lagos), January 24, 2008.

50. Kunle Adeyemi, Ibanga Isine, and Kayode Ketefe, "Police Deploy Anti-Terrorist Squads in Lagos, FCT, Others," *Punch* (Lagos), May 14, 2008.

51. Sunday Aborisade, "Al-Qaeda: Islamic Groups Warn Okiro against Arrest of Innocent Muslims," *Punch* (Lagos), May 21, 2008.

52. Yusha'u Adamu Ibrahim, "Killing of Islamic Scholars—Religious or Political?" *Daily Trust* (Abuja), December 29, 2007.

53. "A Condolence Message to the Kano Muslim Community on the Death of Sheik Ja'afar," press release from U.S. Diplomatic Mission to Nigeria, April 13, 2007.

5. THE NIGER DELTA

1. For an excellent discussion of this reality, see "The Swamps of Insurgency: Nigeria's Delta Unrest," International Crisis Group, Africa Report No. 115, August 2006, 2–5, http://www.unhcr.org/refworld/docid/44e9a07a4.html.

2. See report by the Commission on Environmental, Economic, and Social Policy, "Niger Delta Natural Resource Damage Assessment and Restoration Project," Federal Ministry of Environment, Abuja and Nigeria Conservation Foundation, Lagos (May 2006).

3. "Nigerian Oil Minister of State (Junior Minister) Odein Ajumogobia Speaking on the Sidelines of the Riyadh OPEC Summit on November 15, 2007," *Platts Commodity News*, November 15, 2007. Because of the pervasiveness of bunkering, it is difficult to determine exactly how much oil Nigeria produces on a daily basis. By and large, bunkered oil is not captured in oil production statistics. In the past, actual Nigerian production has regularly exceeded the Organization of Petroleum Exporting Countries (OPEC)–imposed ceiling.

4. Ogoniland since then has largely disappeared from public consciousness, in part because petroleum production has never resumed.

5. "Politics as War: The Human Rights Impact and Causes of Post-Election Violence in Rivers State, Nigeria," Human Rights Watch Report 20, no. 3 (March 28, 2008), https://www.hrw.org/reports/2008/03/27/politics-war.

6. "The Launching of the Human Rights Watch Report, 'Politics as War,'" *This Day* (Lagos), April 1, 2008.

7. I am grateful to Olav Ljosne for pointing out the importance of population pressure and that the oil companies cannot quantify the alleged damaged caused by oil spills.

8. Foreign involvement in the training of militants in the Delta is regularly alleged in the press and is widely believed. I have seen no convincing evidence one way or the other.

9. Alex Last, "The Growing Power of Nigeria's Gangs," BBC News, February 17, 2007, http://news.bbc.co.uk/2/hi/africa/6370929.stm.

10. I am grateful to Olav Ljosne for this information.

11. I am grateful to Richard Joseph for the reference to Soludo's father.

12. Reuben Abati, "Warlords of the Niger Delta," *Guardian* (Lagos), October 4, 2007.

13. In a similar pattern, the Urhobo are supporting former Delta state governor James Ibori, a member of their ethnic group, who is a byword for personal corruption.

14. Adam Nossiter, "An Accidental Leader Stirs Hopes in Nigeria," *International Herald Tribune*, February 19, 2010. Sitting governors in Nigeria are immune from civil and criminal prosecution under the constitution—not so their spouses.

15. For a discussion of MEND as an umbrella group, see "The Swamps of Insurgency," 1–2. See also "Fuelling the Niger Delta Crisis," International Crisis Group, Africa Report No. 118 (September 28, 2006), http://www.crisisgroup.org/en/regions/africa/west-africa/nigeria/118-fuelling-the-niger-delta-crisis.aspx. The two together provide an excellent analysis of the Delta crisis that parallels this one but is largely based on different sources.

16. Ahamefula Ogbu, "Dokubo: Militants Pledge to Suspend Attacks," *This Day* (Lagos), June 16, 2007.

17. Interview with Muhammed Ajah, *Daily Trust* (Abuja), November 26, 2007.

18. "Why We Struck, by MEND," *Vanguard* (Lagos), March 16, 2010. I am grateful to James Sanders for this reference.

19. In Nigeria, called "oil bunkering."

20. Rueben Abati, "Warlords of the Niger Delta," *Guardian* (Lagos), October 4, 2004.

21. Abati, "Warlords of the Niger Delta"; Okafor Ofiebor, "Nigeria: Portrait of Ateke Tom," *News* (Lagos), September 13, 2004.

22. Nigerian press accounts of Dokubo-Asari have been summarized by Erich Marquardt, "Mujahid Dokubo-Asari: The Niger Delta's Ijaw Leader," *Global Terrorism Analysis* 5, no. 15 (August 2007). See also Asari-Dokubo, "Me, Henry Okah, 'Jomo Gbomo,' and the Niger Delta Insurgency," *Sahara Reporters*, December 31, 2008.

23. "The Emergence of Armed Groups in Rivers State," Human Rights Watch Briefing Paper, February 2005.

24. Tony Ita Etim, "N/Delta: Militants Disagree, Expose Kidnappers," *Daily Champion* (Lagos), May 11, 2007 (prints a "code of conduct" for fighters required by Egbesu).

25. As bunkering is a criminal enterprise, it is shrouded in secrecy and there are wide-ranging estimates as to its magnitude. Before 2005, both the federal government and the oil companies in their public statements minimized it—no longer.

26. "Nigeria's Former Oil Bandits Now Collect Government Cash," *Wall Street Journal*, August 22, 2012.

27. For an analysis of this relationship, see Scott Pegg, "The Cost of Doing Business: Transnational Corporations and Violence in Nigeria." *Security Dialogue* 30, no. 4 (December 1999): 473–84.

28. The federal government collects 90 percent of the profits when oil prices are above $60 per barrel. "The Swamps of Insurgency," i.

29. The Nigerian press is now warning of that possibility. See, for example, "Future of Nigeria's Oil at Risk," *Leadership* (Abuja), May 13, 2008.

30. David Howden, "Militia's Hunt for Guns Renews Fears of Nigeria Violence," *Independent* (London), March 11, 2010.

31. "Niger Delta Militants Warn Boko Haram, Threaten Oil Installations," *Leadership* (Abuja), January 9, 2012.

6. A PRESIDENT FOR LIFE?

1. For an illuminating discussion of the elections of 1993 and the circumstances of their annulment, see David Emelifeonwu, "1993: Crisis and Breakdown of Nigeria's Transition to Democracy," in *Dilemmas of Democracy in Nigeria*, ed. Paul A. Beckett and Crawford Young, 193–216 (Rochester, NY: University of Rochester Press, 1997).

2. In March 2008, the *Daily Trust* (Abuja) reported that Obasanjo, by then the chairman of the PDP Board of Trustees, moved a meeting of the board from the Hilton to the presidential villa because he feared an attack on his person.

3. Though there were other constitutional options, at the time the general assumption was that, if the elections were delayed, Obasanjo would remain in office.

4. Adinoyi Ojo Onukaba, *Olusegun Obasanjo: In the Eyes of Time* (New York: African Legacy Press, 1997), 68–69.

5. Dan Isaacs, "Profile: Olusegun Obasanjo," BBC News, February 6, 2002, http://news.bbc.co.uk/2/hi/africa/1804940.stm.

6. Gowon was born in 1934; Obasanjo and Danjuma, in 1937; Murtala Mohammed, in 1938; Buhari, in 1942; and Abacha and Shehu Yar'Adua, in 1943. President Yar'Adua, the youngest, was born in 1951; he alone was still a child at independence and has always been a civilian.

7. The military governed the country through a committee headed by the chief of state and reflecting the Federal Character principle and including all of the services. This committee was called the Armed Forces Ruling Council from 1985 to 1999. The Supreme Military Council was its bureaucratic ancestor.

8. It is an international myth that he was the first military African chief of state to step down voluntarily. In fact, Ibrahim Abboud in Sudan was obliged to resign following elections in 1964, and in Ghana, General Joseph Ankrah ceded power to a civilian government in 1969. I am grateful to M. Crawford Young for this point.

9. "Nigeria: Want in the Midst of Plenty," International Crisis Group, Africa Report No. 113 (July 19, 2006): 13, http://www.crisisgroup.org/en/regions/africa/west-africa/nigeria/113-nigeria-want-in-the-midst-of-plenty.aspx.

10. In addition, some locally hired USAID staff remained.

11. Abiola's death may, indeed, have been caused by a heart attack. Nevertheless, the circumstances have never been credibly explained. And his departure from the political stage was suspiciously convenient for the military men trying to put together a new regime.

12. Former President Carter, the leader of the National Democratic Institute's election observer delegation, regarded them as so bad that he left the country rather than appearing to endorse them.

13. M. Crawford Young, "Permanent Transition and Changing Conjuncture: Dilemmas of Democracy in Nigeria in Comparative Perspective," in *Dilemmas of Democracy in Nigeria*, ed. Paul A. Beckett and Crawford Young, 65–82 (Rochester, NY: University of Rochester Press, 1997), 66.

14. For Obasanjo's unpopularity and growing popular disillusionment with democracy, see Michael Bratton and Peter Lewis, "The Durability of Political Goods? Evidence from Nigeria's New Democracy," Afrobarometer Working Paper No. 48, 2005, http://www.afrobarometer.org/publications/working-papers/81-wp-48.

15. The judiciary's much more expeditious pace following the elections of 2007, as ordered by President Yar'Adua, counters the argument that it is Nigeria's legal procedures that predestine the slow rate of justice.

16. The "luxury" category reflected that they had guards, who were routinely killed by armed robbers.

17. One of the options Shell's corporate planners posited for Nigeria was "the road to Kinshasa"—characterized by strife, dictatorship, little cohesion of the social fabric, and so forth. My National Assembly interlocutors were familiar with this model. For a discussion of it and its context, see John N. Paden, *Faith and Politics in Nigeria: Nigeria as a Pivotal State in the Muslim World* (Washington, DC: U.S. Institute of Peace Press, 2008), 76–78.

18. "Abdulsalami: I'm Afraid for Nigeria," *This Day* (Lagos), January 31, 2008. Abdulsalami Abubakar's context was that the violence then occurring in Kenya could also happen in Nigeria.

19. Major Joseph Haydon, U.S. Army, an outstanding officer universally liked by Nigerians and Americans and marked for much greater future responsibilities.

20. Her attending physician has subsequently been convicted of malpractice in a Spanish court with respect to a different patient.

21. This was a central point in Maduekwe's officially sponsored 2004 National Day lecture.

22. "Third Term" was in common use by 2005 to refer to the question of Obasanjo remaining in power.

23. Friday Olokor, "At Last! EFCC Probes Obasanjo," *Daily Champion* (Lagos), March 27, 2008.

24. But not all of the Christian clergy, some of whom feared the consequences of a return to a Muslim presidency.

25. American ambassadors have the option of celebrating the U.S. National Day either on July 4 or on President's Day in February. Especially in tropical countries, the latter date is often selected because of the better weather.

26. I also acknowledged that Franklin D. Roosevelt had been elected to four terms, though against a background of economic depression and world war. I recalled that subsequently a constitutional amendment formally imposed a two-term limit on the U.S. presidency.

27. U.S. Embassy in Nigeria, "Third Term," press release, April 30, 2006.

28. "U.S. Cautions Nigeria on Third Term," BBC News, May 1, 2006, http://news.bbc.co.uk/2/hi/africa/4962616.stm.

29. For the Conference of Nigerian Political Parties, see Onuka Nzweshi, "Nigeria: CNPP Hails U.S. on 3rd Term," *This Day* (Lagos), May 3, 2006.

30. This point was made explicitly to me by the organizers of an art exhibit commemorating the tenth anniversary of the establishment of the state of Bayelsa, an exhibit that I "closed" in Abuja in January 2007.

7. THE "ELECTION-LIKE EVENT" OF 2007

1. I could never find any evidence that a presidential letter was prepared and signed for that specific event.

2. I never saw any evidence of religious fanaticism or extremism on the part of Buhari or any of the other Muslim presidential candidates.

3. The title signifies that the holder has made the pilgrimage to Mecca.

4. American University, Washington, DC, supplies certain management services under contract for the American University in Yola. The latter's management is almost entirely American, as is a significant part of its faculty and staff. Board members include former Anglican primate of Southern Africa Archbishop Desmond Tutu, former head of United Nations peacekeeping Sir Marrack Goulding, and me.

5. This is plausible; Nigeria has one of the highest maternal mortality rates in the world.

6. National Democratic Institute, "Statement of the National Democratic Institute International Election Observer Delegation to Nigeria's April 21 Presidential and National Assembly Elections," Abuja, Nigeria, April 23, 2007, 3, http://www.ndi.org/node/17435. The International Republican Institute (IRI) expressed similar concerns.

7. For a biographic sketch of Iwu, see Senan Murray, "Keeping Nigeria in Poll Position," BBC News, April 12, 2007, http://news.bbc.co.uk/2/hi/africa/6546443.stm. For Iwu's ties with the Uba brothers, see Ochereome Nnanna, "Is Iwu Finally Unraveling?" *Vanguard* (Lagos), March 15, 2007. For Iwu as Obasanjo's person, see, for example, Mabiru Mato, "Maurice Iwu—Time to Go to School," *Leadership* (Abuja), January 15, 2008.

8. The National Democratic Institute and the IRI both noted this in their pre-election-day survey of preparations for the 2007 elections. I am grateful to Pauline H. Baker for this fact.

9. See Ben Rawlence and Christopher Albin-Lackey for an insightful discussion of the numbers, in their "Briefing: Nigeria's 2007 General Elections: Democracy in Retreat," *African Affairs* 106, no. 424 (2007): 502–3.

10. Transitional Monitoring Group, "An Election Programmed to Fail: Final Report of the April 2007 General Elections in Nigeria," July 2007.

11. European Union Elections Observation Mission, "Nigeria: Final Report of the Presidential and National Assembly Elections," April 21, 2007.

12. National Democratic Institute, "Statement of the National Democratic Institute International Election Observer Delegation to Nigeria's April 21 Presidential and National Assembly Elections," Abuja, April 23, 2007, 3, http://www.ndi.org/node/17435.

13. International Republican Institute, "Nigeria's Elections below Acceptable Standards," April 22, 2007, http://www.iri.org/news-events-press-center/news/nigeria%E2%80%99s-elections-below-acceptable-standards.

14. Commonwealth Election Observers Group, "2007 Nigerian Elections Departure Statement," Commonwealth Secretariat, Abuja, 2007; ECOWAS Observer Mission to the Federal Republic of Nigeria in Connection with the April 2007 General Elections, "Preliminary Declaration of the Presidential and National Assembly Elections," Abuja, 2007, 8.

15. Readily available open-source evaluations of the 2007 elections follow: National Democratic Institute, "Final NDI Report on Nigeria's 2007 Elections," May 8, 2008, http://www.ndi.org/node/14493; International Republican Institute, "Nigeria's Elections below Acceptable Standards; Preliminary Findings of IRI's International Election Observation Mission," Abuja, Nigeria, April 22, 2007, http://www.iri.org/news-events-press-center/news/nigeria%E2%80%99s-elections-below-acceptable-standards; European Union Election Observation Mission, "Nigeria: Final Report: Gubernatorial and State Houses of Assembly Elections 14 April 2007 and Presidential and National Assembly Elections 21 April 2007," Abuja, Nigeria, April 21, 2007, http://eeas.europa.eu/human_rights/election_observation/nigeria/final_report_en.pdf; Commonwealth Election Observer Group, "2007 Nigeria Elections Departure Statement," Commonwealth Secretariat, Abuja, Nigeria, 2007, http://www.thecommonwealth.org/document/190591/191180/176283/177345/162848/270407nigeriadepstatement.htm. An excellent summary of the findings of national and international observer missions is Rawlence and Albin-Lackey, "Briefing," 502–3. U.S. mission reporting—not significantly different from the references cited above—was all in classified channels.

16. Tom Casey, "U.S. Department of State Press Release on Nigeria's Elections," April 27, 2007, http://nigeriavillagesquare.com/newsflash/us-state-department-press-release-on-nigerian-elections.html.

17. Casey, "U.S. Department of State Press Release."

18. Nobody knows how many died. Violence was greater around the April 14 polling than that of April 21. April 14 was, of course, the greater focus of local rivalries. For a discussion of violence, see Rawlence and Albin-Lackey, "Briefing," 499; European Union Election Observation Mission, "Nigeria: Final Report," 2.

19. Press coverage of the Court of Appeals decision was voluminous. See Funso Maraina, "Yar'Adua Floors Buhari, Atiku," *This Day* (Lagos), February 27, 2008; Tunde Rahman, "Tribunal Judgment—No Surprises," *This Day* (Lagos), February 17, 2008; Aliyu Machika, "Verdict a Disaster—TMG, I'm Vindicated—Obasanjo," *Daily Trust* (Abuja), February 27, 2008.

20. Will Connors, "Judges Uphold Nigeria's Presidential Election," *New York Times*, February 27, 2008.

21. Peter Lewis, "Identity, Institutions and Democracy in Nigeria," Afrobarometer Working Paper No. 68, March 2007, http://www.afrobarometer.org/publications/working-papers/115-wp-68; Michael Bratton and Peter Lewis, "The Durability of Political Goods? Evidence from Nigeria's New Democracy," Afrobarometer Working Paper No. 48, April 2005, http://www.afrobarometer.org/publications/working-papers/81-wp-48.

22. The official U.S. delegation to the Yar'Adua inauguration consisted of the assistant secretary for African affairs and me. There were no cabinet members and no U.S. congressional delegation.

23. The 1993 elections did not make use of the secret ballot, nor of prior registration of voters. Voters publicly lined up at polling places behind the standard of the candidate they supported. So, while there was nothing private about how an individual voted, everybody knew which candidate won the most votes. This method has also been used in elections elsewhere in Africa (e.g., Kenya). Perhaps because of this public dimension, however, turnout was only about 35 percent of the estimated eligible voters. For polling data on growing popular disillusionment with democracy, see Bratton and Lewis, "The Durability of Political Goods?"

24. Obasanjo develops his arguments, which are thoughtful, in his *Constitution for National Integration and Development* (Lagos, Nigeria: Friends Foundation Publishers, 1989), esp. 67–86. See also the interesting exchange between Obasanjo and Arthur Nwankwo on a single-party state in the latter's *Before I Die: Olusegun Obasanjo/Arthur Nwankwo Correspondence on the One-Party State* (Enugu, Nigeria: Fourth Dimension Publishing, 1989). Obasanjo published his arguments when he was out of office, and, I think, they reflect his views as to what would be best for Nigeria, rather than merely what would be expedient for himself.

25. See, for example, Kunle Akogun, "On Gbenga—Moji Obasanjo's Expose," *This Day* (Lagos), January 21, 2008.

26. Reuben Abati, "A Dysfunctional Family," *Guardian* (Lagos), January 18, 2008. See also Oti Iiroegbu, "Gbenga Obasanjo Vows to Expose More," Point Blank News, January 18, 2008, http://www.pointblanknews.com/os744.html.

27. See, for example, "A Rebel in the House of Oduduwa," *This Day* (Lagos), January 19, 2008; and Obi Nwakanma, "The Obasanjo Family Saga," *Vanguard* (Lagos), January 20, 2008.

28. In Nigeria, he is commonly referred to as Obasanjo's oldest son. But *This Day* says he is junior to Olusegun Obasanjo Jr. See "A Rebel in the House of Oduduwa."

29. Abacha and his family were also publicly vilified throughout the years of the Obasanjo presidency.

30. Nigerian press commentary on the scandal is voluminous. For Lar's call for Obasanjo's resignation, see Mariam Aleshinloye Agboola, "Obasanjo an Embarrassment to PDP—Lar," *Daily Sun* (Lagos), January 23, 2008.

8. THE BREAKDOWN OF THE NIGERIAN POLITICAL SYSTEM

1. Sanusi was quoted in "Nigeria: Financial Faultlines," *Africa Confidential* 53, no. 12 (October 5, 2012).

2. "Nigeria President Umaru Yar'Adua Has Heart Problem," BBC News, November 26, 2009, http://news.bbc.co.uk/2/hi/africa/8380520.stm.

3. "Nigeria Profile: President Goodluck Jonathan," *BBC News,* April 18, 2t__ "http://www.bbc.co.uk/news/world-africa-13949548"http://www.bbc.co.uk/news/world-africa-13949548.

4. "Nigeria Profile: President Goodluck Jonathan."

5. Imam Imam, Chuks Okocha, Onyebuchi Ezeigbo, and John Shiklam, "Nigeria: Revealed—Atiku Defeated Babangida by Just One Vote!" *This Day* (Lagos), November 23, 2010.

6. U.S. Commission on International Religious Freedom, "Annual Report 2011," May 2011,http://www.uscirf.gov/images/book%20with%20cover%20for%20web.pdf, p. 98.

7. John Paden, *Postelection Conflict Management in Nigeria: The Challenges of National Unity* (Fairfax, VA: George Mason University School for Conflict Analysis and Resolution, 2012), 20.

8. "Annual Report 2011," 98 (quote repeated on p. 99).

9. H.E. Judge Prince Bola Ajibola, quoted in "Report on the Inter-Religious Tensions and Crisis in Nigeria," International Joint Delegation of The World Council of Churches and The Royal Aal al-Bayt Institute for Islamic Thought, May 2012, p. 9,http://www.oikoumene.org/en/ resources/documents/wcc-programmes/interreligious-dialogue-and-cooperation/accompanying -churches-in-conflict-situations/report-on-the-inter-religious-tensions-in-nigeria.html.

10. Paden, *Postelection Conflict Management,* 17.

11. "Civil Society Election Situation Room: Final Statement on the Presidential Elections," Enough is Enough Nigeria (website), April 19, 2011,http://eienigeria.org/reports/others/2011-04-21-civil-society-election-situation-room-final-statement-presidential. Numerous observers estimated the South Kaduna casualties as more than a thousand; however, others applied that figure to the entire country. Seehttp://www.hrw.org/news2011/15/16/nigeria-post-election-vilence-killed-800.

12. "Spiraling Violence: Boko Haram Attacks and Security Force Abuses in Nigeria," Human Rights Watch Report, October 2012,http://www.hrw.org/sites/default/files/reports/nigeria1012webwcover.pdf.

13. Quoted in Gbola Subair, "Nigeria's Poverty Level Rises, Hits 71.5%, Sokoto, Niger Top List of Poorest States," *Nigerian Tribune,* February 13, 2012.

9. BOKO HARAM

1. As always, official sources said only a handful of terrorists escaped, while the media provides the 150 number.

2. "Previously Unknown Islamic Sect Claims Responsibility for Assault on SARS Headquarters in Abuja," *Sahara Reporters,* November 27, 2012.

3. "Spiraling Violence: Boko Haram Attacks and Security Force Abuses in Nigeria," Human Rights Watch Report, October 2012,http://www.hrw.org/sites/default/files/reports/nigeria1012webwcover.pdf, 9.

4. Most information about Boko Haram comes from Nigerian media. However, the following provide an excellent introduction for the general reader: "Spiraling Violence"; Andrew Walker, "What Is Boko Haram," U.S. Institute of Peace, USIP Special Report 308, June 2012; Jacob Zenn, "Boko Haram's Dangerous Expansion into Northwest Nigeria," *CTC Sentinel* 5, no. 10 (October 2012); Jacob Zenn, "Northern Nigeria's Boko Haram: The Prize in al-Qaeda's Africa Strategy," Jamestown Foundation Occasional Paper, November 2012.

5. An extensive discussion of Boko Haram splinters and other groups is in Zenn, "Northern Nigeria's Boko Haram."

6. Udamu Kalu argues this point in "Mohammed Yusuf: Life and Times of a New Maitatsineat Leader," *Vanguard* (Lagos), July 31, 2009.

7. JTF sources quoted by Kingsley Omonobi, "Nigeria: Army Blocks Move by Boko Haram to Hoist Flag in Damaturu," *Vanguard* (Lagos), October 26, 2012.

8. Joe Boyle, "Nigeria's 'Taliban' Enigma," BBC News, July 31, 2009.

9. Tajudeen Suleiman, "A Disciple of Bin Laden?" *Tell,* January 23, 2012.

10. Zenn, in "Northern Nigeria's Boko Haram," argues credibly that many fled over the border into Niger and Cameroon.

11. "Profile of Nigeria's Boko Haram Leader Abubakar Shekau," BBC News, June 22, 2012.

12. "Profile of Nigeria's Boko Haram Leader Abubakar Shekau."

13. "Profile of Nigeria's Boko Haram Leader Abubakar Shekau."

14. However, prohibitions of alcohol in sharia states did not apply to federal installations.

15. Zenn, "Boko Haram's Dangerous Expansion into Northwest Nigeria," 3, citing press statements by ostensible Boko Haram spokesmen published in *This Day* and *Vanguard*.

16. Quoted by A. M. Bashir Shuwa, "Matter Arising from the Arrest of Shu'Aibu Muhammed Bama, a Boko Haram Commander in Maiduguri," *Sahara Reporters*, October 20, 2012.

17. However, it has not been established that Bama was "high-ranking" in Boko Haram—or even that he was in Boko Haram at all. It is the security forces that have so characterized him. See Zenn, "Boko Haram's Dangerous Expansion into Northwest Nigeria," 3, note 16.

18. Ikechukwu Nnochiri, "Terrorism Trial: Intrigues as Ndume Names VP Namadi Sambo," *Vanguard* (Lagos), March 25, 2012.

19. For examples, see A. M. Bashir Shuwa, "Matter Arising."

20. Henry Umoru, "Nigeria: PDP Behind Killings in Borno—State Govt," *Vanguard* (Lagos), November 12, 2012. Umoru lists the following prominent ANPP Borno politicians who have been murdered: Awana Ngala, chairman of the ANPP; Modu Gubio, ANPP gubernatorial candidate; Goni Sheriff, younger brother to Sen. Ali Sheriff; Lawan Yarayi, former chairman of the Kukawa Local Government Area; Lawan Kabu, former chairman of the Damboa Local Government Area; and Kadiri Kaza, former chairman of Mongumo Local Government Area. He goes on to list eight more, including two women.

21. The Fulani herdsmen were Muslim, while the Christian farmers were often Baroum, a small ethnic group formerly preyed upon by the Fulani for the slave trade.

22. Danladi Bature, "Boko Haram: Real Leader Unmasked," *National Daily*, November 5, 2012.

23. Zenn, "Boko Haram's Dangerous Expansion into Northwest Nigeria," 5.

24. Zenn, "Boko Haram's Dangerous Expansion into Northwest Nigeria," 3. In note 17, Zenn cites Boko Haram statements to this effect quoted in *This Day*, March 8, 2012.

25. "Niger Police Arrest 5 Suspected Boko Haram Members," *Vanguard* (Lagos), September 27, 2012.

26. M. J. Smith, "Boko Haram Leader Salutes Global Jihadists in Video: SITE," *Agence France-Presse*, November 29, 2012.

27. This argument is best developed by Zenn's "Boko Haram's Dangerous Expansion into Northwest Nigeria." See also his "Northern Nigeria's Boko Haram: The Prize in al-Qaeda's Africa Strategy," Jamestown Foundation Occasional Paper, November 2012.

28. Hamza Idris and Abdul-Rahman Abubakar, "Nigeria: Boko Haram Offers Conditional Ceasefire," *Daily Trust*, November 2, 2012; Emmanuel Aziken, Ben Agande, and Ndahi Marama, "Boko Haram Names Buhari, 5 Others as Mediators," *Vanguard* (Lagos), November 1, 2012.

29. On the relationship between Boko Haram and the security forces, see "Spiraling Violence."

10. WASHINGTON AND ABUJA

1. Charles Snyder was a career civil servant and Africa expert who served for a year as acting assistant secretary.

2. The efficiency reports for ambassadors were usually drafted by desk officers rather than by assistant secretaries.

3. As with assistant secretaries, my contact with principal deputy assistant secretaries varied. With one, I never had a substantive conversation. With another, telephone and email contact was daily.

4. The division of countries among offices in the Bureau of African Affairs was usually based on administrative convenience or personnel availability. Some desks covered multiple countries.

5. However, the junior of the two positions was usually vacant.

6. Colin Powell was secretary of state during Bush's first term; Condoleezza Rice, during his second. Charles Snyder was acting assistant secretary, 2003–4; Constance Newman was assistant secretary, 2004–5; and Jendayi Frazer was assistant secretary from 2005 to the end of the Bush administration.

7. Donald Easum, U.S. ambassador to Nigeria from 1975 to 1979, served the longest since the U.S. embassy was established in 1960.

8. South Africa, Mauritius, and Tanzania had political appointee ambassadors during the second George W. Bush administration.

9. The Department of Defense assisted the Nigerian military with its response to HIV/AIDS through the President's Emergency Plan for AIDS Relief (PEPFAR). It also had a variety of small humanitarian or development projects. For example, it had a small program to dig boreholes.

10. American men who marry Nigerian women usually keep their families in the United States.

11. "Mapping Sub-Saharan Africa's Future," National Intelligence Council Conference Report, March 2005, http://www.zl50.com/200710049793274.html.

12. Olusegun Adeniyi, "Nigeria/U.S.: But Not Always as Friends," *This Day* (Lagos), June 30, 2005.

13. Adeniyi became President Yar'Adua's press spokesman.

14. Nigeria had been a founder of ECOWAS and on my watch contributed most of the organization's budget. Much of the ECOWAS permanent cadre was Nigerian, and the organization's headquarters is in Abuja. Some West African diplomats told me that they viewed ECOWAS as an instrument of Nigeria's regional hegemony. I was the first U.S. ambassador accredited to ECOWAS, and the practice continues that the ambassador to Nigeria is also accredited to ECOWAS.

15. Acting President Goodluck Jonathan fired Muktar and reappointed Gusau as national security advisor in 2010 as part of his own effort to consolidate his hold on the presidency.

16. Constance Ikokwu, "US: Nigeria Fit for Permanent Member of UN Security Council," *This Day* (Lagos), September 28, 2007.

17. Emeka Mamah, "16 West African Countries Establish Standby Brigade," *Vanguard* (Lagos), January 11, 2008.

18. That reality was conveyed to me in clear terms by a deputy assistant secretary in the Africa bureau when there was suspicion that I might block a high-ranked military visit that I saw as potentially counterproductive.

19. In October 2001, militia from the Tiv ethnic group abducted and murdered nineteen soldiers, whose mutilated bodies were found in the village of Zaki Biam. About ten days later, soldiers from the 23rd Armored Brigade of the 3rd Armored Division rounded up residents for a "meeting." The soldiers made the villagers sit on the ground, separated the men from the others, and then opened fire upon the men. See Frisky Larr, "Odi, Zaki Biam and Bola Ige: Some Credible Weapons for the President's Enemies," *Nigerian Village Square*, May 27, 2007, http://nigeriavillagesquare.com/articles/frisky-larr/some-credible-weapons-for-the-presidents-enemies.html.

20. For a fascinating discussion of Obasanjo's soil-for-infrastructure proposals to the Chinese, see Lillian Wong, "Asian National Oil Companies in Nigeria," in "Thirst for African Oil: Asian National Oil Companies in Nigeria and Angola," by Alex Vines, Lillian Wong, Markus Weimer, and Indira Campos, Chatham House Report, Royal Institute of International Affairs, August 2009, 7–26, http://www.chathamhouse.org/publications/papers/view/109110.

11. DANCING ON THE BRINK

1. Ujudud Shariff, "The Coming Anarchy," *Daily Trust* (Abuja), January 20, 2004.

2. Pauline H. Baker, "June 1, 2006: The Failed States Index: A Discussion with Pauline Baker," *Voices on Genocide Prevention*, a podcasting service of the U.S. Holocaust Memorial Museum, June 2006.

3. The Failed States Index 2009, The Fund for Peace, http://www.fundforpeace.org/global/?q=fsi-grid2009.

4. Stephen Ellis, "How to Rebuild Africa," *Foreign Affairs* 84, no. 5 (September/October 2005): 135–48.

5. The Biafra flag is now flown from many private buildings in the old territory of Biafra.

6. Some argue that as a collective Awolowo, Azikiwe, and Bello were heroes to the nation as a whole. My view is that, while that might have been so in the first decade after independence, it is no longer true.

7. For example, see Daniel Howden, "Militia's Hunt for Guns Renews Fears of Nigeria Violence," *Independent* (London), March 11, 2010.

8. The conference was covered by the Lagos press. See, for example, Ibe Uwaleke, Clifford Ndujihe, and Cornelius Onuoha, "How to Save Nigeria from Collapse, by Atiku, Ex-govs, Others," *Guardian* (Lagos), April 4, 2008. The event was a book launch for Nwabueze.

9. With Yar'Adua's death in May 2010, Jonathan's presidency became fully constitutional.

Selected Bibliography

BOOKS

Adeyi, Olusoji, Phyllis J. Kanki, Oluwole Odutolu, and John Idako, eds. *Aids in Nigeria*. Cambridge, MA: Harvard University Press, 2006.

Ake, Claude. *The Feasibility of Democracy in Africa*. Dakar, Senegal: Council for the Development of Social Science Research in Africa, 2003.

Baker, Pauline H. *Urbanization and Political Changes: The Politics of Lagos, 1917–1967*. Berkeley: University of California Press, 1975.

Barrett, David B., George T. Kurian, and Todd M. Johnson, eds. *World Christian Encyclopedia: A Comparative Survey of Churches and Religions*. 2nd ed. New York: Oxford University Press, 2001.

Beckett, Paul A., and Crawford Young, eds. *Dilemmas of Democracy in Nigeria*. Rochester, NY: University of Rochester Press, 1997.

Brautigam, Deborah. *The Dragon's Gift: The Real Story of China in Africa*. Oxford: Oxford University Press, 2009.

Carland, John M. *The Colonial Office and Nigeria, 1898–1914*. Stanford, CA: Hoover Institution Press, 1985.

Cooke, Jennifer, and J. Stephen Morrison, eds. *U.S. Africa Policy beyond the Bush Years: Critical Challenges for the Obama Administration*. Washington, DC: CSIS Press, 2009.

Dahl, Robert A. *Polyarchy: Participation and Opposition*. New Haven, CT: Yale University Press, 1971.

De Montclos, Marc-Antoine. *Le Nigeria*. Paris: Karthala Press, 1994.

Diamond, Larry. *Class, Ethnicity, and Democracy in Nigeria: The Failure of the First Republic*. Syracuse, NY: Syracuse University Press, 1988.

Farris, Jacqueline, and Mohammed Bornoi, eds. *Shehu Musa Yar'Adua: A Life of Service*. Abuja, Nigeria: Shehu Musa Yar'Adua Foundation, 2004.

Garba, Joe. *Diplomatic Soldiering: Nigerian Foreign Policy 1975–79*. Ibadan, Nigeria: Spectrum Books, 1979.

Ghazvinian, John. *Untapped: The Scramble for Africa's Oil*. Orlando, FL: Houghton Mifflin Harcourt, 2007.

Gifford, Prosser, and W. Roger Louis, eds. *Decolonization and African Independence: The Transfers of Power, 1960–1980*. New Haven, CT: Yale University Press, 1988.

Graf, William. *The Nigerian State: Political Economy, State, Class, and Political System in the Post-colonial Era*. London: James Currey Press, 1988.

Guest, Robert. *The Shackled Continent: Africa's Past, Present and Future*. London: Macmillan, 2004.

Hambolu, M. O., ed. *Perspectives on Kano-British Relations*. Kano, Nigeria: Gidan Makama Museum, 2003.

Hargreaves, John D. *Decolonization in Africa*. 2nd ed. London: Longman, 1996.

Jenkins, Philip. *The Next Christendom: The Coming of Global Christianity*. Oxford: Oxford University Press, 2002.

Joseph, Richard. *Democracy and Prebendal Politics in Nigeria: The Rise and Fall of the Second Republic*. Cambridge: Cambridge University Press, 1987.

Lewis, Peter M. *Growing Apart: Oil, Politics, and Economic Change in Indonesia and Nigeria*. Ann Arbor: University of Michigan Press, 2007.

Low, David A. *The End of the British Empire in Africa*. Cambridge: Cambridge University Press, 1993.

Lugard, Frederick. *The Dual Mandate in British Tropical Africa*. 5th ed. Abingdon, Oxon, UK: F. Cass, 2005.

Maier, Karl. *This House Has Fallen: Nigeria in Crisis*. Boulder, CO: Westview Press, 2002.

Meredith, Martin. *The State of Africa: A History of Fifty Years of Independence*. London: Free Press, 2005.

Metz, Helen Chapin, ed. *Nigeria: A Country Study*. Washington, DC: Federal Research Division, Library of Congress, 1992.

Moss, Todd. *African Development*. Boulder, CO: Lynne Rienner, 2007.

Obasanjo, Olusegun. *Constitution for National Integration and Development*. Lagos, Nigeria: Friends Foundation Publishers, 1989.

Obasanjo, Olusegun, and Arthur Nwankwo. *Before I Die: Olusegun Obasanjo/Arthur Nwankwo Correspondence on the One-Party State*. Enugu, Nigeria: Fourth Dimension Publishing, 1989.

Obiozor, George A. *Uneasy Friendship: Nigeria/U.S. Relations*. 2nd ed. Enugu, Nigeria: Fourth Dimension Publishing, 2003.

Onukaba, Adinoyi Ojo. *Olusegun Obasanjo: In the Eyes of Time*. New York: African Legacy Press, 1997.

Osaghae, Eghosa E. *Crippled Giant: Nigeria since Independence*. Bloomington: Indiana University Press, 1998.

Oshanugor, Frank. *Terrorism: The Nigerian Experience, 1885–1998*. Lagos, Nigeria: Advent Communications, 2004.

Ostien, Philip. *Sharia Implementation in Northern Nigeria, 1999–2006: A Sourcebook*. 5 vols. Ibadan, Nigeria: Spectrum Books, 2007.

Paden, John N. *Ahmadu Bello: Sardauna of Sokoto*. Zaria, Nigeria: Hudahuda Publishing, 1986.

———. *Faith and Politics in Nigeria: Nigeria as a Pivotal State in the Muslim World*. Washington, DC: U.S. Institute of Peace Press, 2008.

———. *Muslim Civic Cultures and Conflict Resolution: The Challenge of Democratic Federalism in Nigeria*. Washington, DC: Brookings Institution Press, 2005.

———. *Postelection Conflict Management in Nigeria: The Challenges of National Unity*. Fairfax, VA: George Mason University School for Conflict Analysis and Resolution, 2012.

Peel, J. D. Y., ed. *Popular Islam South of the Sahara*. Manchester, UK: Manchester University Press, 1985.

———. *Religious Encounter and the Making of the Yoruba*. Bloomington: Indiana University Press, 2000.

Reader, John. *Africa: A Biography of the Continent*. New York: Knopf, 1998.

Smith, Daniel J. *A Culture of Corruption: Everyday Deception and Popular Discontent in Nigeria*. Princeton, NJ: Princeton University Press, 2007.

St. Jorre, John de. *The Brothers' War: Biafra and Nigeria*. Boston: Houghton Mifflin, 1972.

Tomes, Robert R., Angela Mancini, and James T. Kirkhope, eds. *Cross Roads Africa: Perspectives of U.S.-China-Africa Security Affairs*. Washington, DC: Council for Emerging National Security Affairs, 2009.

Young, M. Crawford. *The Politics of Cultural Pluralism*. Madison: University of Wisconsin Press, 1979.

ARTICLES AND REPORTS

Abaku, Tamuno. "Nearer to Peace." *PeaceWorks News* 6, no. 1 (May 2006).
"Africa Union Elections Report: Nigeria 2007." Africa Union Elections Observer Mission (April 2007).
Akeni, Kingsley. "Constructive Engagement with Niger Delta Youths." *PeaceWorksNews* 7, no. 1 (May 2007).
"America's Image Slips, but Allies Share U.S. Concerns over Iran, Hamas." Global Attitudes Project, Pew Research Center (June 2006), http://www.pewglobal.org/2006/06/13/americas-image-slips-but-allies-share-us-concerns-over-iran-hamas.
"Annual Report." U.S. Commission on International Religious Freedom (May 2009). http://www.uscirf.gov/reports-and-briefs/annual-report.html.
"Arbitrary Killings by Security Forces: Submission to the Investigative Bodies on the November 28–29, 2008, Violence in Jos, Plateau State, Nigeria." Human Rights Watch Report (July 20, 2009). http://www.hrw.org/reports/2009/07/20/arbitrary-killings-security-forces-0.
Asuni, Judith. "Blood Oil in the Niger Delta." U.S. Institute of Peace Special Report No. 229 (August 2009): 2–16. http://www.usip.org/publications/blood-oil-in-the-niger-delta.
———. "Peace and Security Strategy for the Niger Delta." *PeaceWorks News* 5, no. 1 (October 2007).
Baker, Pauline H. "June 1, 2006: The Failed States Index: A Discussion with Pauline Baker." Voices on Genocide Prevention, a podcasting service of the U.S. Holocaust Memorial Museum (June 2006).
Bratton, Michael, and Peter Lewis. "The Durability of Political Goods? Evidence from Nigeria's New Democracy." Afrobarometer Working Paper No. 48 (April 2005). http:/www.afrobarometer.org/publications/working-papers/81-wp-48.
Budina, Nina, Gaobo Pang, and Sweder Van Wijnbergen. "Nigeria's Growth Record: Dutch Disease or Debt Overhang?" World Bank Policy Research Working Paper No. 4256 (June 2007). http://elibrary.worldbank.org/content/workingpaper/10.1596/1813-9450-4256.
"Chop Fine: The Human Rights Impact of Local Government Corruption and Mismanagement in Rivers State, Nigeria." Human Rights Watch Report 19, no. 2 (January 2007). http://www.hrw.org/reports/2007/01/30/chop-fine.
"Doing Business Project 2010: Reforming through Difficult Times." World Bank Group (September 9, 2010), http://www.doingbusiness.org/reports/global-reports/Doing%20Business%202010.
"Election Observation Report: Nigeria's 2007 Elections." International Republican Institute (April 2007).
Ellis, Stephen. "How to Rebuild Africa." *Foreign Affairs* 84, no. 5 (September/October 2005): 135–48.
"EU Election Observation Mission: Nigeria 2007." European Union Observation Mission (August 2007). http://www.eueom.eu/files.../final-report-nigeria2011_en.pdf.
"The Failed States Index." Foreign Policy and the Fund for Peace (2005, 2006, 2007, 2009). http://www.fundforpeace.org/global/?q=fsi.
Federal Office of Statistics (Nigeria). "Nigeria Poverty Assessment: Quantitative Aspect." Nigeria Living Standards Survey 2003–2004.
"Final Report on Nigeria's 2007 Elections." National Democratic Institute (May 2008). http://www.ndi.org/node/14493.
"Fuelling the Niger Delta Crisis." International Crisis Group Report No. 118 (September 28, 2006), http://www.crisisgroup.org/en/regions/africa/west-africa/nigeria/118-fuelling-the-niger-delta-crisis.aspx.
Herskovits, Jean. "Nigeria's Rigged Democracy." *Foreign Affairs* 86, no. 4 (July/August 2007): 115–30.

————. "The Real Tragedy in Nigeria's Violence." *Foreign Policy* (Online Edition) (August 2009), http://www.foreignpolicy.com/articles/2009/08/03/the_real_tragedy_in_nigerias_violence.

Hiskett, Mervyn. "The Maitatsine Riots in Kano, 1980: An Assessment." *Journal of Religion in Africa* 17, no. 3 (1987): 209–23.

Ibrahim, Hauwa, and Princeton Lyman. "Reflections on the New Sharia Law in Nigeria." Council on Foreign Relations (2004).

"Islamist Terrorism in the Sahel: Fact or Fiction." International Crisis Group Africa Report No. 92 (March 31, 2005). http://www.crisisgroup.org/en/regions/africa/west-africa/092-islamist-terrorism-in-the-sahel-fact-or-fiction.aspx.

Joseph, Richard, and Alexandra Gillies. "Nigeria's Season of Uncertainty." *Current History* (May 2010): 179–85.

Kaufmann, Judith R., and Harley Feldbaum. "Diplomacy and the Polio Immunization Boycott in Northern Nigeria." *Health Affairs* 28, no. 4 (2009): 1091–1101.

Lewis, Peter. "Identity, Institutions and Democracy in Nigeria." Afrobarometer Working Paper No. 68 (March 2007). http://www.afrobarometer.org/publications/working-papers/115-wp-68.

Lubeck, Paul. "Islamic Protest under Semi-Industrial Capitalism: Yan Tatsine Explained." In *Popular Islam South of the Sahara*, ed. J. D. Y. Peel, 369–89. Manchester, UK: Manchester University Press, 1985.

Lyman, Princeton, and J. Stephen Morrison. "The Terrorist Threat in Africa." *Foreign Affairs* (January/February 2004): 75–86.

"Mapping Sub-Saharan Africa's Future." National Intelligence Council Conference Report (March 2005). http://www.zl50.com/200710049793274.html.

Marquardt, Erich. "Mujahid Dokubo-Asari: The Niger Delta's Ijaw Leader." *Global Terrorism Analysis* 5, no. 15 (August 2007).

Muzan, Allswell. "Partnering in the Niger Delta." *PeaceWorks News* 4, no. 3 (February 2004): 7.

"Nigeria: Criminal Politics: Violence, 'Godfathers' and Corruption in Nigeria." Human Rights Watch Report 19, no. 16(A) (October 2007). http://www.hrw.org/reports/2007/10/11/criminal-politics.

"Nigeria Demographic and Health Survey." National Population Commission of Nigeria (2003).

"Nigeria: Opinion of the United States." Pew Research Center (2009).

"Nigeria: Want in the Midst of Plenty." International Crisis Group Report No. 113 (July 19, 2006): 13. http://www.crisisgroup.org/en/regions/africa/west-africa/nigeria/113-nigeria-want-in-the-midst-of-plenty.aspx.

"Nigeria's Faltering Federal Experiment." International Crisis Group Report No. 119 (October 2006), http://www.crisisgroup.org/en/regions/africa/west-africa/nigeria/119-nigerias-faltering-federal-experiment.aspx.

Okonjo-Iweala, Ngozi, and Philip Osafo-Kwaako. "Nigeria's Economic Reforms Progress and Challenge." Brookings Institution Working Paper No. 6 (March 26, 2007). http://www.brookings.edu/research/papers/2007/03/23globaleconomics-okonjo-iweala.

Oronto, Douglas. "The Road to Justice and Prosperity in the Niger Delta." *PeaceWorks News* 4, no. 4 (September 2004).

Packer, George. "The Megacity: Decoding the Chaos of Lagos." *New Yorker,* November 2006, 62–75.

Pegg, Scott. "The Cost of Doing Business: Transnational Corporations and Violence in Nigeria." *Security Dialogue* 30, no. 4 (December 1999): 473–84.

"Politics as War: The Human Rights Impact and Causes of Post-election Violence in Rivers State, Nigeria." Human Rights Watch Report 20, no. 3 (March 2008), https://www.hrw.org/reports/2008/03/27/politics-war.

"Preliminary Declaration on the Presidential and National Assembly Elections." ECOWAS Observer Mission to the Federal Republic of Nigeria (April 2007).

Rawlence, Ben, and Christopher Albin-Lackey. "Briefing: Nigeria's 2007 General Elections: Democracy in Retreat." *African Affairs* 106, no. 424 (2007): 497–506.

"Report of the Commonwealth Observer Group: Nigeria 2007." Commonwealth Elections Observer Group (June 2007).

"Report of the Niger Delta Youths: Stakeholders Workshop." Academic Associates Peace-Works, Port Harcourt, April 15–17, 2004. http://www.aapw.org/nnpcreport.pdf.

Rotberg, Robert I. "Nigeria: Elections and Continuing Challenges." Council on Foreign Relations, CSR no. 27 (2007). http://www.cfr.org/nigeria/nigeria/p12926.

Ruby, Robert, and Timothy Samuel Shah. "Nigeria's Presidential Election: The Christian-Muslim Divide." Pew Research Center (March 21, 2007). http://www.pewforum.org/Politics-and-Elections/Nigerias-Presidential-Election-The-Christian-Muslim-Divide.aspx.

Shaxston, Nicholas. "Nigeria's Extractive Industries Transparency Initiative: Just a Glorious Audit?" Chatham House Report, Royal Institute of International Affairs (November 2009). http://eiti.org/document/shaxson-neiti-glorious-audit.

"Spiraling Violence: Boko Haram Attacks and Security Force Abuses in Nigeria," Human Rights Watch (October 2012). http://www.hrw.org/sites/default/files/reports/nigeria1012webwcover.pdf.

"Spirit and Power: 10-Country Survey of Pentecostals." Pew Forum on Religion and Public Life (October 5, 2006). http://www.pewforum.org/Christian/Evangelical-Protestant-Churches/Spirit-and-Power.aspx.

Starr, Joel E. "'What Do You Have for Me Today?': Observing the 1999 Nigerian Presidential Election." *Stanford Journal of International Law* 35, no. 2 (1999): 389–97.

"The Swamps of Insurgency: Nigeria's Delta Unrest." International Crisis Group Report No. 115 (August 2006): 2–5, http://www.unhcr.org/refworld/docid/44e9a07a4.html.

"Tolerance and Tension: Islam and Christianity in Sub-Saharan Africa." Pew Research Center's Forum on Religion and Public Life (April 15, 2010). http://www.pewforum.org/Africa-Transcript.aspx.

Vines, Alex, Lillian Wong, Markus Weimer, and Indira Campos. "Thirst for African Oil: Asian National Oil Companies in Nigeria and Angola." Chatham House Report, Royal Institute of International Affairs (August 2009), http://www.chathamhouse.org/publications/papers/view/109110.

Walker, Andrew. "What Is Boko Haram?" U.S. Institute for Peace Special Report (May 2012). http://www.usip.org/publications/what-boko-haram.

Young, M. Crawford. "Permanent Transition and Changing Conjuncture: Dilemmas of Democracy in Nigeria in Comparative Perspective." In *Dilemmas of Democracy in Nigeria*, ed. Paul A. Beckett and Crawford Young, 65–82. Rochester, NY: University of Rochester Press, 1997.

Zenn, Jacob. "Northern Nigeria's Boko Haram: The Prize in al-Qaeda's African Strategy." The Jamestown Foundation (November 2012). http://www.jamestown.org/single/?tx_ttnews%5Btt_news%5D=40153&cHash=d1183de5ee9485fa56f69ac4d0ef93c4.

NEWSPAPERS, MAGAZINES, AND NEWS SERVICES

Daily Champion (Lagos)
Daily Trust (Abuja)
Economist (London)
Elendu Reports (Michigan)
Financial Times (London)
Forbes (New York)
Guardian (Lagos)
Independent (London)
International Herald Tribune (Paris)
Leadership (Abuja)
Nation (Lagos)
News (Lagos)
New York Times (New York)
Nigerian Village Square

Punch (Lagos)
Sahara Reporters (New York)
Sun News (Lagos)
This Day (Lagos)
UN Integrated Regional Information Networks (IRIN)
U.S. Diplomatic Missions to Nigeria press releases (2004–7)
Vanguard (Lagos)
Wall Street Journal (New York)
Weekly Trust (Kaduna)

Index

About the Author

Ambassador John Campbell is the Ralph Bunche Senior Fellow for Africa Policy Studies at the Council on Foreign Relations.

From 1975 to 2007, Campbell served as a U.S. Department of State foreign service officer. He served twice in Nigeria, as political counselor from 1988 to 1990 during the military dictatorship of General Ibrahim Babangida, and as ambassador from 2004 to 2007 during the civilian presidency of General Olusegun Obasanjo.

Campbell's additional overseas postings include Lyon, Paris, Geneva, and Pretoria during South Africa's transition to nonracial democracy from 1993 to 1996. Past domestic assignments in the U.S. Department of State include deputy assistant secretary, Bureau for Human Resources; dean, School of Language Studies, Foreign Service Institute; and director, Office of UN Political Affairs.

From 2007 to 2008, he was a visiting professor of international relations at the University of Wisconsin, Madison. He was also a Department of State midcareer fellow at the Woodrow Wilson School, Princeton University. Prior to his career in the Foreign Service, he taught British and French history at Mary Baldwin College in Staunton, Virginia.

Campbell received a BA and MA from the University of Virginia as well as a PhD in seventeenth-century English history from the University of Wisconsin, Madison.